Novel Cuisine

Recipes that Recreate the Culinary Highlights of Favorite Novels

Elaine Borish, an American living in London, was born in New York City. She holds degrees from Rutgers, Boston University, and Northeastern University and has taught at universities in New England. In old England, she has lectured in English and American literature at Morley College in London. Her numerous articles have appeared in leading newspapers and magazines.

Also by Elaine Borish

A Legacy of Names
Literary Lodgings
Unpublishable!

Elaine Borish

Novel Cuisine

Recipes that Recreate the Culinary Highlights of Favorite Novels

Fidelio Press

Boulder · London

To Sarah, who loves good books—and *good* food!
And Adam, who loves good food—and *good* books!

Published by
Fidelio Press, Inc.
61 Pine Tree Lane
Boulder, Colorado 80304

Library of Congress Catalog Card Number: 98-094128

ISBN 0-952488-3-2

Printed in the United States of America

Cover design by Kate Chitham

ACKNOWLEDGMENTS

The author and publisher would like to thank the following for their permission to use quotations in this book: The Society of Authors as literary representative of the Estate of Virginia Woolf; The Provost and Scholars of King's College, Cambridge, and The Society of Authors as the literary representatives of the E.M. Forster Estate; The Society of Authors as literary representative of the Estate of John Galsworthy; The Society of Authors on behalf of the Bernard Shaw Estate; quotes from *Rumpole of the Bailey* by John Mortimer reprinted by permission of the Peters Fraser & Dunlop Group Ltd.; Constable, publishers of *The Age of Innocence* by Edith Wharton and the short stories of Katherine Mansfield; A.M. Heath & Co. for *Nineteen Eighty-four* by George Orwell; Chapman & Hall for Arnold Bennett quotations; A.P. Watt Ltd. on behalf of the Trustees of the Wodehouse Estate and on behalf the Literary Executors of the Estate of H.G. Wells; excerpts from *The Five Red Herrings* and *The Nine Tailors* by Dorothy L. Sayers published by Harper Collins reprinted by permission of David Higham Associates; excerpt from *Portrait of the Artist as a Young Dog* by Dylan Thomas published by J.M. Dent reprinted by permission of David Higham Associates; *Room at the Top* by John Braine published by Eyre & Spottiswoode; Mrs. Laura Huxley for *Brave New World* by Aldous Huxley published by Chatto & Windus; Random House for *Family History* by V. Sackville-West; excerpts from *The Good Companions* copyright by the estate of J.B. Priestly and with permission of Peters, Fraser and Dunlop Group Ltd.; Laurence Pollinger Ltd. for the estate of Frieda Lawrence Ravagli for quotations from *The White Peacock* and *Sons and Lovers* by D.H. Lawrence; *Frenchman's Creek* and *Rebecca* reproduced with permission of Curtis Brown Ltd, London, on behalf of the Estate of Daphne du Maurier. Copyright the Chichester Partnership; *The Art of British Cookery* by Theodora FitzGibbon published by J.M. Dent.

The publisher would also like to acknowledge the following sources from which short quotations have been taken: *Babbitt* by Sinclair Lewis (Charles Scribner's Sons); *Pomp and Circumstance* by Noël Coward (Heinemann, 1960); *Howards End* by E.M. Forster (Alfred A. Knopf); *The Return of the Soldier* by Rebecca West (Victor Gollancz); *Dubliners* and *Ulysses* by James Joyce; *Memoirs of A Fox-Hunting Man* by Siegfried Sassoon; *The Wise Virgins* by Leonard Woolf; *Brideshead Revisited* and *Decline and Fall* by Evelyn Waugh; *Good English Food* and *Good Things in England* by Florence White.

CONTENTS

PREFACE

SOUPS

APPETIZERS AND LUNCH

FISH AND SEAFOOD

POULTRY AND GAME

MEAT DISHES

ACCOMPANIMENTS

DESSERTS

PREFACE

Food, essential to life, often serves an essential role in the life of a novel. Food can offer insight into character, decide the outcome of a plot, or add meaning. Mrs. Ramsay's dinner of *beouf en daube* in *To the Lighthouse*. . . Becky Sharpe's first experience in tasting curry in *Vanity Fair*. . . the gypsy stew offered to Maggie in *The Mill on the Floss*. . . the ratiocination of Sherlock Holmes after dining on partridge—all of these dishes are vital to the novels in which they appear.

The novelist must have given more than a modicum of thought to the particular food chosen to enhance the story or make revelations. Perhaps the selected food represents a typical meal of members of a particular social class. It may be a choice made within the constrictions of poverty, or one dictated by a higher and more luxurious standard. Perhaps it was eaten with enormous gusto by an exuberant character, or unthinkingly by an introspective one. In any case, eating is often done during a hiatus in the action when something of importance is expressed that develops the plot or theme.

The various dishes which appear as fictional food existed also in fact and might well have been prepared according to actual recipes known at the time the novel was written. *Novel Cuisine* focuses on descriptions of food mentioned in important novels and provides recipes for those dishes taken from contemporary cookery books, thereby adding an exciting dimension to the current popular interest in new cuisine.

Imagine a dinner party at which the host, complimented on a dish, is able to add a literary touch to a culinary delight and boast that the dish is the very one served in a particular classic—Jane Austen's *Pride and Prejudice* or Charles Dickens' *Great Expectations*, for example.

A story added to a meal is a worthy embellishment of any dinner, and *Novel Cuisine* makes it possible. Each chapter has an epigraph quoting the passage in which the particular food mentioned or extolled in the novel appears. It explains the significance of the food described and its place in the story before going on to offer the actual recipe taken from a cook book published before the novel appeared. How did the author use that particular dish? What are the events which lead up to it? What emanates from its use? How is it appropriate to the characters or plot?

For authentic recipes of the period, available when the novel was written, I have tried to include those old recipes which can be duplicated today from understandable directions, with available ingredients. In some cases, ingredients are no longer obtainable, instructions are outmoded, or words are not understandable. But the recipes have been included for their interest and, wherever possible, modifications or "updates" allow for the recreation of the original recipe.

Each chapter presents literary explication as well as cooking directions. With over one hundred recipes based on literary sources, the book offers good reading and good eating as it appeals to countless numbers who enjoy cookbooks of a specialized nature or those with an interest in literature.

Soups

Julienne Soup

A PASSAGE TO INDIA (1924) by E. M. Forster

The menu was: Julienne soup full of bullety bottled peas . . . the menu of Anglo-India . . . the food of exiles, cooked by servants who did not understand it.

Fourteen years elapsed between the appearance of *Howards End* and E. M. Forster's next novel, *A Passage to India.* (Actually, Forster had completed *Maurice* in 1914, but it was not published until after his death.) *A Passage to India* is considered by many to be one of the great English novels by a major writer of this century.

The theme concerns man's attempt to find order and a basis for lasting values of friendship and truth in a disordered world. Forster uses sympathetic characters to explore the varieties of races, creeds, peoples, and classes with their conflicting needs and aims.

In honor of Mrs. Moore and Miss Quested, newly arrived in India, a Bridge Party is given—not the card game, but the attempt "to bridge the gulf between East and West." Predictably, the party is a failure. The barrier between the two worlds proves impenetrable. Adela Quested envisions married life with Ronny as a round of social calls centered on the club, with no entry into the real India. She would never capture its spirit. Indeed, the two women are to find

3

themselves greatly disappointed in their search for confirmation of a belief in an ordered world, as they become involved in a series of catastrophic incidents.

After the unsuccessful party, they leave the club and go to dinner. Julienne soup starts the meal and significantly underscores the fact that neither side understands the other. The English try to duplicate their traditional home cooking in a foreign environment which cannot adapt to strange ingredients. The result is "the food of exiles, cooked by servants who did not understand it." The menu also includes "pseudo-cottage bread, fish full of branching bones, pretending to be plaice, more bottled peas with the cutlets, trifle, sardines on toast: the menu of Anglo-India."

Just as the food fails, so the experiences of the two women trying to delve into the essence of India and pierce its meaning is doomed to failure. Forster's India remains full of unfathomable mystery and muddle.

Julienne Soup

The mystery of good Julienne soup is simple to reveal. Its name is derived from the months of June and July, when vegetables are in full season. This recipe, derived from J.L.W. Thudichum's *The Spirit of Cookery* of 1895 will still work today:

Take equal quantities or numbers of each—carrots, turnips, leeks, onions, and heads of celery (English leaf-stalk celery, not celeriac; in case celeriac be available take half a root); cut them into thin slices an inch in length; put them into a stewpan with 2 oz. of butter, some salt, and a teaspoonful of powdered sugar. Braise the vegetables slowly until they begin to colour; then pour over them from three pints to three quarts, according to the quantity of vegetables taken, of standard broth, or blond de veau, or mutton-broth, or good mixed stock; let the soup boil, skim off the fat, add the white leaves of two cabbage lettuces, some sorrel, tarragon, and chervil, and boil the whole for ten minutes more. You may avoid the frying and subsequent removal of the fat, although at the cost of some gravy flavour, by boiling the vegetables, including some white or savoy cabbage, or Brussels-sprouts, directly with the desirable quantity of standard broth for one hour, or until they be perfectly tender.

Onion Soup

DEATH COMES FOR THE ARCHBISHOP (1927) by
Willa Cather

*Father Joseph lifted the cover and ladled the soup into
the plates, a dark onion soup with croutons.*

When Sinclair Lewis was awarded the Nobel Prize, he is
reported to have said that Willa Cather should have had the
coveted honor and that he would give nine Nobel prizes to
have written *Death Comes for the Archbishop*.

Born on 7 December 1873 in Virginia, Willa Cather
nevertheless belongs to Nebraska. Her family moved there in
1883, and the young girl grew up in Red Cloud. A year after
receiving her degree from the University of Nebraska, she left
for an editorial position in Pittsburgh and eventually found
her way to New York, where she made the decision to devote
herself to her writing.

With *O Pioneers!* (1913), she turned to her Nebraska background and depicted the heroic qualities of the frontier and its
immigrant people. *My Ántonia* (1918) tells of a Bohemian immigrant girl's life on the frontier and the pioneer strength
with which she triumphs over adversities. *The Professor's
House* (1925), which involves the discovery of an ancient cliff
city in New Mexico, foreshadows the setting of *Death Comes
for the Archbishop*, a novel that concerns the spiritual pio-
neering of the Catholic Church in New Mexico.

6

Bishop Jean Latour and his vicar, Father Joseph Vaillant, lifelong friends since their childhood in the Auvergne in France, are united now in their purpose of creating the new diocese of New Mexico. They work together to overcome the apathy of the Indians and the corruption of Spanish priests as well as insalubrious topographic conditions.

Father Latour needs to secure necessary documents for establishing his diocese. After a dangerous journey with a miraculous rescue, he returns to the Santa Fé settlement, which has been readied by his devoted friend. A quiet scene follows as Father Joseph prepares Christmas dinner and Latour anticipates an excellent meal.

The kitchen is used by Cather for establishing order and ritual, and Father Joseph seems to practice an ancient art of cookery as he goes about the task of producing a dinner featuring a special treat—an onion soup in the French manner. When he lifts the cover and ladles the dark onion soup into the plates, the Bishop tastes it and makes his critical pronouncement: "In all this vast country between the Mississippi and the Pacific Ocean, there is probably not another human being who could make a soup like this." Although Father Joseph laments that a proper soup cannot be made without leeks, and that they "cannot go on eating onions for ever," the dinner is a huge success. Latour makes the point that the soup is "the result of a constantly refined tradition. There are nearly a thousand years of history in this soup." Order has been established and their missionary work proceeds.

Onion Soup

Cather, a great lover of food, has likened writing to eating, explaining that creative inspiration made her write just as food makes a hungry person want to eat. She equated her love for cooking and good cuisine with her creative well being. The good food that Father Joseph prepared paved the way for success in the building of a cathedral and in the missionary work of her two hero-priests.

Before the novel appeared, Fannie Merritt Farmer's *A New Book of Cookery* (1912) included this recipe for onion soup:

Wipe and make several gashes through the meat of a six-pound piece cut from a shin of beef. Put in kettle, add three quarts cold water, cover, heat slowly to the boiling point and let simmer six hours. Wipe, peel, and thinly slice five small onions; put in a frying pan and cook in enough butter to prevent burning (stirring constantly) until soft. Strain stock; there should be six cups. Add two and one-half teaspoons beef extract, onions, and salt to taste. Cut stale bread in one-third-inch slices and remove crusts. Toast on both sides. Place in tureen, sprinkle with three tablespoons grated Parmesan cheese and pour soup over bread just before sending to table.

However, I doubt that Father Joseph would have referred to a Boston cook book. Here is a modern French version:

8

# French Onion Soup

4 large onions, cut in half
2 oz. butter
1 clove garlic
1 ½ quarts beef stock
salt and freshly ground black pepper
4 slices toasted French bread
4 oz. grated Parmesan cheese

Cut halved onions into thin slices and sauté in butter with finely-chopped garlic for 10-15 minutes, until the onions are soft and transparent. Add stock and boil for ten minutes. Season with salt and pepper.

Place toasted French bread in four small oven-proof casseroles (or one large one), ladle the soup into them, and sprinkle with grated cheese.

Bake in preheated hot oven (400°) until top is golden brown.

Note: A good, rich beef stock is the secret to the success of this recipe.

Bouillon

DIANA OF THE CROSSWAYS (1885) by George Meredith

*"This bouillon is consummate. . . . I never tasted
anything so good. I could become a glutton."*

A writer of poetry and fiction, George Meredith produced a
number of works of great originality, including his well-
known novel, *The Egoist* (1879). But he met with little public
enthusiasm for his early volumes and had no financial success
until he took up the cause of the beautiful young Diana, who
struggles against unjust laws and tries to achieve independence in a world dominated by men.

When *Diana of the Crossways* was published in 1885, it
went through three editions in the first year. Meredith
reached the peak of his popularity and came to be accepted as
the greatest living Victorian novelist. Visitors—Robert Louis
Stevenson, Thomas Hardy, George Gissing—made pilgrim-
ages to his home in Box Hill in Surrey to listen to the words of
the revered master, the sage of Box Hill. A year before his
death in 1909, on his eightieth birthday, he received messages
of tribute from both King Edward and President Theodore
Roosevelt.

For his so-called feminist novel, Meredith used several
scandalous incidents from the life of a real person to depict
the vulnerable and precarious position of women who try to

depend on their own resources. As a spokesman for modern ideas, he produced a sympathetic portrait of the woman's problem, and his novel came to be linked with the feminist movement. The resurgence of interest in recent times has resulted in the printing of new editions.

Diana is a spirited young lady, alone in the world with no one to protect her. At a Dublin ball, she meets her old and dear friend, Lady Emma Dunstane; and she is introduced to Thomas Redworth, whose unfavorable pecuniary position prevents him from making any serious commitment. Due to her exceptional beauty and charm, Diana is plagued by unpleasant advances of male admirers. Even when she visits her good friend at Copsley, Lady Dunstane's philandering husband makes an attempt at seduction. To escape male persecution, the heroine enters into a loveless marriage with Mr. Augustus Warwick, nearly fifteen years her senior.

The marriage is a disaster, and the name of her house in England—"The Crossways"—becomes symbolic of her situation. When her unreasonably jealous husband suspects her of an indiscretion and sues for divorce, Diana tries to avoid public scandal by leaving England. But Lady Dunstane sends Redworth to stop her from an action that would make her appear guilty. Diana wins the case but goes abroad to circumvent the law demanding that she return to her insufferable husband. On her travels, she meets a rising young politician, Percy Dacier.

Back in London, she turns to writing fiction to support herself while she lives an extravagant social life. When Warwick renews his threats to enforce his marital rights, Diana agrees to elope to France with Dacier. The plan is thwarted when Redworth again intervenes to report that Lady Dunstane is dangerously ill. Diana rushes to Copsley to be with her friend, who recovers while her repentant husband laments his dastardly behavior.

The relationship with Dacier comes to an abrupt end when Diana betrays the political secret he has entrusted to her. His prompt and vengeful proposal to another woman causes Diana to suffer a complete collapse. She is reprieved from the near-fatal illness by Lady Dunstane, who nurses her back to health. All ends happily. Warwick has conveniently died, and Diana marries the patient and loyal Redworth who has remained devoted to her throughout and has by now made his financial fortune.

It is due to the ministrations of Lady Dunstane at her friend's bedside that Diana's life is saved. Lady Dunstane arrives to find Diana in a dark and cold room, motionless, and deaf to entreaties to take food or drink. Without nourishment, her demise is imminent. Scheming to get the invalid to eat something, Lady Dunstane makes a request to the Frenchwoman in the kitchen below with predictably positive results: "Within ten minutes an appetizing bouillon sent its odour over the bedroom. . . .The bouillon smelt pleasantly." Lady Dunstane sips on it, praises it ("consummate. . .I never tasted anything so good."), and cunningly induces her friend to take a spoonful. With the first swallow, Diana's complete recovery is insured.

Bouillon (Veal Broth)

That Diana recovers to live happily ever after with Redworth is directly attributable to bouillon, for bouillon is often recommended in Victorian cookery books as particularly salubrious for invalids. In his *Hand-Book of Practical Cookery* of 1875, Pierre Blot informs his readers that "broth is called bouillon in France." After giving the recipe, the practical author notes its value for convalescence.

Veal.—Procure two pounds of veal, from the neck or breast piece. Put the meat in a soup-kettle with two quarts of cold water and a little salt; set it on a good fire, and skim off the scum as soon as it gathers on the surface. When skimmed, add a head of lettuce, a leek and a few stalks of chewil (see 'Update' below) if handy; simmer for about three hours; strain and use.

This broth, as well as chicken and turkey broth, is excellent for convalescent persons.

It may be made richer by putting a little more meat, according to taste; but generally the physician gives directions.

UPDATE: Yes, 'chewil'—undoubtedly a mistake, even in pre-computer-spell-check days. The author must surely mean the plant known as 'chervil' which is commonly used in soups.

Turtle Soup

THE YOUNG VISITERS (1919) by Daisy Ashford

Well said Mr Salteena lapping up his turtle soup you have a very sumpshous house Bernard.

A remarkable little volume written by Daisy Ashford in 1890, when she was just nine years old, has become a little classic. A notebook found nearly three decades after it was written was passed from person to person until it turned up in the hands of Sir James Barrie. Enchanted with the penciled manuscript, the eminent author eventually agreed to write a preface, and publication followed in 1919. Undoubtedly, his name helped to insure a successful reception for *The Young Visiters*.

The authoress had begun her writing career when she was four years of age, dictating stories to her father. But for some unknown reason, unknown even to the mature Daisy Ashford, she stopped writing after her school days. When she entered the adult world, she has said, her ambition simply vanished. Several additional works survived and were also published, but it is the little masterpiece in her own handwriting that continues to delight new generations with its charming phrases and misspellings, spontaneous humor and innocence, fascinating Victorian characters, and suspenseful story.

Ethel Monticue is a guest in the home of Mr. Salteena, "an elderly man of 42." Her host receives an invitation to visit

Bernard and bring along a young and pretty lady. Together, they leave for Bernard's elegant country home, which is filled with servants, ancestral portraits, winding stairways, and posh dinners. When the young authoress wanted to indicate the height of luxurious dining, it was turtle soup that came to her mind. Although Mr. Salteena is beginning to be very jealous, he laps up the lavish turtle soup and compliments the house.

Mr. Salteena exhibits more than a twinge of jealousy, as well he might, for Ethel and Bernard go to theatre in London and stay at a hotel. The humble Mr. Salteena desires to enter the gay world of London society but lacks social finesse. He is "flustered with his forks" at dinner and does not know what a finger bowl is. He has to roll up his trousers because he has no knickerbockers for the levee at Buckingham Palace. A final humiliation comes when Ethel turns down his marriage proposal. Bernard's proposal she accepts with alacrity and responds to it like a proper Victorian heroine; she promptly faints from the sheer joy of it all. A bit of champagne hastens a speedy recovery.

The wedding at Westminster Abbey is a grand affair with a wedding cake of great height and sparkling wines, followed by a honeymoon in Egypt. It all ends a bit cynically for Mr. Salteena, however. He is married to "one of the maids in waiting at Buckingham palace" and has "a large family of 10 five of each"; but he never stops dreaming of Ethel.

Never mind. He enjoyed the turtle soup.

15

Turtle Soup

I include a turtle soup recipe for its interest. Pierre Blot, in *What to Eat, and How To Cook It* (1863), does not indicate where to procure it. Perhaps he should have started with the classic injunction, first catch your turtle.

Cut the turtle in dice, throw it in boiling water for two or three minutes, and drain; put it in a stewpan with onions and ham, also cut in dice; season with thyme, parsley, bay leaf, salt, pepper, and a wine glass of Madeira wine or good brandy; wet with Espagnole sauce or with consomme, set on a good fire, boil about half an hour. Ten minutes before taking from the fire, chop the eggs of the turtle, after having boiled them, and put them in a stewpan; if the turtle has none, chop and use hard boiled eggs instead. When done, throw away parsley, thyme, and bay leaf, turn in bowls, add a little chopped chervil, and a quarter of a rind of lemon, also chopped; the latter is enough for six persons. Serve warm.

It may be strained before putting it in bowls, according to taste.

Turtle steaks are prepared like beefsteaks.

Mock Turtle Soup

ALICE'S ADVENTURES IN WONDERLAND (1865) by Lewis Carroll

Beautiful Soup, so rich and green,
Waiting in a hot tureen!
Who for such dainties would not stoop?
Soup of the evening, beautiful Soup!

So sings the Mock Turtle in a story which emanates from one of the most significant picnics in literary history. On 4 July 1862, the Reverend Charles Lutwidge Dodgson, a young mathematics lecturer at Christ Church, Oxford, embarked on a river excursion. With him went his friend Robinson Duckworth and the three daughters of Dean Liddell of Christ Church: Lorina, aged thirteen; Alice, ten; and Edith, eight.

From Folly Bridge, the party set off on their journey up the Isis to Godstow. For amusement, Dodgson told the story of Alice's adventures. "Dodgson, is this an extempore romance of yours?" Duckworth asked. The reply was, "Yes, I'm inventing as we go along." Three miles up the river the group disembarked to enjoy tea on the bank at a pretty site with the romantic ruins of Godstow Nunnery nearby and the Oxford skyline in the distance. The historic picnic ended with a dessert that the world has been enjoying ever since, for the heroine fell into a rabbit hole, and the author fell into a whole new literary world in which he was to become better known as Lewis Carroll.

Back at the Deanery, Alice requested, "Oh, Mr. Dodgson, I wish you would write out Alice's adventures for me." To oblige the young lady, he sat up nearly all night. Duckworth, the "Duck" of the story, later persuaded him to publish it, and exactly three years after the famous river expedition, the book telling of Alice's adventures appeared.

Alice dreams of pursuing a White Rabbit down a rabbit hole where she meets with odd characters—the Duchess and the Cheshire Cat, the Mad Hatter and the March Hare, the King and Queen of hearts, and the Mock Turtle. As she encounters happenings that become curiouser and curiouser, food plays no small role. She can expand or contract by popping into her mouth some delicious eatable.

From the catalogue of food which comes to the fore—currant cake, tea with bread and butter, soup with too much pepper in it, tarts—Mock Turtle Soup is selected to pay tribute to this triumphant little classic. The Mock Turtle—"the thing Mock Turtle Soup is made from" (says the Queen)—concludes his story by singing "Turtle Soup."

 # A Mock Turtle Soup

Just as the Mock Turtle was once a real turtle, so turtle soup can be made of the real or mock eponymous ingredient. John Armstrong offers a mock turtle soup recipe in his early Victorian volume of about 1817 with the promising title, *Young Woman's Guide to Virtue, Economy, and Happiness*. The volume includes instructions not only on how to write letters but how to make ink (start with "six quarts of rain water. . .") and a pen—and ends with advice to women on such diverse topics as rules for conversation, novel reading, choice of a husband, advice after marriage, and matrimonial happiness (which may be secured by discharging "the duties peculiar to the situation of a married woman"). The recipe itself is less promising but provides interesting reading.

Take a calf's head with the skin on, and after scalding off the hair, cut the horny part into pieces about an inch square. Wash and clean them well, and put them into a stew-pan, with four quarts of broth made in the following manner:

Take six pounds of lean beef, two calf's feet, two pair of goose giblets, one onion, two carrots, a turnip, a shank of ham, a head of celery, some cloves, and whole white pepper, a bunch of sweet herbs, a little lemon-peel, a few truffles, and eight quarts of water. Stew these till the broth be reduced to four quarts, then strain, and put in the head cut into pieces, with some marjoram, thyme, and parsley chopped small, a few cloves and mace, some cayenne pepper, a few green onions, a shalot chopped, a few fresh mushrooms, or mushroom powder, and a pint of Madeira. Stew gently till reduced to two quarts. Then heat some broth, thickened with flour, and the yolks of two eggs, and keep stirring it till it nearly boil. Add any quantity of this broth to the other

19

soup, and stew together for an hour. When taken from the fire, add some lemon or orange juice, and a few forcemeat-balls, heated in water, but not fried. The quantity of the additional broth determines the strength of the soup, so that much is left to the taste and discretion of the cook.

Vegetable Mullagatawny

FRENCHMAN'S CREEK (1941) by Daphne du Maurier

From the forward part of the ship, where the men lived she supposed, came the good hunger-making smell of vegetable soup.

Frenchman's Creek is set in Cornwall in the romantic past. The narrow inlet of the Helford River, called Frenchman's Creek, offers refuge and escape to the two unrestrained and flamboyant main characters. Dona St. Columb arrives at the family home of Navron ready to take up a quiet existence away from the scandalous and superficial life style she had been living in London.

Out on a solitary walk from Navron House, Dona is astonished to discover a ship anchored at the widening of the creek where it is completely hidden from view. In this silent and remote refuge, it cannot be seen from the open river. Then she hears French spoken, and she understands. She has come upon the hiding place of the dangerous French pirate about whom she had been warned. She lingers for a moment as she thinks about what to do, and she decides to do and say nothing in order to preserve the peace of her Navron sanctuary. But she has hesitated too long, for suddenly a figure emerges from the woods. She is seized, bound, and abducted.

Taken on board the ship, Lady St. Columb is determined to behave with dignity and calmly plan her escape. But she is baffled. The men on board do not look like stereotyped pirates with rings in their ears. They are not dirty or greasy and do not go about swearing wild oaths. Nor is the ship filthy, disordered, or evil-smelling. On the contrary, it is clean and freshly scrubbed, and a "good hunger-making smell of vegetable soup" greets her nostrils.

She is taken to the cabin of the lawless Frenchman, and a rather pleasant discourse ensues between them. During the interview, one of the captain's men enters with "a great bowl of soup on a tray. It smelt rich and good. The hot steam rose in the air." Dona finds it impossible to resist. "The smell of the soup was very tempting, and she was hungry."

As they eat the meal, which is embellished with freshly baked French bread and good wine, she feels as if she is going through the movements of a dream. Suddenly there is a further recognition. It was this very man, this criminal, who had entered Navron when she was away in London and had the audacity to use her bedroom and actually sleep in her bed! Nevertheless, when he asks her to sign her name to the list of the ship's company—it must be the influence of the good soup—she very willingly consents.

The soup is a very powerful impetus indeed, for their friendship continues, and she has many secret and illicit meetings with him, full of pleasure and inevitable love. The plot, reading like a Hollywood scenario, shows Lady St. Columb dressed as a cabin boy as she joins the Frenchman in adventures to end all adventures—filled with acts of piracy, daring escapades, and breathless escapes. Dona's craving for action is fully and finally satisfied, and she is content at the end to settle down with her family to a life of uneventful domesticity.

 # Vegetable Mullagatawny

It is guaranteed that romance and adventure will overtake the life of anyone who partakes of Eliza Acton's vegetable soup recipe (from *Modern Cookery* of 1845), provided the soup is accompanied with wine and with one essential ingredient: a handsome French pirate.

It is also guaranteed that her recipe, which dates back to British rule in India, will emit a pleasant smell and be a worthy dish for an adventurous Frenchman. Eliza Acton tested it in her own kitchen and gave a variant spelling to the soup designed to conjure up the "hunger-making smell" that was so strongly emphasized in the novel, causing the heroine to succumb to the hero's charms.

Butter, 4 ozs.; vegetable marrow, pared and scooped, 3 lbs.; large mild onions, 4; large cucumbers, 4; or middling sized, 6; apples, or tomatas, 3 to 6: thirty to forty minutes. Mild currie-powder, 3 heaped tablespoonsful; salt, one small tablespoonful: twenty to thirty minutes. Water, broth, or good stock, 2 quarts.

Dissolve in a large stewpan, or thick iron saucepan, four ounces of butter, and when it is on the point of browning, throw in four large mild onions sliced, three pounds weight of young vegetable marrow, cut in large dice, and cleared from the skin and seeds, four large, or six moderate-sized cucumbers, pared, split, and emptied likewise of their seeds, and from three to six large acid apples, according to the taste; shake the pan often, and stew these over a gentle fire until they are tolerably tender; then strew lightly over, and mix well amongst them, three heaped tablespoonsful of mild currie-powder, with nearly a third as much of salt, and let the vegetables stew from twenty to thirty minutes longer; then pour to them gradually sufficient boiling water (broth or stock if preferred), to just cover them, and when they are reduced almost to a pulp press the whole through a hair-sieve with a fine wooden spoon, and heat it in a clean stewpan with as much additional liquid as will make two quarts with that which was first added. Give any further flavouring that may be needed, whether of salt, cayenne, or acid, and serve the soup extremely hot. Should any butter appear on the surface, let it be carefully skimmed off, or stir in a small dessertspoonful of arrow-root, (smoothly mixed with a little cold broth or water) to absorb it. Rice may be served with this soup at pleasure, but as it is of the consistency of winter peas soup, it scarcely requires any addition. The currie-powder may be altogether omitted for variety, and the whole converted into a plain vegetable potage; or it may be rendered one of high savour, by browning all the vegetables lightly, and adding to them rich brown stock. Tomatas, when in season, may be substituted for the apples, after being divided, and freed from their seeds.

UPDATE: If you wish to use arrow-root (cornstarch may be substitued), a dessertspoonful is equivalent to two teaspoons.

Haricot Bean Soup

NINETEEN EIGHTY-FOUR (1949) by George Orwell

*The stuff they were eating was a thin stew, actually a
soup, of haricot beans.*

George Orwell completed his last novel, *Nineteen Eighty-Four*,
shortly before his death on January 23, 1950. Writing in the
last, painful year of his life when he was ill with tuberculosis,
Orwell produced what most people would agree is a very
gloomy novel with a horrific view of a totalitarian world.
Indeed, it was his intention to frighten the reader by warning
of dangers to existence in such a world of the future.

The setting is London. Trafalgar Square has been re-
named Victory Square, and Big Brother has replaced Nelson
atop his column. It is a filthy and decrepit environment, with
air raids and underground shelters. In this atmosphere of
decay and fear, a continuous state of war exists. Rationing,
shortages of essential items, and black market are the norm in
the state of Oceania with its motto, "Big Brother Is Watching
You."

In Orwell's vision, meaningful human relationships are
not possible. The Party bans love and undisciplined sexual
activity as dangerous. It controls all thought and action
through power attained by inflicting pain and humiliation, by
degrading each human being. The loneliness of the frightened

individual is the condition sought by leaders of this oppressed world. Things go awry for Winston Smith when he begins to feel attracted to one of his co-workers and develops an illicit feeling.

Winston Smith is a clerk in the Ministry of Truth, the Ministry whose work it is to propagate lies. He rewrites *The Times* and other such literature in a way that makes it impossible to detect falsification. At thirty-nine, he cannot remember a time when his country had not been at war.

By keeping a diary, Winston is committing a crime. But his private attempt to record history is doomed to failure. The Thought Police examine the diary when he is out, carefully replacing the speck of dust he places on the cover in the belief that it would be shaken off if moved. He has curiosity and imagination and wonders about the past. He goes into the forbidden area of town in an attempt to establish contact with the proles, the working caste of Oceania. The prostitute he patronizes turns out by daylight to be an aged and disgusting hag, and his search for an old man who can recall what life was like in the past also ends in failure. The old man he questions is feeble and full of clichés; he cannot remember.

The relationship of Winston and Julia, the subject of Part II, is also doomed to failure. At the Ministry where he works, he notices the young girl who has seemed to seek him out on several different occasions, finding opportunities to sit near him. At first, he fears she is an agent of the Thought Police spying on him. Then, in one particular encounter, she manages to slip a note to him, which he later reads. Written on the scrap of paper are the words, "I love you."

He is stunned. He wants desperately to arrange a meeting and determines that the canteen is the safest place. More than a week elapses before he is able to contrive to sit at her table. Overcome with fear, they eat their soup with a great show of concentration as they arrange the time and place for a meeting, while spooning the watery soup into their mouths.

26

Julia arranges a liaison in the countryside and subsequently changes the venue to avoid detection. Her attempt to be circumspect does not matter. They have been under surveillance all along, and their love affair is doomed. They are eventually captured in the room above an antique shop owned by the seemingly sympathetic Mr. Charrington, who is actually an officer in the Thought Police. Their freedom ends.

Actually, their freedom never existed. It was mere illusion, for the two-way telescreen in their bedroom recorded every act and word; and the woodland of their idyllic country setting was bugged with microphones. Now it is only left for them to be converted and restored to the world of Oceania. Winston Smith must surrender his heart and mind to Big Brother and believe anything that the Party would like him to believe—that two and two equal five. Reintegrated and reindoctrinated, he is ready to die. In his struggles against his threatening and dehumanized world, he is finally a defeated man.

If there is hope, we are repeatedly told, it lay with the proles. But there is hope for members of the Party too. The picture is not one of unrelieved gloom. Winston took an enormous risk in writing a diary to express his ideas and thoughts. He did rebel, and he did desire freedom. As long as the need for individuality exists, there is hope.

Haricot Bean Soup

Ⅰn the world of cabbage smells and food described as slop, the existence of good cuisine, or the possibility for pleasurably satisfying the appetite, is unknown. Yet, when the couple first meet in a disgusting canteen, with its sour smell and overcrowded condition, the food they eat is—or can be—more than merely acceptable sustenance. Although Winston Smith has started his inexorable descent over it, haricot bean soup can be an appetizing course. Designed to appeal to the masses, *High Class and Economical Cookery Recipes* (1907) by E. Roberta Rees is a good source.

1 pint haricot beans
1 oz. butter or dripping
2 quarts of water

1 teaspoonful celery seeds, tied in
   muslin
1 onion (sliced)
1 pint milk
Salt and pepper

Soak the beans in water for twenty-four hours if possible, then put them into a saucepan with the butter, onion, celery seeds, and the water. Allow all to boil gently for three hours or longer till soft, then rub through a sieve, and return to the saucepan with the milk, and pepper and salt to taste. Stir till the soup boils, and serve with little dice of fried bread.

Vermicelli Soup

HUMPHRY CLINKER (1771) by Tobias Smollett

*From the bookseller's shop, we . . . commonly stop at
Mr. Gill's, the pastry-cook, to take a jelly, a tart, or a
small bason of vermicelli.*

Born in Scotland in 1721, Tobias George Smollett studied
medicine at Glasgow University and eventually became a
surgeon in the navy. He sailed with the West India fleet and
took part in the unsuccessful attack on Cartagena. His first
novel, *The Adventures of Roderick Random,* based on his
experiences at sea, was published in 1748 after his return to
London. It made him famous, and he tried to combine a career
of writing with that of medicine.

Smollett wrote in almost every conceivable genre—plays,
poetry, travel and history, translations, and a variety of
journalistic articles. But his fame rests on his accomplish-
ments as a novelist, and *Humphry Clinker* establishes his
permanent claim to literary fame.

Smollett left London to establish a medical practice in
Bath. Failing to attract many patients, he soon abandoned his
unsuccessful attempt. Before returning to London, he wrote a
pamphlet denigrating the salubrious effects of the waters. In
poor health, he returned to Bath in 1766, this time as a
patient, despite the condemnation he issued some fifteen

years earlier. It was at this time that he probably accumulated material for *Humphrey Clinker*. But continuing poor health obliged him to leave England. He settled in Italy, near Leghorn, where he wrote his fifth and final novel, *Humphrey Clinker*, published in the year of his death.

The Expedition of Humphrey Clinker is the most widely read and admired of the novels of Smollett. Written in epistolary form, the novel relates the travels of Mr. Matthew Bramble and his family, consisting of his sister and a servant, his nephew and his niece. Letters from different characters give diverse views of incidents that occur on the expedition that takes them to Bath, London, Harrogate, Durham, Edinburgh, and the Highlands. There is little plot, but amusing episodes convey interesting information about contemporary customs and give a valuable view of eighteenth-century life.

From his frequent visits to Bath, Smollett knew the resort well; the Bath episode supplies one of the richest segments of the novel. Part of the panorama of life is revealed by Matthew Bramble's niece Lydia, who writes a letter from Bath in which she discusses the activities and customs of the time. Lydia finds the social world and whirl of Bath gay and exciting. Her letter is full of breathless and imaginative description, full of the vigor of youth and romance. She writes, "Bath is to me a new world. All is gaiety, good-humour, and diversion." She enjoys everything—the music in the Pump-room, balls, concerts, people. She calls Bath "an earthly paradise" made up of "sumptuous palaces." Buildings are likened to "enchanted castles."

Of course, her exuberant descriptions are in direct contrast to the viewpoint of her uncle. Matthew Bramble finds "nothing but disappointment at Bath" which is full of "noise, tumult, and hurry"—a place for "lunatics." His scathing indictment extends even to the architecture, which he describes as the construction of "some Gothic devil." Matthew's violent reactions are tempered by those of his more moderate nephew Jeremy, who finds the chaos "a source of infinite amusement." From multiple points of view, a unified picture emerges of the social customs of Bath.

Young ladies must behave with propriety, and Lydia is not permitted to enter the ladies' coffee-house near the Pump-room. She is too young, her aunt says, to understand the ongoing conversations on such subjects as politics, scandal, and philosophy. But her aunt does allow her to go to the booksellers' shops where, writes Lydia, "we read novels, plays, pamphlets, and news-papers." That activity is followed by a "tour through the milliners and toy-men" before stopping at the pastry-cook's for a "bason of vermicelli."

With food and drink as a focal point of socializing at this fashionable resort, vermicelli soup represents a highlight of the day's activities. It allows for Smollett's witty observations on Bath and signifies an aspect of eighteenth-century English life.

Vermicelli Soup

Smollett mentions other food in other places, often in disparaging terms. The haggis of Scotland is a completely nasty experience: "A mess of minced lights, livers, suet, oat-meal, onions, and pepper, inclosed in a sheep's stomach, had a very sudden effect upon mine." We come back to the pleasantries of vermicelli.

Lydia might have found Ann Peckham's *The Complete English Cook* of 1771 at the booksellers', and it might have enabled her to reproduce the culinary highlight of a day in Bath.

To Make Vermicelli Soup

Take a knuckle of veal, the scrag-end of a neck of mutton, put them into a kettle with as much water as will cover them, a bit of lean ham, and an onion; let it boil; and skim it well, and put in a little mace and salt; when the meat is boiled down, strain it, put it into your clean kettle, and skim the top clean off; then put in two ounces of vermicelli, let it have a boil, and then pour it into your terreen. You may throw in the top of a French roll if you chuse.

Appetizers

and

Lunch

Kedgeree

FAMILY HISTORY (1932) by Vita Sackville-West

"What will you have to eat, my dear? Sausage, egg, porridge, kidneys, haddock, kedgeree?"

Victoria Sackville-West was born in 1892 in Knole, a vast fifteenth-century house in the Kentish countryside. Bestowed by Queen Elizabeth I upon her illustrious ancestor, Sir Thomas Sackville, the great house, with its fairy-tale turrets and towers and its 365 rooms, is now in the care of the National Trust and open to the public.

When she was eighteen, Vita met Harold Nicholson. She married him in 1913 and traveled with him to Constantinople, Persia and other countries that required his presence as a diplomat. He eventually gave up his diplomatic career, and the couple settled happily in Sissinghurst, a ruined romantic castle in Kent with family associations.

They restored the high square sixteenth-century tower and created exquisite gardens as well as literary works. Vita selected the first floor of the octagonal turret as her own library and writing retreat. In this room she worked on the many volumes which confirm her reputation as a significant writer of the twentieth century. Also now open to the public, Sissinghurst reveals the beloved home and the famous gardens of someone with a permanent place in English literature.

The writing career of V. Sackville-West was initiated with a book of poems published in 1917. Years later, she won the coveted Hawthornden Prize for her long poem, *The Land* (1929). Her first novel, *Heritage* (1919), established her reputation as a novelist. In addition to poetry and novels, she wrote travel books and short stories as well as history and biography, producing a total of some fifty volumes. Her three Edwardian novels—*The Edwardians* (1930), *All Passion Spent* (1931), and *Family History* (1932)—are her best known and finest.

Family History presents a satirical view of English society in the early 1920s. It tells the story of Evelyn Jarrold, an attractive widow of nearly forty whose husband has been killed in the war. Like old William Jarrold, the self-made head of the family, Evelyn is herself also from the middle class. She enjoys the luxuries to be had with money and prestige but is caught in the incompatibility of two worlds. She meets a young man, fifteen years younger than herself, and they fall in love. But Miles Vane-Merrick comes from a different realm, and the problems are insurmountable.

He is a Member of Parliament, an author and intellectual, a liberal, and a lover of the arts. In the country, at his Sissinghurst-like ruined castle, their love flourishes. In London, their spheres collide. He is distracted from his love by many activities and ideas, by his commitment to his work. In a Bohemian society (reminiscent of the Bloomsbury circle into which Vita also came), Evelyn is uncomfortable. She remains a product of Victorianism with a belief in appearance and respectability, wanting an idyllic romance and adhering to a world that clashes irrevocably with that of her handsome young man.

An excellent description of the rich and aristocratic country home that is part of the glamorous life style occurs when Evelyn goes down to breakfast one New Year's Day, and Mr. Jarrold offers her something to eat—sausage, egg, porridge, kidneys, haddock, kedgeree:

On the sideboard a row of silver dishes sizzled over little lamps. Cups stood grouped round the teapot and the urn. The long French windows revealed the Surrey view in the bright, cold winter sunshine. Dogs lay stretched in front of the fire. So the Jarrolds sat at breakfast, and William Jarrold felt himself at peace with the world.

Thus is the breakfast scene a reflection of a rich man's country home.

Kedgeree

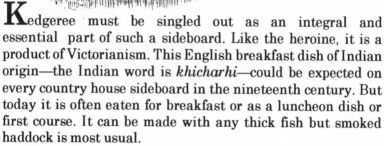

Kedgeree must be singled out as an integral and essential part of such a sideboard. Like the heroine, it is a product of Victorianism. This English breakfast dish of Indian origin—the Indian word is *khicharhi*—could be expected on every country house sideboard in the nineteenth century. But today it is often eaten for breakfast or as a luncheon dish or first course. It can be made with any thick fish but smoked haddock is most usual.

Recipes for this traditional dish continue to appear with various adaptations. A Victorian volume by Matilda Lees Dods, *Handbook of Practical Cookery* (1886), offers this version:

KEDGEREE.—For this will be required one pound of cold boiled fish, two ounces of butter, two eggs, one tea-cupful of rice, one tea-spoonful of salt, one half salt-spoonful of pepper.

Boil the eggs for ten minutes, and the rice for a quarter of an hour. Chop the eggs into irregular pieces, and removing the skin and bone of the fish, melt the butter in a sauce-pan, and add thereto the hard-boiled eggs, the fish, and rice. Stir all now together over the fire until it is very hot, taking care that the mixture does not burn, it being very dry and apt to spoil, since the only moisture in it is the butter.

Add, just before serving, the curry powder, pepper, and salt; and piling it very high in the middle of a hot dish, garnish the preparations with a little fresh parsley, and serve very hot.

Note.—Instead of garnishing this dish with sprigs of parsley, the parsley may be chopped and sprinkled over the top.

Kidney Omelet

HELEN WITH THE HIGH HAND (1908)
by Arnold Bennett

Could it be that there existed women, light and light-handed creatures, creatures of originality and resource, who were capable of producing prodigies like this kidney omelette on the spur of the moment?

Subtitled "An Idyllic Diversion," *Helen With the High Hand* is a slight novel probably written as diversion from the strenuous work Arnold Bennett entailed in producing his great novel, *The Old Wives' Tale.*

The young Helen goes to Bursley to live with her rich and miserly bachelor uncle, James Ollerenshaw. The elderly Potteries business man, one of the wealthiest people in Bursley, has the characteristic Five Towns trait of stinginess, which is reflected in his unfashionable dress and shabby home. He is nevertheless lovable, and Helen sets about to win him over to a richer life style, using her high-handed ways to give the amusing story a predictably happy ending.

She schemes and manipulates and uses her skills at cooking to bring about the final triumph. It is a kidney omelet in particular that does the trick, for that is the dish she cooks for him when she first comes to visit. He watches her chop the kidney, beat the eggs, and stroke the ingredients in a saucepan. Then she magically serves up something that looks to him a little like Yorkshire pudding. He is astonished to be told that it is a kidney omelet, never having tasted, or even seen, anything as fancy as an omelet in his entire life. The taste drives him into raptures. "Had she really made this marvel, this dream, this idyll, this indescribable bliss, out of four common eggs and a veal kidney that Mrs. Butt had dropped on the floor?"

Helen comes to keep house for her uncle, and that requires the expenditure of money. He balks, but the lingering memory of kidney omelet comes to her rescue: "His mouth remembered its first taste of the incomparable kidney omelet. What an ecstasy!" Continuing to impose her own values on Uncle James, she schemes to get him to buy Wilbraham Hall, and she leaves when he adamantly refuses. Kidney omelet again comes to the rescue; he is haunted by memories of it and dreads losing Helen and her cooking. She returns to say a final good-bye to him and cook a farewell supper. But they both know the power of her cooking, and they both win.

Naturally, James Ollerenshaw buys the house. He marries Mrs. Procktor, and Helen marries Andrew Dean. They all live happily ever after—no doubt with his dream come true of "gourmandizing over the meals that Helen alone could cook."

Kidney Omelet

The very title of this 1907 cookery book by E. Roberta Rees—*High-Class and Economical Cookery Recipes*—suggests Helen (High-Class) and her uncle (Economical), while the recipe itself suggests an "incomparable" dish.

Kidney Omelet

2 eggs
½ oz. butter
1 teaspoonful water
pepper and salt

Put the eggs, water, pepper, and salt into a basin and whisk all together till just mixed. Melt the butter in an omelet pan, and when just beginning to get hot pour in the egg mixture. Stir a little for a few seconds till just beginning to set, then allow to cook for another second or two, and while still quite soft and moist on the inside, add a tablespoonful of cooked and chopped kidney, just before folding the omelet over in halves. Turn out on to a hot dish. Serve at once.

Fried Kidney

ULYSSES (1922) by James Joyce

. . . dropped the kidney [into the pan]

James Joyce retells an old fable in *Ulysses* employing episodes
which correspond to those in Homer's *Odyssey*. He follows
Leopold Bloom (Odysseus) through a single day—16 June
1904—in contemporary Dublin, beginning at eight o'clock in
the morning, with Bloom's breakfast, and continuing until
midnight.

The first three episodes concern Stephen Dedalus
(Telemachus), whose day begins at the same time. The same
cloud that hides the sun from Stephen Dedalus when he is in
the tower hides the sun from Leopold Bloom on his walk to the
butcher to buy a kidney for breakfast. Stephen and Bloom
cross paths in the course of the day.

As Bloom prepares breakfast for his wife (Penelope), he
has kidneys on his mind, for, we are told, he ate the inner
organs of animals with gusto. He goes out to the pork butcher
for a kidney, which he cooks while the kettle is boiling for tea.
He arranges things on a tray and brings Molly breakfast in
bed. He converses with her while the kidney is cooking, rushes
downstairs to save it from being irretrievably burned, and

finally eats it with delight. He soaks pieces of bread in the gravy, thoroughly enjoying his repast.

Thus begins a day in the life of Bloom, the wandering Jew, now ready to go out on his quest, to embark on his wanderings on the day known in literary circles as "Bloomsday."

In its rendering of events, *Ulysses* makes the adventures of the ordinary Leopold Bloom a symbolic picture of all experience and all history and makes Dublin a microcosm. Every action has overtones of meaning. It is easy to get caught up in the allusions and suggestions and devices that go beyond the brilliantly realistic surface meaning. (Why does Joyce make his hero an Irish Jew? Does his Jewishness emphasize that he is a rootless alien in the city in which he was born? Although Jewish, why does he fry himself a pork kidney in butter?)

The formidable work is organized around an intricate pattern of motifs which bind the episodes together. Each chapter has a Homeric parallel and each deals with a specific time and theme. Various organs of the body are also associated with each chapter, and the kidney is a prominent symbol of the fourth chapter which starts Bloom's day. Later on in the book, it is used for the Utopian emblem of Bloomusalem, an immense building that is described as having the form of a pork kidney.

The complicated motifs, the labyrinth of words and meanings, the bewildering variety of critical approaches—all contribute to enjoyment of the epic adventures of Leopold Bloom which began, significantly, with his culinary tastes.

Fried Kidney

All that is needed for full understanding is a rendition of Bloom's cooked kidney. The famous Mrs. Beeton's *Book of Household Management* (1861) obliges.

INGREDIENTS. —*Kidneys, butter, pepper and salt to taste.*

Mode.—Cut the kidneys open without quite dividing them, remove the skin, and put a small piece of butter in the frying-pan. When the butter is melted, lay in the kidneys the flat side downwards, and fry them for 7 or 8 minutes, turning them when they are half-done. Serve on a piece of dry toast, season with pepper and salt, and put a small piece of butter in each kidney; pour the gravy from the pan over them, and serve very hot.

Time.—7 or 8 minutes. *Average cost,* 1½ d. each.

Sufficient.—Allow 1 kidney to each person.

Seasonable at any time.

Anchovy Toast

KIPPS, THE STORY OF A SIMPLE SOUL (1905)
by H. G. Wells

*And after Chitterlow had . . . given him some anchovy
paste piping hot on buttered toast, which he preferred
to all other remedies he had encountered, Kipps . . .
prepared to face Mr. Shalford and the reckoning for
this wild, unprecedented night—the first 'night out'
that ever he had taken.*

Young Kipps has been apprenticed as a draper to Mr. Shalford
of Folkstone. While learning the retail trade, he leads a dull
life with no possibility of bettering himself or escaping from
his place in the system. Then he meets Chitterlow. Having
run into Kipps with his bicycle, Chitterlow takes him home
and tries to make amends for causing the mishap. He offers
him whiskey and befriends him. They talk. Kipps, pleased
with the worldly appearance he is making with the would-be
playwright, accepts more whiskey. Fortified by the quantities
of drink in which they indulge, the two become great and
important people and even the shabby room takes on a
glamorous appearance.

Kipps fails to leave on time and is locked out of his
premises above the drapery emporium. He must spend the
night out, with loss of his job as an inevitable consequence.

When he awakens in the morning with a hangover, Chitterlow has the remedy—anchovy on toast—to restore him to sobriety.

Although Kipps has learned about the pleasant, carefree, and oblivious state produced by alcohol, he will never succumb to drunkenness. He agonizes over his dismissal and considers his life irrevocably ruined by Chitterlow but does not resort to the consolation that might be found in a retreat to a state of total intoxication. Kipps knows, knows instinctively, that he has had enough.

At the commercial establishment, he explains to a fellow worker the effect of anchovy toast, taken to rectify his physical condition. He was in bad shape, he admits, before his energizer: "Anchovy on 'ot buttered toast. It's the very best pick-me-up there is." Anchovy toast becomes part of a scene vital to the understanding of the hero's inner traits. The scene shows Kipps as "one of those who always know when they have had enough."

By chance, Chitterlow brings fortune into the life of Kipps when he tells him of a newspaper item he has seen searching for a missing heir. As matters turn out, Kipps is the illegitimate son of a man whose father prevented him from marrying. To make amends, the old man has left a very substantial legacy for his grandson. Now Kipps can abandon the life of drudgery and the bleak future for which he had seemed destined.

He returns home to New Romney to regale his aunt and uncle with the unbelievably good news. At the simple supper table, Kipps convinces them of the authenticity of his claims. He retires after a supper of Welsh rarebit and considers his new life.

Anchovy Toast

That anchovy toast was an accepted method of curbing the ill effects of alcohol in Victorian times, seems to be corroborated by the redoubtable Mrs. Beeton in her *Book of Household Management* of 1861. In a note following her recipe, she warns against adulteration of the anchovy delicacy and adds that anchovy paste spread on toast is eaten by gentlemen at wine parties thus enabling them to "enjoy their port with redoubled gusto."

In any case, anchovy toast goes well with wine and would make a fine hors d'oeuvre.

Anchovy Butter or Paste.

INGREDIENTS.—*2 dozen anchovies, ½ lb. of fresh butter.*

Mode.—Wash the anchovies thoroughly; bone and dry them, and pound them in a mortar to a paste. Mix the butter gradually with them, and rub the whole through a sieve. Put it by in small pots for use, and carefully exclude the air with a bladder, as it soon changes the colour of anchovies, besides spoiling them.

Average cost for this quantity, 2 s.

Anchovy Toast.

INGREDIENTS.—Toast 2 or 3 slices of bread, or, if wanted very savoury, fry them in clarified butter, and spread on them the paste. Made mustard, or a few grains of cayenne, may be added to the paste before laying it on the toast.

Welsh Rarebit

See: KIPPS (1905) by H. G. Wells, page 45.

He had also eaten two Welsh rarebits–an unusual supper.

It is over a supper of Welsh rarebit that Kipps takes into account the full significance of his legacy. A recipe for Welsh rarebit, with its alternative spelling, is taken from *Warne's Model Cookery and Housekeeping Book* of 1869 by Mary Jewry.

Welsh Rabbit

Time, ten minutes

Half a pound of cheese; three tablespoonfuls of ale; a thin slice of toast.

Grate the cheese fine, put to it the ale, and work it in a small saucepan over a slow fire till it is melted. Spread it on toast, and send it up boiling hot.

Macaroni Cheese

POMP AND CIRCUMSTANCE (1960) by Noël Coward

"As a matter of fact I rather like macaroni cheese."

Noël Coward, a complete man of the theatre, achieved universal fame early in life as a playwright, actor, director, and composer. His plays range from serious drama to farce and include revues and musical comedies. A man of tremendous variety and talent, he also wrote screenplays, autobiography, and fiction. His short stories were collected in five volumes, and a novel, *Pomp and Circumstance,* was published in 1960, when he was sixty. A popular writer with a prolific and varied output, he was knighted in 1969 and awarded a Doctorate of Letters from the University of Sussex in 1972.

Noël Coward loved country house living. He felt very much at ease with the upper classes and their comfortable life style and used that setting frequently in his writing. In *Pomp and Circumstance,* his lovely "English country house" is located on the island of Samola, where the Queen is about to pay a visit.

In one of the many incidents which make up the plot of this comic novel, the narrator is having lunch at Government House. Her friend and hostess, Sandra (Lady Alexandra), suddenly complains about the food which, she says, would be more suited to a shabby hotel in the Cromwell Road; the cook will simply have to be dismissed. But Sandra's husband, the governor of the island, looks up from his plate of macaroni cheese and offers a mild objection: "It tastes all right to me." Fortunately, he rather likes macaroni cheese.

The conversation centers on Thelma the cook, who must go, Sandra insists. Although Sandra has plied her with fancy cookbooks and recipes taken from American magazines, "all we get is this everlasting macaroni cheese." She rings her little silver bell and requests that cold ham or tongue and salad be brought. But the ham turns out to be less palatable than the macaroni.

All of the fuss and palaver about food leads to discussion of luncheon arrangements for the Queen and inevitable complications; the forthcoming visit of the Queen and Prince Philip to this island is at the core of the story. Coward produces comic scenes filled with witty dialogue in his inimitable style. Without undue concern for whether the plot is progressing steadily, he throws barbs at such topics as English class distinctions, current fashionable literature, and pretentious American women's journals.

Macaroni Cheese

Instead of cutting recipes with impossibly high standards from glossy magazines, Lady Alexandra ought to have given the cook a recipe from *A Handbook of Cookery* (1923) compiled by Jessie Conrad. The volume might have appealed to her snobbish sense by using the French translation, *Macaroni au Gratin*. It might also have allowed her to feed her penchant for name dropping since Jessie Conrad was the wife of the well-known author, Joseph Conrad. Lady Alexandra might have been pleased to know that although macaroni itself came from medieval Italy, the word probably emanates from the Greek *makaria*, meaning barley-broth. Moreover, macaroni cheese appears regularly in English cook books of the eighteenth century. Armed with these facts of culinary history and tradition, perhaps she could comfortably have served macaroni cheese even at the Queen's luncheon.

Macaroni au Gratin

Have ready three pints of freshly boiling water with a good pinch of salt in a saucepan for about half a pound of straight macaroni which must be broken up to a convenient size. Macaroni should always be put straight into boiling water. Boil gently for forty minutes to an hour but be careful not to let it boil over, adding boiling water from time to time as the macaroni swells. Strain the water off with the lid, and stir into the saucepan a breakfast-cupful of grated Gruyère cheese (a little grated Parmesan cheese is a great improvement added to the Gruyère). Turn into a stone dish. Dust a little more cheese over the top, put a piece of butter about the size of two good-sized walnuts and place in a quick oven to brown slightly.

Potato Scones

THE FIVE RED HERRINGS (1931) by Dorothy L. Sayers

He... while voraciously filling himself up with potato-scones and ginger-cake, made out a rough list of possible suspects.

The five red herrings of the title refer, not to a Scottish gourmet delight, but to a list of murder suspects drawn up by Lord Peter Wimsey. On one of his periodic visits to Galloway, in the fishing and artistic center of Kirkcudbright, Lord Peter Wimsey applies his own artistic flair and skill for unraveling murder mysteries.

The routine of the fishing and painting community is shattered when a belligerent and offensive painter, generally disliked by the residents of the area, is found dead. Told of the discovery of the body, Wimsey leaves immediately to view the scene of the accident. The painter had apparently fallen from the cliff when he stood back from the canvas to assess his work. Wimsey surveys the body and the setting, taking in even the minutest details, before returning to his hotel in Kirkudbright.

Wimsey knows that it is a clear case of murder. He also knows that it is time for tea. At the Anwoth Hotel, he partakes of potato scones while pondering the various aspects of the case. The puzzle pieces begin to be pieced together over the devouring of the scones. Other foods and other meals may be mentioned in other parts of the novel, but it is over a tea featuring potato scones that the plot sets off on its inexorable course towards solution of the mystery.

It is of great significance that the savory Scottish speciality is particularly satisfying also to the author. In the Foreword to her book, Dorothy Sayers thanks the landlord of the hotel for his help and adds, "We shall come back next summer to eat some more potato-scones at the Anwoth."

 # Potato Scones

A recipe from *The Scots Kitchen* (1929) by Florence Marian McNeill could obviate the author's need to return to Scotland. But that might leave a murder unsolved—or a novel unwritten.

Cooked Potatoes, flour, salt, sweet milk

Mash half a pound of boiled potatoes and add, if necessary, a pinch of salt. Knead in as much flour as it will take up (about two ounces) and add about half a gill of sweet milk or enough to make a very stiff dough. Roll out very thiny on a floured board. Cut into rounds and prick with a fork. Bake on a hot girdle for about five minutes, turning when half cooked. When baked, butter the scones, roll up, and serve very hot.

UPDATE: The measurement "about half a gill" may be rendered as "about two fluid ounces."

Ravioli

REBECCA (1938) by Daphne du Maurier

*I could tell from the way the sauce ran down her chin
that her dish of ravioli pleased her.*

"Last night I dreamt I went to Manderley again." With that
suspenseful opening line of *Rebecca*, begins the story of
Manderley and its mistress, the second Mrs. de Winter. But
the heroine's rise to that position started many years earlier
when she was the shy, insecure, and impecunious companion
to the wealthy, snobby Mrs. Van Hopper.

On one "unforgettable afternoon," she sits at luncheon in a
Monte Carlo hotel dining room watching Mrs. Hopper's "fat
bejewelled fingers questing a plate heaped high with ravioli."
She herself, her inferior status apparent to all, is given an
unappetizing plate of leftover ham and tongue, which she is
too timid to refuse. When a new arrival sits down at a nearby
table, Mrs. Van Hopper puts down her fork in order to
impolitely peer at him with her lorgnette; she recognizes Max
de Winter, the owner of Manderley and its scandalous secrets.

Eager for gossip and social opportunity, Mrs. Van Hopper
arranges to introduce herself to him, and soon the three join
for coffee in the lounge. Mr. de Winter is kind to the young,
ill-treated companion and takes her usual hard chair, thereby
forcing her to seat herself on the comfortable sofa. He makes

unkind barbs at the callous and interfering Mrs. Van Hopper, who does not even understand the insults she well deserves.

The friendship which develops between the two younger people broadens into romance. Circumstances quickly lead to marriage and to a future full of anxiety over the mysterious Rebecca. As the plot thickens, it is easy to forget the dish of ravioli over which the master of Manderley is first recognized.

Ravioli

The dish that sets off meetings and events might have come from the pages of *Senn's Century Cook Book* (1923) in which Charles Herman Senn offers a recipe for Raviolis à l'Italienne.

½ lb. nouille paste, salt and pepper, about 6 oz. fish or liver farce, 1½ gills good tomato sauce, 2 oz. Parmesan cheese, and ½ oz. butter.

Prepare the paste as in "Nouilles au Gratin." Roll it out as thinly as possible, stamp out some rounds about the size of a half-crown piece, put about a teaspoonful of farce (liver or fish forcemeat richly seasoned and mixed with Parmesan) on the center of a round, wet the edges of the paste, and cover with another round of paste, press the edges well together, drop these into fast-boiling and slightly salted water, boil for about 15 or 20 minutes, and drain on a sieve. Dress them on a dish in layers with tomato sauce and grated Parmesan cheese between the layers. Sauce over well with tomato sauce, sprinkle over with cheese, and place a few tiny bits of fresh butter here and there. Set the dish in a brisk oven for 10 minutes, and serve quickly.

Nouilles au Gratin.—Prepare a stiff but smoothly kneaded paste with ½ lb. flour, ½ oz. butter, 3 yolks of eggs, and a pinch of salt. Allow the paste to stand for at least 1 hour, roll out as thinly as possible.

UPDATE: A half-crown piece is 1 ¼ inches in diameter.
A gill is equal to 4 fluid ounces.

Rissoles

THE DAUGHTER OF TIME (1951) by Josephine Tey

"Both rissoles all eaten up to the last crumb!"

The Daughter of Time is destined to remain one of the most remarkable and unorthodox detective novels ever written, for in it Josephine Tey has created an engaging mystery over King Richard the Third.

Alan Grant, a Scotland Yard detective, is confined to a hospital bed while recuperating from the effects of a recent accident. Having suffered the indignity of falling through a trap-door while chasing a criminal, Grant now suffers the effects of boredom. Everything—books, puzzles, games—he finds tedious. Relief is limited to the perverse pleasures found in staring at the ceiling and in relentless teasing of his nurses, referred to as The Midget and The Amazon.

The situation changes drastically when a visitor arrives with an envelope full of pictures for his amusement and suggests that the portraits will appeal to his passion for studying faces. He had in the past exhibited shrewd ability to discern the personality and nature of an individual merely from scrutiny of the face. He now finds himself intrigued with one portrait in particular, which he analyzes as that of a man full of worry and responsibility and illness. When he learns that it is the face of Richard the Third, the scene is set for an unusual kind of mystery.

Was Richard the Third a villain? Did he actually kill his two nephews in the tower? Could that suffering face of the photograph possibly belong to a murderer? Or is he a maligned king who has been subjected to undeserved infamy, partly due to Shakespeare's inaccurate but unforgettable characterization of a deformed and evil king? Ought Richard the Third to be finally exonerated from the accusation of murder?

With consummate skill, the author allows Grant to delve into history and into the sources to uncover facts concerning the hapless king. Suspense mounts.

Indeed, as the mystery increases, we can sympathize with the bed-ridden detective who is so involved in the baffling details of the case that he eats his supper mechanically, "without for one moment being conscious either of its taste or its nature." To the extreme pleasure of The Amazon, he has completely devoured his meal of rissoles.

Rissoles

It is a pity that the detective missed the flavor, as Sir Francis Colchester-Wemyss would confirm. In *The Pleasures of the Table* of 1931, he extols the possibility of using leftovers to create, not a mediocre gallimaufry, but a very pleasant dish of rissoles.

Remove all gristle and hard skin from three or four ounces of leftover cold mutton, chop the meat and pound it; season with pepper and salt, make a roux with flour and butter, add a little stock if available, or failing that a few spoonfuls of milk. Mix the pounded meat with the sauce, working it till thoroughly incorporated. Make the mixture into rissoles, and leave, if possible, for 3 or 4 hours before cooking. Roll in egg and bread crumbs and fry in deep fat in a basket.

The result is a dainty little dish fit to put before any good judge, which certainly costs no more than the usual dreadful ball of meat.

It is not of course necessary to use only one sort of meat, any scraps—beef, mutton, ham, chicken—go quite well together, and fish can be used instead of meat.

Faggots

NEW GRUB STREET (1891) by George Gissing

*"Excellent faggots they have there, too. I'll give you a
supper of them some night before you go."*

George Gissing died in 1903 at the age of forty-six without
having achieved the wide public recognition that many
contemporary critics feel he fully deserved. Nevertheless,
periodic revivals of interest in Gissing continue to this day.
New Grub Street, his ninth of twenty-two novels, is his most
popular and enduring work.

The extreme poverty which George Gissing himself
experienced is reflected in many of his novels. *New Grub
Street* depicts the struggles and intrigues of the literary world
of his day and the destructive effect of poverty on artistic
creation. The mercenary Jasper Milvain is a clever but
superficial writer of reviews who accepts the commercial
conditions of success. He is contrasted with literary idealists
such as Edwin Reardon, an author who is hindered by poverty
and by an unsympathetic, ambitious wife. Harold Biffen is an
earnest writer of novels so realistic that he wants them to
reproduce life "verbatim, without one single impertinent
suggestion of any point of view save that of honest reporting."

In the morally shabby world, the poor who are governed
by artistic temperament and integrity are doomed to failure,

while the unscrupulous, self-aggrandizing manipulators inherit the literary world. The novel follows the increasing misfortunes of Reardon and Biffen. But before disaster strikes, the two men are seen together in happier, though impoverished, times.

Reardon calls on his friend Biffen at his lodgings, a small and dreary third-floor garret where they share literary ideas. Reardon tells him of his plans to leave the city for a quiet country place in which to recuperate and write. Before going out together to visit a friend, Biffen has a hungry desire for a mouthful to eat. Desperately poor, he finds nourishment in bread and dripping with salt and pepper—economical fare for an impecunious person—and endows his meal with dignity by using a knife and fork. Then Biffen, thinking of faggots with enthusiasm, promises a supper of excellent faggots the night before Reardon is to leave London. They visit a friend. They part, but not before Biffen renews the invitation to a garret supper and receives a positive response.

The fascinating picture of the London literary world of the 1880s has been called a unique study of the business aspects of literature. Only Jasper Milvain succeeds because he recognizes that he is no genius and accepts literature as a trade, doing what he feels is appropriate to the world as he sees it, a commercial world in which art cannot transcend materialism. He is calculating and determined to succeed. Reardon preserves his integrity and experiences a nervous breakdown when he fails to earn a living with his pen; he alienates his wife who cannot abide poverty or the agonies of failure. Biffen, a connoisseur of bread and dripping, tries to get on by taking pupils for sixpence a session while he cheerfully writes his realistic but unprofitable novel. It is a powerful presentation of grim human truth.

Faggots

Bread and dripping is hardly the stuff that gourmet food is made of; and faggots, which can be quite tasty and are highly regarded as pub food, are included here primarily for the sake of their interest. Traditionally shaped into small domed portions, faggots are also sometimes known as savory ducks, particularly in the north of England. They are made from the liver, heart, sweetbread, and offal of the pig, seasoned with herbs, and with the addition of oatmeal or breadcrumbs. Once again, Mrs. Beeton supplies the recipe.

INGREDIENTS.—*1 ½ lbs. of pig's liver, ½ a lb. of fat pork, 3 eggs, I large onion, breadcrumbs, pig's caul, nutmeg, sage, thyme, basil, salt, pepper.*

Method.—Chop the liver and onion rather finely and cut the pork into small dice. Put all together in a stewpan, add salt, pepper, sage, thyme, and basil to taste, cover closely, and cook slowly for about ½ an hour, but it must not be allowed to brown. Drain off the fat, let the preparation cool slightly, then beat and add the eggs, nutmeg to taste, and sufficient breadcrumbs to form a fairly stiff mixture. Mix thoroughly, then form into squares and enclose each one in a piece of caul. Place them in a baking-tin, add a little good gravy and bake until nicely browned. Serve with a good gravy. If preferred the mixture may be pressed into a well-greased baking-tin, covered with caul, and cut into squares when cooked.

Sweetbread

MOLL FLANDERS (1722) by Daniel Defoe

The maid had orders to make me some chocolate in the morning before she came away, and at noon she brought me the sweetbread of a breast of veal, whole.

Moll Flanders was perhaps the first novel ever to consider the misfortunes of unprotected women with sympathy and intelligence. Defoe held unusually liberal ideas for his time about the status of women, believing that they were at a distinct disadvantage legally and economically. His autobiographical narrative, which sees life through the eyes of a woman, was a huge success when it was first published in 1722 and is still highly regarded.

Born in Newgate Prison, and left with no resources, Moll Flanders is on a continuous quest for security. The circumstances of her early life, together with her beauty and intelligence, drive her to seek escape from a life of drudgery. But Moll wants more than mere security. She acquires a desperate desire for a life of gentility, which she has learned about from the Colchester household into which she had been taken after being abandoned as an infant. It is a hopeless aspiration, for Moll lacks the background and the money necessary for marriage to a gentleman.

Moll has ambition, however, as well as a large capacity for adapting to circumstances, and she goes through an amazing series of adventures and catastrophes. The title page tells it all: "The Fortunes and Misfortunes of the Famous Moll Flanders, &c. Who was Born in Newgate, and during a Life of continu'd Variety for Threescore Years, besides her Childhood, was Twelve Year a Whore, five times a Wife (whereof once to her own Brother) Twelve Year a Thief, Eight Year a Transported Felon in Virginia, at last grew Rich, liv'd Honest, and died a Penitent. Written from her own Memorandums."

Like Robinson Crusoe, Defoe's other famous hero, Moll is full of vitality and determination to survive. She knows that a woman must use her wits and even deception if necessary to secure a good husband. She is out to obtain for herself the highest economic and social rewards possible, and she derives pleasure out of life.

Married to a man she truly loves, Moll finds that she must nevertheless leave her dashing Lancashire husband, for they are mutually deceived. Each has put on a show of wealth, and each has mistakenly believed that the other was rich. They part. Her Lancashire highwayman husband is to reappear towards the end of the story, amidst a resurgence of love, when both are imprisoned in Newgate and transported to Virginia, where together they prosper. But immediate economic necessity forces her to turn to a banker she had previously met and kept in abeyance, who is now free to marry her and provide the solid comforts she requires.

However, before Moll can be united with the banker, one obstacle to the marriage must be settled. Moll is expecting a child. She opts to give birth to the inconvenient child of her Lancashire husband, rather than undergo an abortion, and arranges to be secretly cared for by a midwife who manages a lying-in home. Afterwards, she muses over the fate of the infant.

65

Moll has little alternative if she is to extricate herself from her predicament. Assured that her son will not be abused if she parts with him, she accepts the argument that nurses have stronger motives for giving better care than mothers; after all, their professional reputations are at stake. The argument may seem specious and Moll may seem callous, but she has considered her son's welfare and she is moved: "It touch'd my heart so forcibly to think of parting entirely with the child." But part with him she does, for circumstances have forced her to become obsessed with security. The child would have been an impossible encumbrance and must be farmed out to a foster mother.

It is her craving for the fine accouterments of a lady that is illustrated when she dines on a sweetbread while awaiting the birth of her child. Moll knows how to get good service, and she fully appreciates the sweetbread of a breast of veal which has been brought to her while she is receiving maternity care. She is "mightily well pleas'd" and recovers quickly from her state of dejection. She is not merely staving off hunger but is thoroughly enjoying the good food and treatment she receives. It suits her scheme for a life of luxuries, well above mere subsistence level.

After years of hard work and good fortune abroad, Moll is able to return to England with wealth and respectability. She lives a life of repentance and writes a book of memoirs. Her confessions assuage her guilt and allow her to savor her past, as once she savored sweetbread. In telling her story, Moll often suppresses feelings, justifies certain deeds, or conceals particular facts. She never even reveals her real name. But her greatest error of omission is in not telling how her meal of sweetbread was prepared. Fortunately, that lapse may be corrected.

Sweetbread

Most recipes of the day call for cutting up or chopping the sweetbread. Moll's account makes the special point that it was served whole. A recipe from John Murrell's *A New Book of Cookerie* (new when it was written in 1617) will suffice as an illustration of what she might have eaten. Note the charming use of archaic words and spellings; a manchet is a small loaf of fine white bread.

A made dish of a Sweet-bread

Boyle or roast your Sweet-bread, and put into it a few parboyled Currans, a minst Date, the yolkes of two new-laid Egges, a peece of a Manchet grated fine. Season it with a little Pepper, Salt, Nutmeg, and Sugar, wring in the juyce of an Orenge or Lemmon, & put it betweene two sheets of puft-paste, or any other good paste: and eyther bake it, or frye it, whether you please.

Mutton Pasty

LORNA DOONE (1869) by R. D. Blackmore

*Hot mutton pasty was a thing I had often heard of from
very wealthy boys and men, who made a dessert of
dinner; and to hear them talk of it made my lips smack,
and my ribs come inwards. . . . and the smell of it was
enough to make an empty man thank God for the room
there was inside him. Fifty years have passed me
quicker than the taste of that gravy.*

Richard Doddridge Blackmore, born in 1825, spent unhappy
years at Blundell's School at Tiverton in Devon which he
entered at the age of twelve. Abused and maltreated by other
boys, he showed no bitterness when he later wrote about his
old school in *Lorna Doone*.

After Oxford, Blackmore abandoned a career in law for
the sake of his health. Fortunately, a bequest from his uncle
enabled him to indulge in his passion for horticulture. He
purchased an eleven-acre estate in Teddington, where he
settled for the rest of his life as a market gardener and writer.
He spent mornings planting, pruning and cultivating fruit,
taking special pride in his peaches. Afterwards, in his upstairs
study, he produced literary fruit. His work as a farmer did not
yield financial success, but his literary efforts yielded a lucra-
tive crop, *Lorna Doone* in particular. As the century drew to a
close, so did his life. Old and frail, he died on 20 January 1900.

Altogether, Blackmore produced twenty-one books, including a book of short stories and seven volumes of poetry. The third of his fourteen novels is the single volume by which he is still remembered. *Lorna Doone*, a romance set in realistic Exmoor soil in the seventeenth century, was an extraordinarily successful best seller in its time and has remained a favorite.

John Ridd narrates the story when he is well along in years. Also the main character, he begins with events at his school in Tiverton. Fighting has been an integral part of school life, and the hero is victorious in a fight which takes place just as John Fry has arrived, having been sent to fetch the young lad home. Taken out of school early, just before the holidays have begun, young John suspects that something is amiss.

On the way home, they stop at a hostel in Dulverton to dine on "the rarest and choicest victuals that ever I did taste." As John Ridd looks back over the past, he recalls the mutton pasty in the most superlative terms: "Even now, at my time of life, to think of it gives me appetite, as once and awhile to think of my first love makes me love all goodness." Well may he remember the taste in childhood of that delicacy, for it marks the end of his youth. Home at last, he learns that his father has been killed by the clan of Doone, a marauding band of robbers and murderers from a neighboring valley. Nothing can ever be the same again for John Ridd; innocence and security are lost. He must seek revenge for his father's murder.

The narration takes up John's search for vengeance and the complications which ensue because of his love for Lorna Doone. He rescues Lorna from the villains, but marriage is not possible since her putative father is responsible for the murder of John's father. When it is revealed that she is really the daughter of a Scottish nobleman, stolen as a child by the Doones, it remains only for the disparity in their social positions to be resolved. When John renders valuable service to the king and to Lorna's guardian and is rewarded with a knighthood, a happy ending is in store for the young lovers.

Among so many sensational and melodramatic events, the eating of a mutton pasty figures as an action indelibly impressed on the narrator, who finds it worth singling out decades later when he is relating his story. Such a mutton pasty must be very worthy indeed.

Mutton Pasty

Cornish pasties, with their vast varieties of fillings, are held in the hand and eaten without utensils as suitable snacks or light collations. Mrs. Martha Bradley's recipe, however, more like a traditional English mutton pie, more accurately duplicates the delicacy described and relished by the hero of *Lorna Doone*.

Her recipe, which appeared in about 1770 in *The British Housewife*, attempts to imitate a venison taste and seems to apologize for being mere mutton. No doubt, John Ridd's judgment would brook no defense.

A Mutton Pasty.

This is to be made of Mutton in the same Manner as the other is of Venison, and the Mutton is to be managed in a particular Way to give it something of a Venison Flavour.

Chuse a fine large fat Loin of Mutton, hang it four Days, or longer if it will keep, in a cool Place, then take out the Bones, leaving the Meat as whole as possible; mix together a Pint of red Wine and a Pint of Vinegar, put them in a deep earthen Pan, put the Mutton into it, and let it lie four and twenty Hours, turning it two or three times; when it is taken out season it well with Pepper and Salt, put it into a good Crust, and let it be well baked; when it comes home open the Lid, and pour in three quarters of a Pint of rich Gravy, and send it up.

Some pretend this may be taken for a Venison Pasty, and others say it is full as good as Venison; neither is true, but it is a very good Dish.

71

Game Pie

THE DUKE'S CHILDREN (1880) by Anthony Trollope

*In his misery he had recourse to game-pie and a pint of
champagne for his lunch.*

The Duke's Children is the final book of Trollope's famous
Palliser series, which takes its name from the most important
recurrent character of the six novels. Plantagenet Palliser,
later Duke of Omnium, is here presented as a widower with
the responsibility of managing his three grown children, two
sons and a daughter. In the novel which completes the sequence, the emphasis shifts away from the political side of the
Duke's life and concentrates almost entirely on domestic life.

The aristocratic father undergoes struggles with the
younger generation. Each of his children contributes to his
sorrow and grief. He is grieved when Gerald, his younger son,
is expelled from Cambridge for a breach of conduct. He is
disturbed by the imprudent matrimonial choice made by his
daughter, Lady Mary Palliser, who loves a young man who
is neither rich nor noble. He is shocked and disappointed
when his elder son and heir, Lord Silverbridge, abandons the
family political tradition and becomes a Conservative rather
than a Liberal. Moreover, Lord Silverbridge has fallen in love
with an American, Isabel Boncassen, in opposition to his
father's preference for Lady Mabel Grex as a suitable
marriage partner for his son.

The Duke is caught in the throes of a changing society. He loves his children but is loyal to the code by which he has lived his own life. He has his principles, but he must also move forward. A new generation of Pallisers will emerge, and the Duke must learn to live in the new world as best he can. He gives way in the end and thereby achieves greater wisdom and self-knowledge. Lady Mary is allowed to marry her young Cornishman. Silverbridge is united with Boncassen.

As the plot unfolds, Silverbridge, feeling distressed and rebuffed by events, needs to fortify himself with game-pie and champagne. The reason for his misery is that he has called on Isabel Boncassen only to be told that she was not at home. And he had sent a note stating the time of his arrival! Did she mean to slight him? Did she no longer care for him? Did her father disapprove of a match with an English aristocrat?

After lunch, Silverbridge feels a little better. He returns to her home, and Isabel is there to greet him. The reason for her absence earlier is simply explained by the fact that she had never received his letter. In his haste, Silverbridge had mis-addressed the envelope. Now the young couple reach an agreement. It only remains for the Duke to consent to the marriage and accept the lovely young lady as his daughter.

Game Pie

A careful reading will disclose that Silverbridge need not have resorted to game pie for palliation of his misery. Indeed, he need not have been miserable at all had he addressed the letter correctly in the first place. That truism, applied to the eating of game pie, may seem complicated, but it is not as complicated as the preparation of game pie, as a careful reading of Eliza Acton's recipe in *Modern Cookery* (1845) will disclose. Reproduced in its entirety, the recipe is meant to be a revelation rather than an expectation that instructions will be carried out.

A Good Common English Game Pie

Raise the flesh entire from the upper side of the best end of a well-kept neck of venison, trim it to the length of the dish in which the pie is to be served, and rub it with a mixture of salt, cayenne, pounded mace, and nutmeg. Cut down into joints a fine young hare which has hung from eight to fourteen days, bone the back and thighs, and fill them with forcemeat No. 1, but put into it a double portion of butter, and a small quantity of minced eschalots, should their flavour be liked, and the raw liver of the hare, chopped small. Line the dish with a rich short crust, lay the venison in the centre, and the hare closely round and on it; fill the vacant spaces with more forcemeat, add a few spoonsful of well-jellied gravy, fasten on the cover securely, ornament it or not, at pleasure, and bake the pie two hours in a well heated oven. The remnants and bones of the hare and venison may be stewed down into a small quantity of excellent soup, or with a less proportion of water into an admirable gravy, part of which, after having been cleared from fat, may be poured into the pie. The jelly, added to its contents at first, can be made, when no such stock is at hand, of a couple of pounds of shin of beef, boiled down

in a quart of water, which must be reduced quite half, and seasoned only with a good slice of lean ham, a few pepper-corns, seven or eight cloves, a blade of mace, and a little salt. One pound and a half of flour will be sufficient for the crust; this, when it is so preferred, may be laid round the sides of the dish, instead of entirely over it. The prime joints of a second hare may be substituted for the venison when it can be more conveniently procured.
Baked 2 hours.

Obs.—These same ingredients will make an excellent raised pie, if the venison be divided and intermixed with the hare; the whole should be highly seasoned, and all the cavities filled with the forcemeat No. 1. The top, before the paste is laid over, should be covered with slices of fat bacon, or with plenty of butter, to prevent the surface of the meat from becoming hard. No liquid is to be put into the pie until after it is baked, if at all. It will require from half to a full hour more of the oven than if baked in a dish.

Forcemeat No. 1:
Good Common Forcemeat for Roast Veal, Turkeys, Etc.
Grate very lightly into exceedingly fine crumbs, four ounces of the inside of a stale loaf, and mix thoroughly with it, a quarter-ounce of lemon-rind pared as thin as possible, and minced extremely small; the same quantity of savoury herbs, of which two-thirds should be parsley, and one-third thyme,— likewise finely minced, a little grated nutmeg, a half-teaspoonful of salt, and as much common pepper or cayenne as will season the forcemeat sufficiently. Break into these, two ounces of good butter in very small bits, add the unbeaten yolk of one egg, and with the fingers work the whole well together until it is smoothly mixed. It is usual to chop the lemon-rind, but we prefer it lightly grated on a fine grater. It should always be fresh for the purpose, or it will be likely to impart a very unpleasant flavour to the forcemeat. Half the rind of a moderate-sized lemon will be sufficient for this quantity; which for a large turkey must be increased one-half.

75

Bread-crumbs, 4 ozs.; lemon-rind, ¼ oz. (or grated rind of ½ lemon); mixed savoury herbs, minced, ¼ oz.; salt, ½ teaspoonful; pepper, ¼ to 1/3 of teaspoonful; butter, 2 ozs.; yolk I egg.

Obs.—This, to our taste, is a much nicer and more delicate forcemeat than that which is made with chopped suet, and we would recommend it for trial in preference. Any variety of herb or spice may be used to give it flavour, and a little minced onion or eschalot can be added to it also; but these last do not appear to us suited to the meats for which the forcemeat is more particularly intended. Half an ounce of the butter may be omitted on ordinary occasions; and a portion of marjoram or of sweet basil may take the place of part of the thyme and parsley when preferred to them.

Forcemeat No. 18:
Forcemeat for Raised and Other Cold Pies
The very finest sausage-meat, highly seasoned, and made with an equal proportion of fat and lean, is an exceedingly good forcemeat for veal, chicken, rabbit, and some few other pies; savoury herbs minced small, may be added to heighten its flavour, if it be intended for immediate eating; but it will not then remain good quite so long, unless they should have been previously dried. To prevent its being too dry, two or three spoonsful of cold water should be mixed with it before it is put into the pie. One pound of lean veal to one and a quarter of the pork-fat is sometimes used, and smoothly pounded with a high seasoning of spices, herbs, and eschalots, or garlic, but we cannot recommend the introduction of these last into pies unless they are especially ordered; mushrooms may be mixed with any kind of forcemeat with far better effect. Equal parts of veal and fat bacon, will also make a good forcemeat for pies, chopped finely, and well-spiced.

Sausage-meat, well seasoned. Or: veal, I lb.; pork-fat, 1½ lb.; salt, I oz.; pepper, ¼ to ½ oz.; fine herb, spice, etc., as in forcemeat No. I, or sausage meat. Or: veal and bacon, equal weight, seasoned in the same way.

Fish

and

Seafood

Lobster Newburg

BRIDESHEAD REVISITED (1945) by Evelyn Waugh

When the eggs were gone and we were eating the lobster Newburg, the last guest arrived.

Brideshead Revisited, considered by many to be Evelyn Waugh's best novel, has been made even more popular by the television realization. It is a complex story in which the hero, now an infantry captain, returns by coincidence to the great country house known as Brideshead. Charles Ryder recalls his previous association with the house and family in the old days before the war. Using a flashback technique, he relates the events of his life as it became intertwined with the Flyte family.

It all begins at Oxford, where Charles Ryder meets and becomes the friend of Sebastian Flyte, younger son of the Marquis of Marchmain of Brideshead. Charles lives in ground-floor rooms in the front quadrangle of an Oxford college. One evening, an inebriated Sebastian appears at the window and is sick, through the open window, into the narrator's room. He sends a note of apology the following morning, together with a luncheon invitation. Ryder goes, but not without some trepidation.

He feels insecure and apprehensive as he enters alien territory. Nevertheless, he is filled with curiosity at the prospect of opening a door to an unknown world, to "an enchanted garden."

The sense of anticipation is fully satisfied. The luncheon party marks the narrator's entry into the world of Sebastian Flyte and the start of an intimate friendship. It is at the luncheon party, over lobster Newburg, that Charles Ryder enjoys the experience which was to be, as he later summarizes, "the beginning of a new epoch in my life."

Ryder's friendship with Sebastian, the most vivid and sympathetic character of the novel, is the main interest of Book One. As the section ends, Ryder, who has started out with middle-class tastes, goes from a state of innocence to one of awareness with touches of cynicism. By the time the novel ends, he has completely lost the world of "nursery freshness."

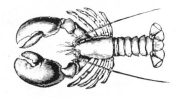 # Lobster Newburg

It is to be noted with prandial pride that all the events and relationships have had their inception at a luncheon featuring lobster Newburg. Here, from *The Pleasures of the Table* (1931) by Sir Francis Colchester-Wemyss, is the recipe that promises to start great friendships:

Take all the meat of a cooked lobster, and cook it in a fireproof casserole with sherry and a fish or fowl stock or broth, half and half, using barely enough to cover the lobster packed close on the bottom. When the liquid has practically all been absorbed, pour on the lobster two yolks of eggs mixed with cream, salt and pepper; adjust with a fork, so that the sauce is distributed evenly among and on the pieces of lobster, and cook watching very carefully till it just sets and serve immediately.

Fish Pie

HOWARDS END (1910) by E. M. Forster

*"Fish pie! Fancy coming for fish pie to Simpson's. It's
not a bit the thing to go for here."*

This extremely complicated fourth novel of E. M. Forster tries
to present the conflict between the outer life and the inner life,
between the Wilcoxes and the Schlegels.

Margaret and Helen Schlegel meet the Wilcoxes in
Germany, and the lives of the two familes become intertwined. Margaret and Mrs. Wilcox achieve a special kind of
understanding and rapport. They agree on conditions of life
which can most easily be met in the country, in a place like
Howards End.

Margaret values the inner life and appreciates Howards
End, the Hertfordshire house of the Wilcoxes, and all that it
stands for—peace, harmony, and stability. It is presented in
total contrast to London, which is in a constant state of flux
and filled with people living harried and anonymous lives. At
Howards End, Margaret is able to forget the fragmented life
of London and its population rushing about, disconnected.
The country landscape symbolizes the steadiness of a life for
centuries rooted in the soil, and Margaret connects its beauty
with a love for England.

The friendship between the families continues to develop after Mrs. Wilcox dies. Her daughter, Evie Wilcox, invites Margaret to Simpson's restaurant in the Strand. Margaret accepts with some misgivings for she does not greatly care about Evie and has no wish to meet Evie's fiancé. At Simpson's, Evie greets her with the news that her father is expected to join the party. Margaret is pleased, and Mr. Wilcox soon dispels her feeling of isolation.

Margaret, who has never before been to Simpson's, is hungry and orders fish pie, only to be told by Mr. Wilcox that saddle of mutton is the correct thing to order in this old English place. She goes along with his suggestion. When they finish lunch, we are told that "he and she were advancing out of their respective families towards a more intimate acquaintance" and that they "were really beginning to know each other."

Henry Wilcox comes to see in Margaret some of the qualities of his late wife. Margaret's respect and love for Henry Wilcox grow, and they eventually marry. The plot grows too, and the unraveling of the plot sounds like modern soap opera. But the characters are alive, and the spirit of Ruth Wilcox dominates. It was she who had seen that Margaret Schlegel would make a worthy successor to her ancestral home, Howards End.

Fish Pie

After Henry and Margaret are married, Margaret is able to resolve crucial matters, matters much more important than fish pie. Had she taken a strong stand in the Strand and insisted on improper fish pie, her lunch might have been based on a 1907 recipe from *High Class and Economical Cookery Recipes* by E. Roberta Rees. Not high class enough for Simpson's in the Strand, this recipe could be made less economical by using more fish.

½ lb. cooked fish
1 lb. cooked potatoes
1 oz. butter
A little milk or fish stock

Salt and pepper
Some white or anchovy or
 parsley sauce

Mash the potatoes, melt the butter in a saucepan and put in the potatoes, add a little milk if not moist enough, and season well with pepper and salt. Spread a layer of the potato in a buttered piedish, break the fish into small pieces, and place it on the top of the potato, with a little more pepper and salt and about three tablespoonfuls of sauce. Cover the pie with the remainder of the potatoes, piling them as high as possible, mark into ridges with a fork, and bake in a hot oven for about half an hour till the potatoes are brown. The pie may be brushed over with egg, before being put into the oven, to glaze it. More fish may be used if liked.

Cod Steaks

THE WISE VIRGINS (1914) by Leonard Woolf

At this moment the parlourmaid came in with a piece of tepid codfish on a plate.

Leonard Woolf, whose posthumous fate it is to be remembered primarily as the husband of Virginia Woolf, was himself a highly regarded writer. Born in London in 1880, he spent seven years in the Ceylon Civil Service but returned to live in England and become a central figure in the Bloomsbury group when he married Virginia Stephen in 1912.

His first novel, *The Village in the Jungle* (1913), used the background and knowledge he had acquired during his years of service in Ceylon. *The Wise Virgins* was published the following year, and *Stories of the East* (1916) returned to the Eastern setting. In addition to the novels, he wrote books on politics and international affairs as well as commendable volumes of autobiography, which are particularly valuable for the information they yield about various members of the Bloomsbury circle.

The fictional characters of *The Wise Virgins* also offer insights into their actual prototypes—Leonard and Virginia Woolf—and their friends and families. The novel tells the love story of Harry Davis and Camilla Lawrence (Leonard Woolf and Virginia Stephen) and explores the gap between their religious and cultural backgrounds. The conventional Davises, whose beliefs and attitudes Harry has outgrown, contrast vividly with the intellectual and free-thinking Lawrences. Among the people belonging to the Lawrence circle are Camilla's sister Katharine (Vanessa) and Arthur Woodhouse (Clive Bell).

Leonard Woolf offended many who recognized their portraits in the novel. He hurt his own mother deeply by representing her in the character of Mrs. Davis as a fat, elderly, overbearing, and demanding Jewish mother.

Leonard depicted himself also in harsh terms. Harry Davis, an unpleasant and egotistical young man who does not get along well with others, finds himself strongly attracted to the intelligent, imaginative, and beautiful Camilla. One Sunday, he and Camilla part after a stroll, and Harry, filled with deep emotion and thought, knows for a certainty that he is in love with her. Hurrying home to dinner, he finds that he is late and that dinner has already commenced.

His mother prods him for information ("Where have you been, Harry?"), his father surveys him mechanically, and his sister pokes at her pudding. Harry feels disgust. He gulps down the fish which is brought to him, wondering whether Camilla returns his love and thinking of the intolerable family situation in which he now finds himself. The fish may be tepid, but the conversation is hot.

Camilla Lawrence is accurately portrayed as a passionless person who is unable to respond to Harry's warmth and love. Her frigidity keeps the courtship from progressing. The novel may offer a brave and correct characterization, but its conclusion has been altered; Harry is made to marry the young girl he has compromised.

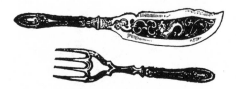# Cod Steaks

In any case, this codfish course, taken from *The Practice of Cookery and Pastry* (1887) by D. Williamson, is meant to be eaten hot and enjoyed over pleasant conversation, possibly about the Bloomsbury background of the book that suggested it.

Cut from the tail end of a fresh cod three or four slices rather more than half an inch thick, remove the skin from them, and lay them on a dish. Mix two table-spoonfuls of salad oil with the same of vinegar, a few sprigs of parsley, and a little pepper and salt, with a spoon, pour this over the steaks, and let them remain in it for two hours. When wanted, wipe them with a clean cloth, dust some flour on both sides, then brush with beaten egg, coat with bread crumbs, and fry in boiling fat till they become a nice brown colour. Serve hot with maitre d'hotel butter under them and garnished with parsley, or with plain butter sauce in a sauce tureen. For a small party of four or six persons, this way of cooking cod is very much to be preferred to the usual boiling.

Boiled Fish

ALMAYER'S FOLLY (1895) by Joseph Conrad

*Nina Almayer came through the curtained doorway
followed by an old Malay woman, who busied herself
in setting upon the table a plateful of rice and fish.*

Born of Polish parents in 1857, Joseph Conrad was seventeen
when he began a seafaring career on a French vessel. He later
joined an English ship and made his first visit to England in
1878. After becoming a British citizen, he settled in England
and turned to writing; his long voyages provided the settings
and experiences he used in his career as a novelist.

While on a tour of sea duty in 1887, which took him up the
Berau River in eastern Borneo, Conrad met a trader from
Java named Charles Olmeijer. The Dutch trader's story gave
Conrad the impetus for writing a novel about a man called
Kaspar Almayer, and the novel, *Almayer's Folly*, catapulted
the unknown author into fame.

Conrad's first production places Almayer in the terrifying
isolation of a small river settlement in Borneo. The solitary
Dutchman has married a Malay woman in the hope of obtaining an inheritance, and he has gone out to Sambir to manage
a small trading post. The main action takes place some twenty
years later. He has failed to secure the gold and wealth he
covets. His half-caste daughter Nina represents all that is

precious to him, and he longs to leave the scene of his bitter struggle and live with her in Europe, rich and respected by all. The sun is setting as the novel begins. Stranded in Sambir, Almayer thinks of his wrecked dreams of power and riches while awaiting the arrival of a Balinese prince, Dain Maroola, who is expected to supply men and a ship for gold. Almayer is called to dinner, but he lingers and continues anxiously to wait as he surveys the wreckage and debris carried along in the roaring flow of the flooded river.

The scene prefigures his own destiny. Almayer is drifting along toward destruction. He is financially ruined, and his decaying house has been derisively dubbed "Almayer's Folly." The epithet symbolizes also the foolish dream which has controlled his life. His last hope of securing wealth is in Dain, whose lateness is a cause for anxiety.

Dain finally arrives, but only to leave immediately under mysterious and suspicious circumstances. Actually, he is in flight from the Dutch authorities who have just seized his contraband cargo of arms. He explains that he has an urgent need to see the Rajah but promises to return the next day when there will be time to talk about the enterprise. With a sense of relief, Almayer can now go home and eat.

He is greeted by his daughter and admits that he is hungry. The food, fish and rice, is placed before him. "Almayer attacked his rice greedily." He feels happy, believing he is on the verge of being able to leave this place of suffering and misery for a European life of luxury.

The dinner scene, when Almayer feels contented, is full of irony. Having chosen in the past to live only for a life of riches in the future, he does not see that his obsessive dream of prosperity is doomed. He is ultimately an abandoned and piteous figure, his loneliness intensified by his daughter's love affair with Dain, who steals his last hope of wealth and his last human connection—Nina. Almayer tries unsuccessfully to forget, resorts to opium, and eventually dies.

Boiled Fish

It is curious that food does not often appear in the novels of Joseph Conrad, for he was a fastidious host. After he married Jessie George in 1896, the sociable couple entertained frequently and elaborately. Jessie was an excellent cook, and Conrad insisted on high standards for his guests.

Jessie used her talent to produce a little volume called *Simple Cooking Precepts for a Little House*, published in 1921. In the Preface which he wrote to his wife's cook book, Conrad states that the object of a cookery book is "no other than to increase the happiness of mankind." Since the character he created is feeling happy as he eats fish and rice, it follows that a recipe derived from Jessie's book accords with the correct emotional state. Furthermore, since Conrad must have tasted and enjoyed his wife's fish dish creation, it is entirely fitting to resort to her cookery book even though it appeared some years after Almayer ate fish and rice in Conrad's novel.

Boiled Fish and Melted Butter

Plaice. Lay your fish on a perforated white stone strainer in a fish kettle. Cover with cold water, add a teaspoonful of salt and a teaspoonful of vinegar. Put over a quick fire, bring to a boil and keep it boiling for about fifteen minutes. Have ready the following sauce:—

Mix one dessert-spoonful of flour smoothly with one ounce of butter. Add sufficient boiling milk to make up to half a pint, and a little salt. Put it into a double saucepan the bottom half containing boiling water. Stir with a spoon always the same way until it thickens. Chop about six sprigs of parsley (not stalk) and add to the sauce. Dish the fish in a flat dish and serve the sauce in a sauce boat.

Cod may be cooked in the same way only it must boil for fully half an hour after it has been brought to the boil.

UPDATE: A dessertspoonful is equal to two teaspoons.

Boiled Salmon

WESTWARD HO! (1855) by Charles Kingsley

Mr. St. Leger. . . offered a bet of five pounds, that he would find them, out of the pool below Annery, as firm and flaky a salmon as the Appledore one which they had just eaten.

Charles Kingsley lived in Bideford when he wrote his highly successful novel, *Westward Ho!*, in which he described the North Devonshire town with its "many-arched old bridge" over the River Torridge, as well as the surrounding country-side. A stirring adventure story, *Westward Ho!* had the added purpose of inspiring young Englishmen to emulate a heroic tradition. It made effective recruiting propaganda at a time when England was involved in the Crimean War. And it made Charles Kingsley a leading novelist of the time. Indeed, the novel became so popular that a resort town very near Bideford was named Westward Ho! in honor of the successful author.

In the novel, Kingsley refers to Bideford Bridge as the cynosure and soul of Bideford. He goes so far as to call it a "dinner-giving bridge" and explains the epithet by an incident in the plot.

At a dinner once given for the notables of Bideford, an argument arose as to whether salmon caught below the bridge were better than those caught above. A guest, Mr. St.Leger of

Annery, invited the entire company to dinner at his estate to prove that a salmon taken from the pool below Annery would be just as delectable as the one they had just eaten. So a feast takes place in the great hall at Annery. But the reader can only guess which salmon won the wager, for during dinner the story turns to the more mundane topic of love and romance and digresses from the passionate and all-consuming issue of food.

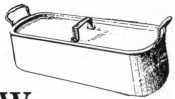

Boiled Salmon

We might guess that the salmon was cooked in a simple style, as good fresh salmon needs no superfluous embellishment. In this recipe lifted from *Modern Cookery* (1845), all the emphasis is on freshness. Eliza Acton advises, "To be eaten in perfection it should be dressed as soon as it is caught, before the curd (or white substance which lies between the flakes of flesh) has melted and rendered the fish oily."

To Boil Salmon

To preserve the fine colour of this fish, and to set the curd when it is quite freshly caught, it is usual to put it into boiling, instead of into cold water. Scale, empty, and wash it with the greatest nicety, and be especially careful to cleanse all the blood from the inside. Stir into the fish-kettle eight ounces of common salt to the gallon of water; let it boil quickly for a minute or two, take off all the scum, put in the salmon and boil it moderately fast, if it be small, but more gently should it be very thick; and assure yourself that it is quite sufficiently done before it is sent to table, for nothing can be more distasteful, even to the eye, than fish which is under dressed.

From two to three pounds of the thick part of a fine salmon will require half an hour to boil it; but eight or ten pounds will be done in little more than double that time; less, in proportion to its weight, should be allowed for a small fish, or for the thin end of a large one. Do not allow the salmon to remain in the water after it is ready to serve, or both its flavour and appearance will be injured. Dish it on a hot napkin, and send dressed cucumber, and anchovy, shrimp, or lobster sauce, and a tureen of plain melted butter to table with it.

To each gallon water, 8 ozs. salt. Salmon, 2 to 3 lbs. (thick) ½ hour; 8 to 10 lbs. 1 hour and ¼; small, or thin fish, less time.

Salmon

MRS. DALLOWAY (1925) by Virginia Woolf

... the salmon, Mrs. Walker knew, as usual underdone, for she always got nervous about the pudding and left it to Jenny; so it happened, the salmon was always underdone.

The action of Virginia Woolf's fourth novel takes place on a single day, between Mrs. Dalloway's morning preparations for a dinner party and the actual event that evening. She begins her day by walking through the streets of the London she loves to buy flowers for the occasion.

As the fashionable Mrs. Dalloway makes her way to her favorite flower shop, she perceives, she muses, she recalls the past. We meet a variety of people because she sees or thinks of them or because they too happen to be out on this lovely June day. She meets an old friend who is coming to the party, and she crosses the paths of people she does not know. The events and actions are trivial but are related to the main character or to the theme. Human beings are part of the flux of life, and Virginia Woolf expresses the idea of the continuous flow of life. As Mrs. Dalloway thinks and soliloquizes, moving back and forth in time, pieces of individual experiences are molded into a unified and satisfactory whole.

Time passes and the party hour arrives—the culminating event and the vehicle for bringing together people whose lives impinge on Clarissa Dalloway. The party becomes the focus for drawing together the principal characters as well as a variety of impressions and experiences of the day. The significance is that the events are not significant, but Virginia Woolf has used the technique of interior monologue for the unfolding of an entire life.

Even Septimus Smith, a character who would never actually be invited to this particular social circle, is present in spirit. Through what happens to him, Mrs. Dalloway, during the happiness and excitement of the party, is made to face the fact of death. Septimus Smith represents Clarissa Dalloway's other self, as she has her private vision in the midst of her social triumph. He has defied those who use power and position for "forcing your soul." He has maintained his independence of soul, but it has cost him his life. Clarissa, by contrast, has made compromises to achieve social success and position.

The heroine is left to consider the need for communion with others as well as the need for individuality, and the novel ends with a moment in the midst of flux. The entertainment and the preparations for it have enabled the author to present life and character in motion.

For the basic dinner preparations, the scene transfers to Mrs. Walker in the kitchen, with one course singled out. Salmon seems to be regular fare on such occasions, and Mrs. Walker seems to be regularly troubled by the thought of its being improperly prepared. We do not know whether the salmon was actually underdone, just that Mrs. Walker worries about it. In fact, one guest is very complimentary about the dinner and asks whether the entrée was really made at home.

Salmon (with Genevese Sauce)

In Mrs. Dalloway's time, salmon was plentiful and even the Thames was full of salmon. Recipes for salmon were plentiful too, and advice from the famous Mrs. Beeton might have prevented undercooking. She warns that "experience alone can teach the cook to fix the time for boiling fish" and instructs that it is done "when the meat separates easily from the bone."

Mrs. Beeton's Book of Household Management has been a basic and popular guide since its first issue in 1861, with new editions continually appearing. The revised 1915 edition offers a recipe more elaborate than simple boiled salmon, as befits the atmosphere of Mrs. Dalloway's elegant dinner party.

(Fr.—Sauman Sauce Genevoise)

INGREDIENTS. —*2 slices of salmon, ½ a pint of good stock, ¼ of a pint of Madeira or other white wine, 2 ozs. of butter, I oz. of flour, I dessertspoonful each of chopped-onion and parsley, I carrot sliced, a bouquet-garni (parsley, thyme, bay-leaf), a blade of mace, the juice of a lemon, a teaspoonful of anchovy-essence, cayenne, salt and pepper.*

Method.—Melt 1 oz. of butter in a stewpan and fry the onion until slightly browned, add the stock, wine, parsley, carrot, bouquet-garni, mace, anchovy-essence and seasoning, and boil gently for 30 minutes, then strain, and return to the stewpan. Bring the sauce to boiling point, put in the slices of fish, and let them simmer gently about 20 minutes, or until the fish separates easily from the bone. Meanwhile melt the remaining oz. of butter in another stewpan, add to it the flour, stir and cook over the fire for 4 or 5 minutes. When the fish is done, remove it carefully to a hot dish, pour the liquor on to the butter and flour, stir until smooth, then simmer for 5 or 6 minutes. Add the lemon-juice to the sauce, season to taste, strain over the fish, and serve.

Time.—From 1 to 1 ¼ hours.
Average Cost, 3s. to 3s.6d.
Sufficient for 6 persons.
Seasonable from April to August.

Stewed Oysters

WASHINGTON SQUARE (1881) by Henry James

*The situation was really thrilling, and it scarcely
seemed to her a false note when her companion asked
for an oyster stew, and proceeded to consume it before
her eyes. Morris, indeed, needed all the satisfaction
that stewed oysters could give him.*

Catherine Sloper is the unfashionable daughter of a fashionable New York physician. Dr. Sloper sees his daughter as
plain, dull, and unmarriageable. Her dominant character
trait is goodness. Indeed, that very quality of goodness, rather
than beauty or intelligence, has been a source of deep
disappointment and irritation to the brilliant and witty
Dr. Sloper, who victimizes his daughter. The simple-minded
Catherine often does not even understand her father's ironic
taunts. Nor does she understand the motives of the fortune-
hunter, Morris Townsend. But Dr. Sloper sees through the
young man's mercenary nature immediately. He sees that
only someone interested in acquiring wealth through mat-
rimony would be interested in his awkward daughter. Alas, he
is right. When Dr. Sloper fights the match by threatening to
disinherit Catherine if she marries without his consent,
Morris Townsend abandons the young lady and marriage
plans. She is left disillusioned by the shattering revelations of
character.

The motherless girl is also exploited by her Aunt Penniman, who lives with them. Dr. Sloper's sister is a foolish, romantic widow without much common sense or shrewdness and with an inordinate penchant for secrets and mysteries. The meddling matron continually oversteps her bounds and acts with duplicity, while Catherine remains unsuspecting. Mrs. Penniman craves a role as the central figure in a drama of the couple's secret marriage and eventual reconciliation with her brother. Although Dr. Sloper has prohibited Morris from entering their home, Mrs. Penniman has continued to keep in touch with the young man.

When Mrs. Penniman arranges to meet with Morris Townsend in an oyster bar, she is taking advantage of Catherine's timid nature and furthering her own desires for romantic intrigue. She selects a particular oyster saloon in Seventh Avenue for a surreptitious meeting with Morris and wears an opaque veil to avoid being recognized. The "tryst" is a "thrilling" diversion for her, but Morris arrives a half hour late. His tardiness and the bad cup of tea she drinks both serve to intensify the pleasure she feels in suffering for a romantic cause. She remains oblivious to the fact that Morris scorns her as a silly old woman whom he has used only to gain entrance into the Washington Square house. While she derives her pleasure from the air of romance, he derives his from stewed oysters.

During the conversation, in which she urges elopement, Morris silently proclaims the woman's idiocy but remains outwardly civil and patient. The meeting over, Mrs. Penniman pays for her cup of tea, and Morris pays for his oyster stew. They leave, walking together through the dusky streets to Washington Square. She has enjoyed a brief sojourn into realms of romance.

This vital scene illustrates the kind of help which Catherine receives from the only person who acts in her behalf, but acts unwisely. With Mrs. Penniman abetting

Morris Townsend and suggesting a secret marriage, as consistent with her own needs, Catherine's future doom is indicated.

Stewed Oysters

This recipe for the oyster stew enjoyed by Morris Townsend is from *The Cook's Oracle* (1860) by William Kitchener:

Large oysters will do for stewing, and by some are preferred; but we love the plump juicy Natives. Stew a couple of dozen of these in their own liquor;—when they are coming to a boil, skim well, take them up and beard them; strain the liquor through a tamis-sieve, and lay the oysters on a dish. Put an ounce of butter into a stew-pan; when it is melted, put to it as much flour as will dry it up, the liquor of the Oysters, and three table-spoonsful of milk or cream, and a little white pepper and salt; to this some Cooks add a little Catchup, or finely chopped Parsley, grated Lemon-peel, and juice; let it boil up for a couple of minutes, till it is smooth, then take it off the fire, put in the Oysters, and let them get warm (they must not themselves be boiled, or they will become hard); line the bottom and sides of a hash-dish with bread-sippets, and pour your oysters and sauce into it.

Carp

THE COMPLEAT ANGLER (1653) by Isaak Walton

I will tell you how to make this Carp, that is so curious to be caught, so curious a dish of meat as shall make him worth all your labour and patience. And though it is not without some trouble and charges, yet it will recompense both.

Isaak Walton is best known for an amazing little volume that appeared when he was a man of sixty and insured his literary immortality. *The Compleat Angler, Or* (to complete its full title) *The Contemplative Man's Recreation, Being A Discourse On Fish And Fishing, Not Unworth The Perusal of Most Anglers* identifies him forever with the sport of fishing.

Written in a humorous, digressive style, the book is not a definitive study of the art of fishing, but rather a discursive escape into leisure activities. It reads like a lively novel. Walton incorporated characters and conversation, folklore, poems, jokes, philosophy, and even recipes into the text, and the recipes reveal that his delight in fishing carried over to the table.

Isaak Walton so captured the hearts and needs of readers that admirers still visit his timber-framed cottage at Shallowford in Staffordshire where he wrote much of *The Compleat Angler*. And followers of Walton also go to

Winchester, where he lived in his later years and where he died in 1683 at the age of ninety. He is buried in Winchester Cathedral, and a stained-glass window in the south transept is a fitting memorial with its pastoral scene of a picnic feast on the banks of the nearby River Itchen, one of the many rivers in which he fished.

Walton angled for escape from the pressures of city life, and he shares with his readers the peaceful pleasures and pure bliss to be derived from the idyllic world of fishing:

> For when the lawyer is swallowed up with business and the statesman is preventing or contriving plots, then we sit on cowslip banks, hear the birds sing and possess ourselves in as much quietness as those silent streams, which we now see glide so quietly by us.

 # Carp

If Walton's evocative passage did not make you dash off immediately and head for the nearest river, you might try one of his own fish dishes. His recipe for Carp is full of promise. But if you dropped everything in search of the contentment he describes, the recipe makes good reading—or a good outdoor fish barbecue.

Take a Carp, alive if possible; scour him, and rub him clean with water and salt, but scale him not: then open him; and put him, with his blood and his liver, which you must save when you open him, into a small pot or kettle: then take sweet marjoram, thyme, and parsley, of each half a handful; a sprig of rosemary, and another of savoury; bind them into two or three small bundles, and put them in your Carp, with four or five whole onions, twenty pickled oysters, and three anchovies. Then pour upon your Carp as much claret wine as will only cover him; and season your claret well with salt, cloves, and mace, and the rinds of oranges and lemons. That done, cover your pot and set it on a quick fire till it be sufficiently boiled. Then take out the Carp; and lay it, with the broth, into the dish; and pour upon it a quarter of a pound of the best fresh butter, melted, and beaten with half a dozen spoonfuls of the broth, the yolks of two or three eggs, and some of the herbs shred: garnish your dish with lemons, and so serve it up. And much good do you!

Salt Herrings

THE LITTLE MINISTER (1891) by J. M. Barrie

He used to run through the streets between his work and his classes. Potatoes and salt fish, which could then be got at twopence the pound if bought by the half-hundred weight, were his food.

After graduating from Edinburgh University in 1882, James Matthew Barrie began his career as a journalist before turning to other forms of writing. Among his first works of fiction were *Better Dead* (1887), *Auld Licht Idylls* (1888), and *A Window in Thrums* (1889). Thrums was his fictional name for Kirriemuir, the town in which he was born in 1860.

Nowadays, the fiction of J. M. Barrie is overshadowed by the plays, and the plays—*Quality Street, What Every Woman Knows, The Admirable Crichton, Dear Brutus*—though still produced and still popular, are overshadowed by the immortal *Peter Pan*. But when it was published in 1891, *The Little Minister* was quite a successful novel. The fantasy of situation and character appealed greatly to the public, although critics today may find it confused and filled with characters lacking credibility. Barrie's dramatization of *The Little Minister* in 1897 was his first stage play to achieve enormous success.

Gavin Dishart, the little minister, lives in Thrums with his mother, Margaret. His only recollection of a distant time

and place, the fishing village of Harvie in which he was born,
is that of the arrival of a fisherman to announce the distress-
ing news that Adam Dishart, his father, has drowned. Gavin
was then four, and mother and son soon leave for Glasgow
where Margaret works as housekeeper for her brother.

From his earliest days, the lad was destined for the
ministry. Margaret encouraged him and continued to work
hard to keep him at school after her brother died. Gavin went
to the university at twelve and also secured a position as
errand boy, sustaining himself on potatoes and salt fish. Such
was their poverty that at evening meal times, Margaret would
tell her son that she had already supped. Gavin would see
through the deception and insist that she have something to
eat together with him. Impatient for better economic times, he
would dream of being a minister so that his mother might
have an egg for breakfast every morning.

One day, appearing for the first time in his ministerial
clothes before his mother, he laments that he is of such small
stature, and the adoring mother comforts him with the
assurance that he is "just the height I like." She accompanies
him to Thrums when he is at last called as a minister to that
weaving town.

Margaret had married Adam Dishart rather than her
preferred choice of Gavin Ogilvy because Adam was the more
forceful rival. With her husband presumed dead, she is free to
marry Gavin Ogilvy. But after six years of marriage, it turns
out that she was not a widow, as had been supposed. Adam
reappears, not drowned after all. Having arranged his own
disappearance in order to indulge in a life of pleasure and
freedom, he now returns to reassert his mastery over the
weak and helpless Margaret. When Adam does actually and
ironically lose his life at sea, Ogilvy decides not to return to
Margaret.

But it is the second generation story that makes up the
main plot. Young Gavin's love for Babbie sets up a rivalry

between the two women of his life, his mother and the enchanting gypsy. A tangled plot is unraveled when a disastrous flood maroons the minister, who performs an unselfish act of bravery. He is rescued, and the townspeople accept his association with a gypsy girl. We learn at the end that Ogilvy has been narrating the story to his eighteen-year-old granddaughter, the child of Gavin and Babbie.

Salt Herrings

Recipes for potatoes and salt fish, the food of the poor, are presented in Mrs. Dalgairns' cookery book of 1842 with the no-nonsense title, *The Practice of Cookery, adapted to the Business of Every Day Life.* (See page 291 for mashed potatoes recipe.)

To Salt Herrings
Cut them open carefully, separating the guts from the milts and roes; throw away the milts, and leave the roes in the fish; wash them, and then put them into a brine, strong enough to bear an egg; let them lie in that from twelve to sixteen hours, take them out and drain them well. In the bottom of a keg or jar, strew a good deal of salt; lay a row of herrings, and then sprinkle over them more salt, and repeat this till all are packed. Cover the top with salt, and stop it very closely, to exclude the air.

When to be dressed, put them on in cold water, and when it boils let them boil for ten minutes. Serve them with mashed potatoes.

Fried Whitebait

THE WHITE PEACOCK (1911) by D. H. Lawrence

"It's fried whitebait," she said.
. . .He poured vinegar freely over the hot fish.

The first novel of D. H. Lawrence, *The White Peacock*, is an immature work, and critics tend to dwell on its callow nature. The author wrote of it years later, "I began it at twenty. Let that be my apology."

Far from a precocious masterpiece, the novel nevertheless provides a powerful study of the choices facing people and the consequences of selecting incorrect alternatives. The main characters make wrong decisions and end up with unfulfilled lives.

The narrator tells about a group of young people with George Saxton as the most deeply imagined character of the group. With all the promise and potential of vital youth, he is first described to the reader with sensuous physicality as he stands with legs apart and with shirt open to reveal "sun-hot skin." He is seen at the end as a pitiful figure suffering from the effects of alcoholism and awaiting death. The contrast is moving. The failure to develop potential is tragic.

George is a handsome young farmer whose portrayal brings the main theme to life. He loves Lettie but is jilted by her. Inarticulate and indecisive, he lacks courage and allows

110

Lettie and her love to slip away. Instead of asserting his will, George capriciously marries Meg, the girl at the Ram Inn; so begins his downfall. He drifts into alcoholism and allows life itself to slip away. Cyril the narrator later tells him, "You should have insisted and made your own destiny."

Unused, his will and his consciousness atrophy. His life has gone drastically wrong, ruined by the wretched marriage into which he willingly entered. The latter part of the novel conveys the degeneration and degradation of a man who denies his potentialities—a classic Lawrentian motif.

When the narrator visits George toward the end of his wasted life, he finds a pitiful person who is offered a plate of whitebait that he takes without appetite and with complete indifference. Cyril again sees the paltry ruin of a man two years later when George, finally defeated, makes the bitter statement, "I shall soon—be out of everybody's way!"

Fried Whitebait

To ignore a good plate of whitebait indicates a state of stupor. Whitebait is a classic English fish dish and is normally, like all fried fish-and-chips, seasoned with vinegar. It is customarily offered on restaurant menus, in season, as an appetizer.

Mrs. Beeton's famous cookery book offers this edifying note on whitebait after presenting a recipe:

WHITEBAIT.—This highly-esteemed little fish appears in innumerable multitudes in the river Thames, near Greenwich and Blackwall, during the month of July, when it forms a tempting dish to vast numbers of Londoners, who flock to the various taverns of these places, in order to gratify their appetites. The fish has been supposed be the fry of the shad, the sprat, the smelt, or the bleak. Mr. Yarrell, however, maintains that it is a species in itself, distinct from every other fish. When fried with flour, it is esteemed a great delicacy. The ministers of the Crown have had a custom, for many years, of having a "whitebait dinner" just before the close of the session. It is invariably the precursor of the prorogation of Parliament, and the repast is provided by the proprietor of the "Trafalgar," Greenwich.

To Dress Whitebait

INGREDIENTS. —*A little flour, hot lard, seasoning of salt.*

Mode.—This fish should be put into iced water as soon as bought, unless they are cooked immediately. Drain them from the water in a colander, and have ready a nice clean dry cloth, over which put 2 good handfuls of flour. Toss in the whitebait, shake them lightly in the cloth, and put them in a wicker sieve to take away the superfluous flour. Throw them into a pan of boiling lard, very few at a time, and let them fry till of a whitey-brown colour. Directly they are done, they must be taken out, and laid before the fire for a minute or two on a sieve reversed, covered with blotting-paper to absorb the fat. Dish them on a hot napkin, arrange the fish very high in the centre, and sprinkle a little salt over the whole.

Time.—3 minutes.

Seasonable from April to August.

Poultry

and Game

Roast Chicken

JANE EYRE (1847) by Charlotte Brontë

The ladle with which she was basting a pair of chickens roasting at the fire, did for some minutes hang suspended in the air.

"Reader, I married him." With that famous line which begins the final chapter of *Jane Eyre*, the narrator takes the reader into her confidence and brings the long episodic story to a satisfying conclusion. Charlotte Brontë had used a powerful creative imagination to present Jane's miserable childhood. The orphan endured cruel treatment by her aunt Mrs. Reed, harsh conditions at Lowood school, tyranny at the hands of Mr. Brocklehurst, and heartbreak with the untimely death of her friend Helen Burns. The promise of an end to her sufferings comes with Jane's acceptance of a postion at Thornfield Hall.

Her experiences as governess at Thornfield constitute the main part of the novel. This portion centers on her relationship with Rochester and encompasses events full of Gothic horrors—dreadful nightmares, the mad woman in the tower, the splitting of the great chestnut tree, a last-minute rescue from a bigamous marriage, the fire which destroys Thornfield, and the maiming of Rochester. Finally, there is the moving reunion of Jane with Rochester.

The reader has been taken through the life of the protagonist, who has struggled toward a decent life and domestic happiness. At last, she reaches a state of self-fulfillment and is at the end a happily married woman.

Immediately after the wedding, Jane returns to her new home to announce her marriage to Mary and John, the housekeeper and her husband, who are in the kitchen. Mary is cooking dinner and John is cleaning knives. They are stunned by the news. Their activities cease and hang suspended for a while in mid-air. Then life continues. Mary bends over the chickens and carries on with her basting. She and John both make appropriate remarks and express their pleasure. Life flows on happily for Jane and Edward Rochester.

Jane Eyre was the first published novel of Charlotte Brontë. *The Professor*, the first to be written, was the last to be published and appeared after Charlotte's death in 1855, just one month short of her thirty-ninth birthday. *Shirley* came in 1849 and *Villette* in 1853. Of the four novels of Charlotte Brontë, *Jane Eyre* achieved a phenomenal and well-deserved success.

Critics may continue to argue and expostulate forever—for the book has become a classic—about the merits and faults of *Jane Eyre*. They may include the flaw of pathetic fallacy which falsifies a description in order to convey sensation. Thus, the spoon ceases to baste the chickens and is arrested in mid-air to indicate how emotionally overcome the servant is when news of Jane's marriage is imparted. Nevertheless, the device is effective.

Presumably, the chickens (usually prepared as a pair) will continue to roast uneventfully until done.

Roast Chicken

When Elizabeth Raffeld wrote this recipe in 1801, it was meant for smaller chickens than the ones to which we are accustomed and took only fifteen minutes to roast in a very hot oven. Allow at least an hour in a moderate oven.

To Roast Young Chickens

When you roast young chickens, pluck them very carefully, draw them, only cut off the claws, truss them, and put them down to a good fire, singe, dust, and baste them with butter; they will take a quarter of an hour roasting, then froth them up, lay them on your dish, pour butter and parsley in your dish, and serve them up hot.

Fried Chicken

BABBITT (1922) by Sinclair Lewis

*"I thought the fried chicken was delicious! ... Fried to
the Queen's taste. Best fried chicken I've tasted for a
coon's age."*

When Sinclair Lewis published *Babbitt* in 1922, he was
denounced as a villain and a traitor for his devastating picture
of middle-class American life. The novel begins with a description of the typical Midwestern city of Zenith, a city for "giants"
in which dwells the typical member of society, George F.
Babbitt. The hero, at age forty-six, believes in middle-class
conventions and in conventional virtues of home life.

So typical is his lifestyle that even his bedroom is described with the "standard bedside book." He respects bigness
in anything, is exceedingly well fed, and follows a routine and
activities that are petty and trivial.

His attempts to cut down on overeating and cigar smoking
are pathetic, as are his efforts at social climbing and civic
boosting. He is devoted to mechanical conveniences, and
gadgets are important. A closely-detailed description of razor
blades and the routine of shaving effectively emphasize the
smallness, meaninglessness, and lack of freedom in the life of
this dull member of a materialistic society for whom the

family car is a status symbol rather than a method of transportation.

Babbitt continually mouths the clichés of his empty and joyless existence. No sooner does he advocate less eating and lighter lunches, than he goes to the Zenith Athletic Club where he indulges in a light lunch of mutton chop, radishes, peas, deep-dish apple pie, cheese, and coffee with cream, plus an extra order of French-fried potatoes.

Politics, clubs, religion, labor, morals, questionable business ethics, marriage and family all expose Babbitt as a product of his environment. His business code allows for bribery, lying, conspiracy—if *he* does it. He dismisses an employee for using the same methods that he has used with impunity. It is the pretense of morality that must prevail. He extols law and order but proudly secures bootleg liquor for his party. As he tries to climb the social ladder, he invites the important McKelveys to dinner in the "best style of women's magazine art"; afterwards he beams at the success of the "best fried chicken I've tasted. . . ." He is snubbed, however, for the invitation is not returned. But he in turn snubs the Overbrooks, less important members of society.

He is not totally despicable. On the positive side, he at least sees glimmerings of something desirable beyond the environment in which he is trapped. His fairy child dream is a saving grace. So is his friendship with Paul, who stands apart from the backslapping, joking friends who are full of affectionate nicknames, hollow congeniality, and forced comradeship. Sympathy goes out to him as he achieves realization of the ludicrousness of his friends and their values, even if it is too late for him to revolt successfully. He returns to their favor but will never be content with them again. The freedom he ultimately finds is in the hope that his son will not make the same mistakes.

Fried Chicken

That quintessential American dish, fried chicken, is a perfect choice; and it seems right to extract a recipe taken from that quintessential cookery book by Francis Merritt Farmer, a revised and enlarged 1913 edition of *The Boston Cooking-School Cook Book.*

Fried Chicken (Southern Style)
Clean, singe, and cut in pieces for serving, two young chickens. Plunge in cold water, drain but do not wipe. Sprinkle with salt and pepper, and coat thickly with flour, having as much flour adhere to chicken as possible. Try out one pound fat salt pork cut in pieces, and cook chicken slowly in fat until tender and well browned.

Chicken Fricassee

CARRY ON, JEEVES (1925) by P. G. Wodehouse

*Fortunately, however, the second course consisted of a
chicken fricassee of such outstanding excellence that
the old boy, after wolfing a plateful, handed up his
dinner-pail for a second instalment and became almost
genial.*

Carry On, Jeeves is a collection of ten stories centered on
Jeeves, the imperturbable, wise old butler. First created in
1916, Jeeves became a beloved series character, much used in
the comic writings of Wodehouse to extricate Bertie Wooster
from a variety of contorted situations. The immortal Bertie
Wooster, Wodehouse's crowning achievement, may be charac-
terized as a likable idiot and a born bachelor, who eats and
drinks a lot. In "The Rummy Affair of Old Biffy," the situation
approaches resolution after a luncheon of chicken fricassee.

Bertie Wooster's old friend, Mr. Charles Edward Biffen,
with possibly the worst memory on record, manages to forget
even the name of the girl to whom he has proposed. Through
careless lethargy, he has now become unhappily engaged to
an overbearing and possessive young woman. Bertie joins
Biffy and Sir Roderick Glossop, the formidable father of the
impossible young lady, for lunch. The terrible Sir Roderick

enjoys the luncheon so enormously—"This is most excellent chicken"—that the forbidding man melts somewhat as he announces his intention to take Charles to the British Empire Exhibition at Wembley.

At the exhibition, Jeeves comes to the rescue, managing to get Biffen disengaged from the undesirable female and reunited with the girl he loves. With a few funny twists and some help from the all-knowing Jeeves, the plot dissolves into sheer happiness, and another work of one of the most prolific and popular writers of the twentieth century comes to a close.

 # Chicken Fricasee

For our purposes, forget the short memory of Old Biffy and remember the luncheon which featured an excellent chicken fricassee, as culled from *High Class and Economical Cookery Recipes* by E. Roberta Rees, 1907.

Fricasee of Chicken

1 fowl	1 bayleaf
1½ pints white stock or water	10 peppercorns
2 oz. butter	1 clove
A blade of mace	a bunch of herbs
1 small onion	2 yolks of eggs
2 tablespoonfuls cream	

Cut the fowl into neat joints and remove the skin. Put the stock, mace, bayleaf, onion, peppercorns, clove, and herbs into a saucepan, with the neck, skin, and trimmings of the fowl, and bring slowly to the boil. When boiling, rub the fowl with lemon juice, and add to the stock. Simmer gently about an hour till the fowl is tender. Melt the butter in a saucepan, add the flour, and fry a little, without browning; then strain the stock, and add nearly all of it to the butter and flour; stir till boiling, and boil four or five minutes, if too thick, add the rest of the stock. Remove from the fire, mix the cream and yolks of eggs together, and stir them quickly to the sauce; cook a little without boiling, put in the pieces of fowl, and let them get hot through, without boiling, stirring carefully. Pile the fowl in the middle of a hot dish, and pour the sauce over and round. If liked, the dish may be garnished with cooked button mushrooms, and the trimmings used to flavor the stock.

Chicken: Poulet Danoise

ROOM AT THE TOP (1957) by John Braine

And that's how it is in all the fairy stories: the princess is always beautiful, and lives in a golden palace... and eats chicken and strawberries and cakes made from honey.

John Braine's first novel was greeted by enthusiastic reviews and outstanding praise. *Room at the Top* related the struggle of an ambitious working-class hero to get to the top. It examined disenchantment with the British class system and delved into central issues of the time. With a setting in postwar Yorkshire, the novel focused on grim realities of the industrial North and developed a new trend in British fiction. The story of a young man spiritually killed by society became representative of the literature of the "Angry Young Men" of the decade of the 1950s.

Joe Lampton sees marriage as the only way to enter the social class that will secure for him the materialistic future he craves. He succeeds in his social climb but loses spiritually when he gives up the woman he loves for a magnate's daughter. Basically a decent person, Joe agonizes over the cost but never considers relinquishing the chance for a life of luxury. He is a deadened man at the end—a "Zombie."

The one food from which Joe derives satisfaction—chicken—is mentioned a number of times. Chicken is served when he first arrives at his new lodging in Warley, the town to which he has come in search of an improved position. He drifts off into pleasurable sleep by dwelling on its pleasant taste. Later, he thinks of the wealthy Susan Brown as the beautiful princess of fairy stories who indulges herself with chicken. It reappears when he and Alice share fried chicken sandwiches. Again, a sumptuous feast at a party he attends includes chicken sandwiches. Significant events occur over a chicken lunch with Mr. Brown.

Mr. Brown's invitation to luncheon at the Leddersford Conservative Club marks the turning point in Joe Lampton's quest for a life of economic security. Over lunch, Mr. Brown arranges for Joe and his daughter Susan, now expecting a child, to wed. The chicken is served just as Mr. Brown explains why he no longer objects to the marriage and why Susan, not wanting Joe to feel obliged to marry, has not told him of her condition.

> Brown looked at the chicken the waiter had just brought him. "Chicken again," he grumbled. "I'll be turning into one soon."

Joe gains access to a world of wealth. His dream of rising to the top has come true.

Chicken: Poulet Danoise

The hero's dream of a princess eating chicken might be realized with the selection of a chicken delicacy fit for a princess and actually created for royalty. Chef Gabriel Tschumi offers, in his *Royal Chef* of 1954, recollections and recipes of royal meals. The great chef came to England from Switzerland in 1898 and served Queen Victoria, King Edward VII, King George V, and Queen Mary. He seems particularly proud of this chicken dish prepared during his service with King Edward VII and gives it a special title: Queen Alexandra's Favourite Dish. This recipe was popular with Edwardians generally.

Poulet Danoise. Take a large Surrey chicken, cleaned and dressed, and put inside it a mixture consisting of ¼ lb. of butter, the juice of ½ lemon and a little chopped parsley. Place it in a casserole dish with a sliced onion, carrot and a bayleaf. Cook in a slow oven for about 1 ½ hours, watching to see it does not brown too much. The juice should be sufficient to cook it. If it becomes too dry add about ½ pint of good white stock to the casserole.

When well cooked, reduce the juice (after removing all fat) with ½ pint of white chicken stock and ½ pint of cream to a good thickness. Season with lemon juice, salt and pepper. Add a small piece of meat glaze.

Cook some home-made nouilles in water, strain, and saute in fresh butter. Season to taste.

Cut chicken as you would a roast chicken, arrange it on a bed of nouilles in a shallow dish, and cover with the sauce. Serve very hot.

It was customary to arrange some nouilles at each end of the dish, garnishing them with small squares of tongue, pieces of chicken and chopped parsley.

Nouilles paste:

These taste a little like macaroni, and can be bought ready prepared. But the recipe for making them at Buckingham Palace about 1902 was as follows:

Take ½ lb. of flour, 12 egg yolks and a pinch of salt, make into a stiff paste and roll out on a board very thinly. Cut in long narrow strips taking care to keep each separate. Cook in boiling water.

Boiled Chicken

THE WOMAN IN WHITE (1860) by Wilkie Collins

"Boiled chicken, is it not? I thought you liked boiled chicken better than cutlet, Mrs. Vesey?"

The immediate and astounding success of *The Woman in White* made Wilkie Collins a great celebrity. Called "the most popular novel of the century" by an envious rival publisher, the bestseller gave the name "Woman in White" to perfumes and toilet accessories, fashionable articles of clothing, and even musical compositions. The dramatic idea for the sensationally successful novel emanated from an actual personal incident, as sensational as anything Collins ever wrote.

One evening, Wilkie Collins and his brother were accompanying their friend Millais home after a dinner given by Mrs. Collins, when a piercing female shriek from a nearby villa broke the peace of the summer evening. A garden gate opened and a beautiful young woman in white flowing drapery materialized. She paused briefly before the three men, then ran off and disappeared into the moonlit night. Wilkie dashed out after the white luminescent figure and did not return to his waiting friends.

The next day, Wilkie related to his friends her story: She had been imprisoned in the house which the threesome chanced to be passing one fateful evening, just as she

130

managed to escape. Entranced and haunted by the mysterious figure, Collins pursued her all night to prevent harm. Caroline Elizabeth Graves, the prototype for the fictional damsel in distress, was to play an influential role in the life and writing of Wilkie Collins.

When the fictional narrative begins, Walter Hartright has accepted an appointment in Cumberland to give drawing lessons to Laura Fairlie and her half-sister, Marian Halcombe. Just before departing from London to take up his new position, he encounters on a lonely road a woman dressed in white, who is said to have escaped from an asylum. At Limmeridge House in Cumberland, he falls in love with Laura, who strongly resembles the woman in white. But Laura is already betrothed to Sir Percival Glyde, the villain who marries her for her money and who is responsible for the imprisonment of the woman in white. When Laura refuses to sign away her wealth, she is herself committed to an asylum. Eventually—and naturally—all the mysteries are untangled, the villains are exposed and justly punished, and Hartright and Laura are happily married.

But when Hartright first arrived at Limmeridge House, he met the young ladies and the other inhabitants of the house at luncheon. The elderly Mrs. Vesey, Laura's former governess, is described as "counting for nothing." She placidly sits her way through life in a tranquil, harmless, vacant, and vegetable existence. It is early in the story that Collins introduces this minor character whose brief part has the quality of dramatic irony:

> Mrs. Vesey looked the personification of human composure and female amiability. A calm enjoyment of a calm existence beamed in drowsy smiles on her plump, placid face. Some of us rush through life, and some of us saunter through life. Mrs. Vesey sat through life. Sat in the house, early and late; sat in the

garden; sat in unexpected window-seats in passages; sat (on a camp-stool) when her friends tried to take her out walking; sat before she looked at anything, before she talked of anything, before she answered Yes, or No, to the commonest question. . . .

Luncheon illustrates her innocuous existence. Offered a cutlet by Miss Halcombe, she accepts. "Yes, dear." Then Miss Halcombe points out that boiled chicken, which Mrs. Vesey likes, is also available. Mrs. Vesey nods at the boiled chicken and responds, "Yes, dear." Pressed to choose between chicken or cutlet, she hesitates drowsily before answering, "Which you please, dear." It takes the forceful and decisive Marian Halcombe to resolve the issue: "Suppose you have a little of both? and suppose you begin with the chicken, because Mr. Hartright looks devoured by anxiety to carve for you."

A vast array of characters appear in the novel, and Mrs. Vesey is a memorable minor one. Carefully individualized, she is an important illustration of human nature. Collins himself, in the Preface to *The Woman in White*, emphasized the vital importance of character delineation. Characters must exist as "recognisable realities, being the sole condition on which the story can be effectively told." While every work of fiction must tell a good story, he insists, its effectiveness depends on the human interest associated with events.

As the plot and complex forces unfold, Mrs. Vesey remains in the background as a necessary adjunct for full interaction of the primary characters. In the foreground, the actions of the resolute and resourceful Marian eventually overthrow the diabolical conspiracy against Laura. But once again, food has come to the fore as a means for depicting character.

Boiled Chicken

As a tribute to the luncheon scene, with its presentation of human nature, here is a recipe for boiled chicken. Or should it be cutlet? The resources of a powerful personality might resolve the issue by simply offering recipes for both cutlet and boiled chicken. A powerful personality might also very strongly suggest beginning with the chicken. It might even go so far as to refer for both dishes to *The English Cookery Book* of 1856 by Frederick W. Davis. (For mutton cutlets see page 200.)

Note that the full title of this volume is: *THE ENGLISH COOKERY BOOK: Comprising Mrs. Rundell's Domestic Cookery, Revised. With several Modern Dishes added thereto, Carefully Selected and Simplified by Frederick W. Davis, Head Cook of the Freemasons' Tavern.* But while the title goes on and on, the recipes themselves do not.

To Boil Fowl

For boiling, choose those that are not black-legged. Pick them nicely, singe, wash, and truss them. Flour them, and put them into boiling water. A chicken will take twenty minutes; a large fowl, forty minutes. Serve with parsley and butter; oyster, lemon, liver, or celery-sauce. If for dinner, ham, tongue, or bacon, is usually served to eat with them, as likewise greens.

UPDATE: More cooking time will now be needed for a well-done chicken. Allow an hour for a small fowl.

Boiled Fowl

GULLIVER'S TRAVELS (1726) by Jonathan Swift

I laid in a stock of boiled Flesh, of Rabbits and Fowls; and took with me two Vessels, one filled with Milk, and the other with Water.

Gulliver's Travels, the most famous work of Jonathan Swift and perhaps the most famous satire in the English language, has remained an enormous success from the time of its publication in 1726. A world classic, it has survived also in abridged and expurgated form as a children's classic. The first two books in particular, relating an imaginative adventure story with a fairy tale atmosphere, have never ceased to delight youthful audiences. Even the noble horses who rule Houyhnhnmland in Book Four appeal greatly to children.

Yet *Gulliver's Travels* was written as a savage indictment of mankind. Consisting of four books in the form of a narrative of journeys, it parodied travel books and travel writers in general, as well as particular people and events. Political satire and personal references were enlisted for the purpose of exposing the evil and idiotic side of human behavior and conveying the message that man is depraved.

Successive sea journeys place Gulliver in strange lands with events that strain the reader's credulity. Gulliver's fantastic travels take him from a land of pygmies to a land of giants and from a flying island to a country of talking horses. But Swift sets out to establish authenticity by using Gulliver's name on the title page and giving biographical details to sustain the illusion of actual travels. Lemuel Gulliver is a Cambridge man, a scientist and linguist with a curiosity about other lands and people. A map faces the opening chapter to further enforce belief in this true voyage of an honest man. In fact, Gulliver's imaginary adventures have a real purpose—the purpose of presenting a scathing account of man's monstrous nature.

In the first book, Lemuel Gulliver is shipwrecked on the island of Lilliput where the diminutive inhabitants, a mere six inches high, emphasize man's pettiness. Their reduced scales make them effective devices for ridiculing the English and their institutions. They are little people who are also morally small and display their petty and mean natures by such trivial arguments as which end of an egg should be broken first. In the second book, the eponymous hero is in Brobdingnag where the inhabitants are giants. The scale is reversed, and the size magnifies human imperfections and horrors.

The voyage to Laputa in the third part takes Gulliver to a flying island inhabited by philosophers and intellectuals and immortal beings and aims its barbs at philosophers, scientists, and historians. The court is so devoted to mathematics that the obsession is imposed on food; dinner includes "a shoulder of mutton, cut into an equilateral triangle, a piece of beef into a rhomboid, and a pudding into a cycloid."

The powerful final book describes the country of the Houyhnhnms, horses with reason, who appear to Gulliver to be perfection. They are contrasted with the repulsive Yahoos, beasts in the shape of humans. Gulliver lives in Houyhnhnmland for three years in admiration of the fantastic horses and in isolation from human company. He resists being classed with Yahoos until a female Yahoo sees him bathing and is overcome with passion, forcing him to face the incontrovertible evidence that he is indeed a member of that bestial species.

His experiences cause him to revile man's depraved nature, and Gulliver returns home a lonely and alienated misanthrope. But in preparation for the journey home, he must lay in a supply of food which will insure his safe return to England. For the real food which will bring him back to the real world, he chooses boiled rabbits and fowls.

On arrival, he is never able to adjust fully to normal humanity. He believes himself to be a horse and acts accordingly, for he is a Houyhnhnm in his inner being. He feels so alienated from the corrupt and vicious human race that he can hardly tolerate dinner with his own wife. Yet he was fully lucid and practical when stocking food for the return to home and family.

Boiled Fowl

Mrs. Gulliver might have weaned her husband back more successfully and promoted his adjustment to human society if she had served boiled rabbit. After all, boiled rabbits and fowls were not mere inferior sailor's food, but graced the elegant tables of the well-to-do, as attested to by the inclusion of recipes for these dishes in old cookery books designed for accomplished ladies and queens: The anonymous *The Accomplisht Ladys Delight* of 1684 supplies instructions for boiling fowl. Instructions for boiling rabbit, taken from *The Queen-Like Closet* of 1670, may be found on page 265.

To boyl a Capon, Pullet, or Chicken.
Boyl them in good Mutton-broath, with Mace, a Faggot of sweet Herbs, Sage, Spinage, Marygold leaves and flowers, white or green Endive, Burrage, Bugloss, Parsley and Sorrel, and serve it on sippets.

137

Roast Fowl

THE WAY OF ALL FLESH (1903) by Samuel Butler

"I think we might have a roast fowl with bread sauce, new potatoes and green peas, and then we will see if they could let us have a cherry tart and some cream."

Of the fifteen books Samuel Butler published in his lifetime, only *Erewhon* received attention. He wrote *The Way of All Flesh*, the title by which he is best known today, in the years 1873 to 1884, scribbling away for the most part in the British Museum Reading Room; but his most famous book was not published until the year after his death in 1902.

The Way of All Flesh is based on his own experiences. Like the hero, Butler was born in 1835. Like the hero, Butler felt deep antipathy to his parents and had an acrimonious relationship with them. When Butler rebelled openly, he was forced to emigrate to New Zealand, returning after five years with a small fortune. The date on which he left England, 30 September 1859, is the very date on which the hero of the novel rejects his parents.

Since various characters were easily identifiable, Butler tried to prevent hurting members of his family by not allowing the novel to be published while any of them were still living. Nevertheless, his sisters were alive when his literary executor permitted publication of the novel in 1903.

The novel was not an immediate success. Butler examined the deep-rooted motives of his characters, tracing the influence of heredity and environment on them. He exposed selfish imposition of parental will and authority on helpless offspring. His attack on family life and society shocked the public. It was simply too far ahead of its time with its story of rebellion against the tyranny of parents and its plea for the rights of the younger generation.

The fame he achieved posthumously is attributed largely to George Bernard Shaw, who praised the novel in his 1907 preface to *Major Barbara*:

> "It drives one almost to despair of English literature when one sees so extraordinary a study of English life as Butler's posthumous *Way of All Flesh* making so little impression."

The story unfolds in simple chronological sequence. Although Theobald Pontifex has no inclination to be ordained, he is cowed into becoming a clergyman by his determined father. He helps a busy minister on Sundays and weakly succumbs to marriage in a family plot to snare him as a husband for one of five unmarried daughters. When he finally attains financial security, he finds himself trapped into marriage to the smug Christina, who has won him in a game of cards with her sisters.

After the wedding ceremony, Theobald and Christina leave the little village of Crampsford to take up married life. The first episode evoking the unpleasant nature of the married pair centers on dinner at a Newmarket inn on their wedding day. Their roles are clarified over the dinner which Christina must order while Theobald must eat and pay for it.

But Christina is full of anxiety. She cannot face anyone, and ordering dinner represents a major ordeal. She has just been married that morning and feels extremely self-conscious at being an unattractive and older bride of thirty-three. Despite her state of consternation, her bridegroom, filled with anger and resentment at the marriage from which he could not extricate himself, insists on being served. She must go through with it. Escape from duty is no more possible for her than it was for him. She cries. He sulks. At last she relents and asks what he would like to eat. Pleased at her submission, he suggests roast fowl with bread sauce as the main course of a full dinner which concludes with cherry tart. She manages to place the order with the landlady and to perform her duty admirably.

The successful dinner has allowed Theobald to assert his authority and be pleased with himself for having established his superior position on the first day of their married life. However, both Theobald and Christina are portrayed as a couple who will prove to be unsuitable parents.

Having suffered from his own father's tyranny, Theobald causes his son Ernest to suffer in turn from parental cruelty. The despicable parents bully and beat their son Ernest, the central character, into spiritless obedience. Their monstrous ways and the ways of the middle-class Victorian world are exposed in this study of the interactions of parents and children. The stage for a parental reign of terror has been set by the dinner taken by the destructive Theobald and Christina.

Roast Fowl

At least the dinner may be constructive, as taken from a variety of Victorian sources: Roast fowl from *Warne's Model Cookery and Housekeeping Book* by Mary Jewry (1869); bread sauce (see page 289) from *The English Cookery Book* by Frederick Davis; new potatoes (see page 290) from *Modern Cookery* by Eliza Acton; green pease (see page 293) from *Handbook of Practical Cookery* by Matilda Lee Dods; and cherry tart (page 304) and short crust for fruit tarts (page 306) from *Mrs. Beeton's Book of Household Management.*

To Roast a Fowl—Family Receipt
Time, one hour.

A large fowl; two or three tablespoonfuls of bread-crumbs, half a pound of butter; pepper and salt.

Draw and truss a fowl for roasting, put into the inside two or three tablespoonfuls of fine bread-crumbs, seasoned with pepper and salt, and a piece of butter the size of a large walnut. Put the fowl down before a clear fire to roast, basting it well with butter; and just before it is done dredge over it a little flour, and baste it with butter to give it a frothy appearance. When done, add a little warm water to the butter in the dripping-pan, or add a little very thin melted butter, and strain it over the fowl. Serve with bread sauce in a tureen, or a little made gravy if preferred.

Roast Guinea Fowls

See: GREAT EXPECTATIONS (1860) by Charles Dickens, page 270.

We were to have a superb dinner, consisting of . . . . a pair of roast stuffed fowls.

Pip does not object to being given "the scaley tips of the drumsticks of the fowls" as much as he objects to being given admonitions to be virtuous and grateful. Charles Elme Francatelli supplies directions for preparation of a pair of roast fowls in *The Modern Cook* (1846). For stuffing, see page 288.

Roast Guinea Fowls
Two of these are generally served for a dish, one of which should be larded, and the other covered with a layer of fat bacon; roast them before a brisk fire for about forty minutes, glaze and dish them up with watercresses; pour some gravy under, and serve bread-sauce separately, in a boat.

UPDATE: Because roast capons, fowls, and guinea fowls are treated in the same manner by Francatelli, this recipe will serve nicely for the "pair of roast stuffed fowls" that are part of Pip's Christmas dinner.

Capon

KENILWORTH (1821) by Sir Walter Scott

. . . a choice capon, so delicately roasted that the lard frothed on it.

Kenilworth is an evocation of sixteenth-century Elizabethan England, with Queen Elizabeth I herself appearing as a powerful figure. The Queen had actually conferred Kenilworth Castle on her favorite, Robert Dudley, Earl of Leicester. When Scott visited the castle in 1815, the red stone fortress was already a ruin, a magnificent and romantic ruin that still stands in the heart of Warwickshire. It is open to tourists who might well imagine, as did Scott, the extravagant festivities of 1575 when Leicester entertained the Queen on her historic visit to Kenilworth.

In addition to the vivid descriptions of the lavish revels held to entertain royalty, the novel offers many glimpses into the Elizabethan court. One incident describes young Walter Raleigh's act of courtesy and reverence as he places his cloak over a muddy spot so that Queen Elizabeth may safely pass with dry feet.

Although Scott is incorrect in many of the historical details, he was highly successful in capturing the flavor and color of Elizabethan England. Queen Elizabeth is not the central character, however, but a dominant force. The story

143

concerns the beautiful Amy Robsart, who is brought to a tragic end through the devious schemes of Richard Varney. The villain persuades her to conceal her secret marriage to the Earl of Leicester in order to avoid incurring the jealous wrath of the Queen. A key character in the story is Amy's rejected suitor, the worthy Cornish gentleman, Edmund Tressilian. His efforts throughout are directed toward trying to save Amy from her tragic fate.

Having left Cumnor, where Amy is being kept out of sight, Tressilian journeys to Devonshire in the company of Wayland Smith, who aids in the attempt to save Amy. Their destination is the home of Sir Hugh Robsart, Amy's father. They stop at an inn in the town of Marlborough as much to refresh the horses as themselves. The guests drink sack while awaiting the arrival of the food, featuring a delicately-roasted capon. Both the master and his attendant sit at the same table while Wayland extols the excellence of the capon. He converses with Tressilian while "the limbs of the capon disappeared before his own exertions."

But Tressilian is eager to resume the journey. As soon as the horses are rested, they carry on as far as Bradford, where they spend the night. Then they cross the counties of Wiltshire and Somerset and arrive in Devonshire at Sir Hugh Robsart's seat of Lidcote Hall. There, he consults on how to proceed in unhappy Amy's cause and soon departs again on his quest.

For a short and simple recipe for capon, let us turn to *A Complete System of Cookery* (1813) by John Simpson, who specialized in huge banquets undoubtedly utilizing larger fires and smaller capons than are today available. The time for roasting should be amended to at least an hour at 375° for a five-pound capon.

A Capon

A capon will take half an hour to roast; baste it with butter, sprinkle salt and flour over it a few minutes before it is taken up; put gravy in the dish, and garnish with water cresses.

Duck and Green Peas

THE RETURN OF THE SOLDIER (1918)
by Rebecca West

*They were very kind when they heard who I was; gave
us duck and green peas for lunch and I did think of dad.*

When Rebecca West began her career as a writer, she changed
her actual name, Cicely Isabel Fairfield, to that of the strong
heroine she had once played on the stage in Ibsens's drama,
Rosmersholm. From the start, she produced powerful literary
essays, vivid travel pieces, and provocative journalistic
articles on politics and on the problems of women. A review of
1912 attacking a new novel by H. G. Wells (*Marriage*) led to
a meeting with the well-known author and the beginning of a
friendship that developed into an intense love relationship
lasting ten years. The tempestuous affair with a married man
was troublesome and complex, and a son was born in August
1914. But the difficult years did bring happy times and
productive writing.

Frequent and joyous meetings occurred at Monkey Island,
a lovely spot that Wells had enjoyed since boyhood. At this
very special place, Rebecca West and H.G. Wells were most
happy. When she wrote her first novel at the age of twenty-
five, it was the site of her love affair, the island in the Thames
near the village of Bray, that became the setting of the idyllic

romance of the young couple. *The Return of the Soldier* established her reputation as a novelist. By the time of her death in 1983 at the age of ninety, she had to her credit eight volumes of fiction as well as ten major works of non-fiction.

The Return of the Soldier deals with the amnesia of a shell-shocked soldier who cannot remember his married life or life in the trenches. He has forgotten completely the ten years of an apparently happy marriage and is fixated on a former love. His wife Kitty and his cousin Jenny are awaiting his arrival when Margaret appears with news of his condition. All three women care about Chris Baldry, who is returning from the war to a life he does not remember.

Neither Kitty nor Jenny can believe that Chris could possibly have been interested in this plain and unfashionable woman who now intrudes into their lives. Margaret's part in the drama turns Kitty into a "broken doll" with more concern for her rights as a wife than compassion for his condition. Jenny is "stunned with jealousy" but recognizes the fine qualities—simplicity and goodness—of Margaret, who comforts Chris and is instrumental in obtaining his cure.

The idyllic romance between Margaret and Chris, with its key setting on Monkey Island, took place some fifteen years earlier. Margaret had lived there happily with her father who managed the inn. She fell in love with Chris when he first landed on their magical island. And they parted over a silly quarrel. Called out of England by a business crisis, and unable to find her on his return, Chris married Kitty a few years later.

Margaret, married to an ineffectual man, apparently cherished loving memories of the past. At one point, she gave way to an obsession to see the site again and returned with her husband. From the new owners of the hotel she received a lunch of duck (not as good as her father's ducks) and green peas—as well as a packet of letters from Chris which never reached her. The Monkey Island she knew and loved in her youth no longer existed for her; the happy past cannot be recaptured and made to replace the actual present.

Margaret knows that the situation into which Chris has escaped is not real and consents to help in restoring him to the present. Truth, as the unselfish Margaret puts it, must be faced at any cost. Chris is indeed cured—brought back to reality and made ordinary. The soldier returns to his world of actuality.

Duck and Green Peas

Without doubt, it is best to leave psychoanalysis to one of the first writers ever to use it in fiction and turn to analysis of the fine dish of duck and green peas offered by Matilda Lees Dods in her *Handbook of Practical Cookery* (1886).

Duck with Green Pease.—*One young duck, one pint of green pease, one tea-spoonful of salt, one half tea-spoonful of pepper, one half pint of stock, two ounces of butter.*

Draw and truss the duck. Melt in a large stewpan the butter, and when it smokes place in the duck breast downwards. When both sides of the breast are browned turn it over, and brown the legs and back; this takes about twenty minutes. Add then the stock, and when it boils skim it well; add the pepper and salt, and allow this to cook for three-quarters of an hour very slowly. Add then the pease, and cook all twenty minutes longer.

Canvas-back Duck

THE AGE OF INNOCENCE (1920) by Edith Wharton

". . . it signified either canvas-backs or terrapin, two soups, a hot and a cold sweet, full décolletage with short sleeves, and guests of a proportionate importance."

Although Edith Wharton, a member of a distinguished and wealthy New York family, had no need to work, she nevertheless made the difficult choice of becoming a writer. Among her novels and stories are *The House of Mirth* (1905), *Ethan Frome* (1911), *The Reef* (1912) and *The Age of Innocence,* for which she won the 1921 Pulitzer Prize.

With a title that suggests a historical novel, her prize-winning book delved into the New York society of the 1870s. Edith Wharton's protagonists are victims of convention who find themselves stunted by the system and subject to the forces of society in which they live.

Newland Archer, a member of the highest circle of New York social life, aspires to break through the barrier of convention but is too weak to escape. Engaged to May Welland, he meets her cousin, Ellen Olenska, and the two fall in love. But Archer cannot break the engagement. He is trapped into marriage with May, as is expected of him, and will spend a lifetime with her, despite his love for Ellen. The ironic handling of social standards in New York high society is skillfully constructed.

In a society that uses even details of the dinner menu to judge others, canvas-back ducks with currant jelly are mentioned a number of times in the novel as the pinnacle of society dining. If you dined with the right people, "you got canvas-back and terrapin and vintage wines." It is simply the most proper choice to grace the most proper dinner table. When the young couple give their first big dinner, canvas-backs are the vital element.

When May gives a farewell dinner party for Ellen Olenska, who is about to depart for Europe, she is following the New York code that is a "tribal rally around a kinswoman about to be eliminated from the tribe." Everything must be done magnificently. Just as the guests are "engaged upon May's canvas-backs" comes the realization to Newland Archer that all assembled around the dinner table harbor the belief that he and Madame Olenska have been lovers, that members of the vast circle believe he has been enjoying the very affair he has not achieved. The dinner was a cover-up for people who "dreaded scandal more than disease."

 **Canvas-back Duck**

And what exactly is a canvas-back? *Mrs. Beeton's Book of Household Management* (1915) offers an explanation: "Among the numerous species and variety of ducks are the Canvas-back duck, a native of North America, and highly esteemed for the table." Fannie Merritt Farmer, principal of the Boston Cooking School, says: "Canvasback Ducks have gained a fine reputation throughout the country, and are found in market from the last of November until March. . . The distinctive flavor . . . is due to the wild celery on which they feed."

The Boston Cooking-School Cook Book of 1896, with its "carefully worked-out measurements and easy to follow directions leaving nothing to chance," might well have been a basic volume in an upper-class New York kitchen. Fannie Farmer's recipe follows.

Roast Wild Duck. Dress and clean a wild duck and truss as goose. Place on rack in dripping-pan, sprinkle with salt and pepper, and cover breast with two very thin slices fat salt pork. Bake twenty to thirty minutes in a very hot oven, basting every five minutes with fat in pan; cut string and remove string and skewers. Serve with Orange or Olive Sauce. Currant jelly should accompany a duck course. Domestic ducks should always be well cooked, requiring little more than twice the time allowed for wild ducks.

Ducks are sometimes stuffed with apples, pared, cored, and cut in quarters, or three small onions may be put in body of duck to improve flavor. Neither apples nor onions are to be served. If a stuffing to be eaten is desired, cover pieces of dry bread with boiling water; as soon as bread has absorbed water, press out the water; season bread with salt, pepper, melted butter, and finely-chopped onion.

Pigeon Pie

EMMA (1815) by Jane Austen

It was now the middle of June, and the weather fine; and Mrs. Elton was growing impatient to name the day, and settle with Mr. Weston as to pigeon-pies and cold lamb.

Jane Austen died at forty-two, at the height of her literary powers. During the last year of her life, she struggled with a painful illness, now known as Addison's disease, for which there was no known cure or treatment. Symptoms worsened, and she was placed in the care of a special doctor in Winchester. There she died on 18 July 1817. *Northanger Abbey* and *Persuasion* were published the following year.

Emma, the last of the novels of Jane Austen to appear in her lifetime, contains one of the famous picnics of literary history. Originally intended as a diversion to satisfy the need for amusement on the part of Mrs. Elton and Mr. Weston, the picnic excursion to Box Hill provides the possibility for disruptive behavior.

"They had a very fine day for Box Hill." Despite such an auspicious beginning, the day not only fails to be pleasurable, but ends in total misery for Emma, who is not a faultless heroine. Full of self-importance, she is so sure of herself that she takes it upon herself to control the destinies of others, particularly as an inveterate matchmaker. But she is often mistaken and misguided. Although Emma has shortcomings, she is also lovely and intelligent. She can be a very likable and lively heroine. She behaves badly, but the picnic is the social occasion which initiates a positive change in Emma's development.

At Box Hill, Emma is rude to Miss Bates, treating her with lack of kindness and humanity. The essential flaw in Emma's character is exposed as she indulges in an act of cruelty. A game is proposed. Miss Bates makes a self-deprecating comment ("I shall be sure to say three dull things as soon as ever I open my mouth. . ."), and Emma seizes upon it to respond with an insult (". . . but you will be limited as to number—only three at once").

Mr. Knightley points out to Emma the moral significance of her lapse in good manners and humanity, and she is immediately filled with remorse and grief. Distressed and contrite, Emma apologizes to Miss Bates the very next morning. Her repentance is genuine, and she achieves self-knowledge through her error. She learns to become more generous and tolerant, to accept change, and to understand her proper social role. In the end, she pays sincere attention to Miss Bates, tries to be helpful to others, and happily changes her own status as she accepts Mr. Knightley's proposal of marriage.

With such vital developments emanating from the excursion to Box Hill, it is no small wonder that the small episode fails to report on what the participants ate—or even that they ate. (Were the pigeon pies actually made and taken along?)

Pigeon Pie

While more realistic than four and twenty blackbirds baked in a pie, pigeon pie is not consistent with modern tastes. Hannah Glasse, in *The Art of Cookery Made Plain and Easy* (1747), offers a recipe which belies the title by making pigeon pie seem neither "plain" nor "easy." But the book was in print when arrangements were being made in the novel for a picnic at Box Hill. A more modern recipe is also offered.

To Make a Pigeon Pye
Make a Puff-paste Crust, cover your Dish, let your Pigeons be very nicely picked and cleaned, season them with Pepper and Salt, and put a good Piece of fine fresh Butter with Pepper and Salt in their Bellies, lay them in your Pan, the Necks, Gizzards, Livers, Pinions and Hearts lay between, with the Yolk of a hard Egg and a Beef Steak in the Middle; put as much Water as will almost fill the Dish, lay on the Top-Crust, and bake it well. This is the best Way to make a Pigeon Pye, but the French fill the Pigeons with a very high Force-Meat, and lay Force-Meat Balls around the Inside, with Asparagus Tops, Artichoke Bottoms, Mushrooms, Truffles and Morels, and season, high, but that is according to different Palates.

Coventry Pigeon Pie
Florence White, in *Good English Food* (1952), expresses the belief that the good things of yesteryear are treasures for today or tomorrow as well, and she proceeds to illustrate that pigeon pie can be a modern day delicacy by offering this recipe, dated 1822 (only seven years after *Emma* appeared in print):

155

Clean and singe the pigeons, cut off heads, and the legs to the first joint, and pinions to the second joint; mix pepper and salt, season them well, and put a bit of butter into each; truss them, but without skewers, and lay them in the pie dish; boil an egg hard, or two, if for six pigeons; take the yolk and cut it in quarters, lay it between the pigeons and a bit of butter on each breast, lay the giblets by the side of each; put a teacupful of water in; then make a rich crust of puff pastry.

Braised Pheasant

DECLINE AND FALL (1928) by Evelyn Waugh

*"I wonder whether I could have just a little more of this
very excellent pheasant?"*

The first published novel of Evelyn Waugh, *Decline and Fall*,
led to the author's being hailed as England's leading satirical
novelist of the 1930s. With a title that suggests the theme of
decay of a civilization, *Decline and Fall* portrays an innocent
young man adrift in a hostile society. Social institutions are
ridiculed as Paul Pennyfeather is initiated into a harsh,
exploiting, and criminal world.

An unfortunate circumstance makes Paul Pennyfeather, a
theological student at Oxford, the victim of the antics of a
group of exuberant students who steal his trousers. He is
unjustly sent down from Oxford for indecent behavior and
becomes a schoolmaster at one of the worst institutions in
existence. Full of greed, corruption, doubt, and indifference,
Llanabba Castle is an appropriate site for his initiation into a
savage society. He becomes friendly with Captain Grimes, a
scoundrel who believes in doing whatever he wants to do, and
Mr. Prendergast, a chaplain riddled by doubt.

Prior to the marriage of Captain Grimes to Flossie Fagan,
daughter of the bogus headmaster (with a bogus Ph.D.), he

invites his two strange colleagues, Grimes and Prendergast, to dinner at the Hotel Metropole. As Paul drinks a champagne toast, he moves closer to the anarchic world of Captain Grimes and further away from a world of discipline and order. The guests partake of soup in little aluminum bowls, followed by "the worst sort of sole" and what is undoubtedly the worst sort of philosophical conversation. A dejected Captain Grimes thinks of his impending marriage and wonders, "What is birth?" On a more practical level, Mr. Prendergast wonders whether he may have more pheasant. The pheasant, unlike the level of discussion, is excellent.

The dinner scene conveys an air of confusion and absurdity as unrelated incidents are arranged in a pattern that eventually establishes the meaning of the novel. Grimes announces that he will get a motor bicycle and is considerably cheered by his decision. Told of a sea lion who juggled with an umbrella and two oranges, Grimes proceeds to surpass that accomplishment by juggling with a bottle, a lump of ice, and two knives. While he demonstrates, a waiter remonstrates. Meanwhile, Mr. Prendergast continues to focus on food and indulges in two pêches Melba.

The scene signals the hapless Paul Pennyfeather's entry into a fantastic and chaotic world in which anarchy emerges victorious. The picaresque hero, essentially a passive victim, is drawn into a series of adventures. He is seduced by the mother of one of the students, arrested while unwittingly arranging transportation for a white slavery operation, imprisoned in an institution given to ineffective experiments in criminal rehabilitation, rescued by arrangement of a false release, and resurrected under a new name to resume his studies at Oxford—where it all began.

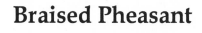

Braised Pheasant

We may as well begin with a recipe for pheasant from *The Gentle Art of Cookery* (by Mrs. C.F. Leyel and Miss Olga Hartley, 1925) before going on to dessert of pêche melba (see page 348).

Braised Pheasant with Chestnut Purée

Pheasant, butter, chestnuts, milk or cream.

Put the pheasant into an earthenware pot with one and a half ounces of butter; rub into the cavity of the pheasant some powdered herbs, salt, pepper, and half a clove of garlic. Brown the bird slightly in the butter, then cover the casserole and put it in the oven, basting it from time to time with good stock in which the bird is cooking. Remove the clove of garlic. Cook for forty-five minutes, and serve it with a puree of chestnuts.

159

Roast Green Goose

WUTHERING HEIGHTS (1847) by Emily Brontë

Mr. Earnshaw carved bountiful platefuls. . . .I was pained to behold Catherine, with dry eyes and an indifferent air, commence cutting up the wing of a goose before her.

When things calm down after Heathcliff has dashed a tureen of hot apple sauce on his adversary, the hungry party continue with the "fragrant feast" featuring roast goose, no doubt without the apple sauce.

Heathcliff, of mysterious origin, is the passionate hero and villain of the novel. Growing up at Wuthering Heights, he makes an enemy of the son of the house, Hindley, who despises and degrades him. Heathcliff is proud, vindictive, and violent, but capable of deep love. He resents and envies his handsome and blue-eyed rival, Edgar Linton, heir of Thrushcross Grange, who later marries his beloved Cathy.

Edgar Linton and his sister are invited to Wuthering Heights for Christmas dinner, an occasion marred by a physical assault as Heathcliff gives vent to the agony within him. When maltreatment by Hindley is followed by insult from Linton, Heathcliff cannot contain his volcanic fury—violence always erupts in Heathcliff's presence—and hurls the tureen of hot apple sauce at his persecutor. While Linton is being cleaned off with a dish cloth, his sister sobs, and Cathy tries to impose order as she defends Heathcliff. It is the sight of the Christmas feast that finally restores peace. Mr. Earnshaw carves the goose, and Catherine begins to cut up her serving. The festivities seem to have commenced.

But Heathcliff has been banished for the day. He is locked up, away from the dinner feast and away from the evening dance. Left alone, he determines to take revenge for all the wrongs done him. He will ruin both families. He will take control of both houses and acquire all the property and wealth of the Earnshaws and the Lintons.

The dinner incident suggests his potential for malevolent behavior. He destroys and debases and inflicts pain on others as he brings his demonic plan of revenge to fruition. Such is the power of the writing that the reader sympathizes with Heathcliff as he pursues his course of vengeful destruction. The reader feels the reasons for his violence. Emily Brontë's single novel has presented a story of extraordinary passion and great emotional intensity.

 # Roast Green Goose

Since the fictional events happened in Yorkshire between 1775 and 1803, it is appropriate for a cookbook of 1801, *The Experienced English Housekeeper* by Elizabeth Raffald, to yield recipes for goose as well as apple sauce. (See page 287 for apple sauce.)

To Roast a Green Goose

When your goose is ready dressed, put in a good lump of butter, spit it, lay it down, singe it well, dust it with flour, baste it well with fresh butter, baste it three or four different times with cold butter, it will make the flesh rise better than if you was to baste it out of the dripping pan; if it is a large one it will take three quarters of an hour to roast it; when you think it is enough, dredge it with flour, baste it till it is in a fine froth, and your goose a nice brown, and dish it up with a little brown gravy under it; garnish with a crust of bread grated round the edge of your dish.

UPDATE: Geese and turkeys were not much larger than fowls, and a green goose is a young one, "one that has not attained its full growth."

Goose and Dumplings

THE VICAR OF WAKEFIELD (1766) by Oliver Goldsmith

Our honest neighbour's goose and dumplings were fine. . . .

Oliver Goldsmith's only novel, *The Vicar of Wakefield*, appeared in 1766 and eventually became one of the most popular novels in circulation. It was translated into many foreign languages, and Goethe hailed it as the finest novel of his day. Dickens was so impressed that he nicknamed his little brother "Moses" after a character from the novel and later used a corrupted form of the name—"Boz"—as his own pseudonym.

Goldsmith, who was also an essayist, dramatist, and poet, incorporated three well-known poems into the novel. Of these, the shortest, "When lovely woman stoops to folly," is regularly anthologized; and "The Deserted Village" is his finest and most loved. Among his plays, *She Stoops to Conquer*, published and acted the year before his death in 1774, is still being produced. And his single novel continues to be widely read and greatly admired.

The sentimental plot of the novel overflows with the sufferings of its characters, and the sentimental reader is expected to respond with a flood of tears. But there is also a satirical level of meaning and a comic spirit in the story told by a very human clergyman.

The vicar has chosen a wife, Deborah, who cannot be excelled in cookery. She is proud of her ability as a housekeeper but has social ambitions and pretentions. Good-natured and generous, they enjoy a particularly good reputation for the gooseberry wine which they offer to visitors who come to their elegant house in Wakefield. Here they live in happiness and prosperity with their six children until forced to move to another area when the vicar loses his fortune through the bankruptcy of a town merchant.

Humbled by misfortune, the couple make another home in a community of simple farmers. When they condescend to accept an invitation from Farmer Flamborough, they find much pleasure in the happy rural games and feasting on Michaelmas Eve. Even Deborah Primrose, proud of her own housekeeping, compliments the fare of goose and dumplings and the lamb's-wool—a drink of hot ale and pulp of roasted apples, sugared and spiced. This friendly party takes place in the calm before the storm. The Primroses are soon to be deluged with disasters and are about to fare less well.

At their lowest ebb of fortune, the vicar is in prison for debt, his home has been destroyed by fire, his eldest daughter, Olivia, is said to have died of grief after a false marriage, Sophia has been abducted, and George is also imprisoned and liable to death on the gallows for having challenged the villainous Squire Thornhill to a duel. Modern critics and readers may deride the piling up of calamities, but all the virtuous characters are relieved of their miseries and restored to former prosperity. The happy outcome of the comic novel has really never been in doubt.

Goose and Dumplings

After their fortunes have declined, the vicar and his wife are served goose and dumplings at a Michaelmas Eve feast. The goose recipe is taken from Hannah Glasse's *The Art of Cookery Made Plain and Easy*, 1747. The recipe for dumplings is from Charles Carter's *The Complete Practical Cook*, 1730. For the gooseberry wine recipe that the Primroses serve at the high point of their success, see page 358.

To Dress a Goose in Ragoo.

Flat the Breast down with a Cleaver, then press it down with your Hand, skin it, dip it into scalding Water, let it be cold, lard it with Bacon, season it well with Pepper, Salt, and a little beaten Mace, then flour it all over, take a Pound of good Beef Sewet cut small, put it into a deep Stew-pan, let it be melted, then put in your Goose, let it be Brown on both Sides, when it is Brown put in a Pint of boiling Water, an Onion or two, a Bundle of Sweet Herbs, a Bay-Leaf, some Whole Pepper, and a few Cloves, cover it close, and let it stew softly till it is tender; about Half an Hour will do it if Small, if a large one three Quarters of an Hour: In the mean Time make a Ragoo, boil some Turnips almost enough, some Carrots and Onions quite enough; cut them all into little Pieces, put them into a Sauce-pan with Half a Pint of good Beef Gravy, a little Pepper and Salt, a Piece of Butter rolled in Flour, and let this stew all together for a Quarter of an Hour; take the Goose and drain it well, then lay it in the Dish, and pour the Ragoo over it.

Dumplings of Sorts.

First, Drop-Dumplings, or Norfolk-Dumplings; To a Pint of Cream or Milk put three Eggs, Whites and all; work it up pretty stiff with fine Flower; season it with salt, Nutmeg and Ginger; put in a Spoonful of good Ale-Yeast, and let it be so stiff that you can drop it by a good Spoonful into the Pot, which must be boiling, and so kept till enough, which will be in a quarter of an Hour: The Sauce is only plain Butter.

Another Way is,

To work a Pint of Cream or Milk up with good Flower and a Pound of good Beef-Suet minc'd, season'd with Salt, Ginger and Nutmeg; work it up very stiff, and divide it in three or four, as you think fit, and boil them well: The Sauce is Butter.

Roast Goose

THE ADVENTURE OF THE BLUE CARBUNCLE (1887)
by Arthur Conan Doyle

"It arrived upon Christmas morning, in company with a good fat goose, which is, I have no doubt, roasting at this moment in front of Peterson's fire."

Arthur Conan Doyle achieved enormous fame and literary success with his creation of one of the most celebrated characters in English literature, Sherlock Holmes. The famous hero-detective relied on deductive reasoning to reconstruct and solve crimes, and the public still clamor for those intriguing mysteries which are ingeniously solved by the detective's application of his special form of logic. Such is the acclaim still given to Sherlock Holmes that aficionados continue to seek out his fictional and non-existent premises in Baker Street.

A Christmas goose is at the heart of this adventure. Sherlock Holmes explains to Dr. Watson how Peterson, the commissionaire, happened to come into the possession of "a most unimpeachable Christmas goose" together with the hat Holmes was examining when Watson arrived to present holiday felicitations.

Peace is suddenly broken on this second morning after Christmas as Peterson rushes into the famous Baker Street

167

venue with the exciting news that Mrs. Peterson has found in the crop of the goose a blue diamond. It is immediately recognized as the Countess of Morcar's precious carbuncle of the title, which had been stolen five days earlier in a hotel robbery.

How the goose has come to swallow the gem and how the perpetrator of the crime is traced make up the elements of this excellent detective story. Meanwhile, the Peterson family enjoy the goose, for "there were signs that, in spite of the slight frost, it would be well that it should be eaten without delay." And a replacement goose is purchased and given to the "gentleman who lost his Christmas dinner."

Roast Goose

A recipe taken from *Mrs. Beeton's Book of Household Management* is extremely appropriate, for Arthur Conan Doyle invokes her name in a relatively unknown and untypical work, *A Duet With an Occasional Chorus*. In this study of married life, the young wife tries to master every page of that volume, and the young husband conjectures that Mrs. Beeton must have been the finest housekeeper in the world. After reading the advice that no criticism of her husband's failings should pass a wife's lips, the husband forms the ironic conclusion, "By Jove, this book has more wisdom to the square inch than any work of man."

INGREDIENTS.—*Goose, 4 large onions, 10 sage-leaves, ¼ lb. of bread crumbs, 1 ½ oz. of butter, salt and pepper to taste, 1 egg.*

Choosing and Trussing.—Select a goose with a clean white skin, plump breast, and yellow feet: if these latter are red, the bird is old. Should the weather permit, let it hang for a few days: by so doing, the flavour will be very much improved. Pluck, singe, draw, and carefully wash and wipe the goose; cut off the neck close to the back, leaving the skin long enough to turn over; cut off the feet at the first joint, and separate the pinions at the first joint. Beat the breast bone flat with a rolling pin, put a skewer through the under part of each wing, and having drawn up the legs closely, put a skewer into the middle of each, and pass the same quite through the body. Insert another skewer into the small of the leg, bring it close down to the side bone, run it through, and do the same to the other side. Now cut off the end of the vent, and make a hole in the skin sufficiently large for the passage of the rump, in order to keep in the seasoning.

169

Mode.—Make a sage and onion stuffing of the above ingredients; put it into the body of the goose, and secure firmly at both ends, by passing the rump through the hole made in the skin, and the other end by tying the skin of the neck to the back; by this means the seasoning will not escape. Put it down to a brisk fire, keep it well basted, and roast from 1 ½ to 2 hours, according to the size. Remove the skewers, and serve with a tureen of good gravy, and one of well-made apple sauce. . . .

Be careful to serve the goose before the breast falls, or its appearance will be spoiled by coming flattened to table. As this is rather a troublesome joint to carve, a *large* quantity of gravy should not be poured round the goose, but sent in a tureen.

Time.—A large goose, 1 ¾ hour; a moderate-sized one, 1 ¾ to 1 ½ hour.

Seasonable from September to March; but in perfection from Michaelmas to Christmas.

Average cost, 5s. 6d. each. *Sufficient* for 8 or 9 persons.

Note.—A teaspoonful of made mustard, a saltspoonful of salt, a few grains of cayenne, mixed with a glass of port wine, are sometimes poured into the goose by a slit made in the apron. This sauce is, by many persons, considered an improvement.

Boiled Partridge

THE ADVENTURE OF THE VEILED LODGER (1896)
by Arthur Conan Doyle

*"There is a cold partridge on the sideboard, Watson,
and a bottle of Montrachet. Let us renew our energies
before we make a fresh call upon them."*

The veiled lodger keeps her face hidden from everyone. The
landlady with whom she has lodged for seven years visits
Sherlock Holmes to enlist his help for the self-imprisoned,
tormented victim. Only once, in a sudden chance encounter,
has the landlady seen the face behind the veil. She presents
the facts of the case on behalf of the mysterious woman who is
now willing to expose her secrets and make a confession to the
right person—to Sherlock Holmes.

Holmes knows something of the history of Mrs. Ronda, as
the veiled lodger is named, and remembers that she had been
a circus lion trainer in partnership with a despicable husband.
He reviews with Watson the details of the case before suggesting a repast designed to refresh their thoughts and actions.

Apparently, cold partridge does the trick. He and Watson
visit Mrs. Ronda, see her mutilated face, and are told the
entire story which has placed her in this plight. The puzzle
pieces are fitted together. Or was it the Montrachet which
brought about a successful conclusion?

 # Boiled Partridge and Sauce

In any case, a recipe for partridge from John Armstrong's *Young Woman's Guide to Virtue, Economy and Happiness* (1817) sounds too interesting to suppose that anything will be left over for serving cold. A sauce is included, just in case there is.

To boil Partridges.
Truss the partridges, as done for boiled fowls. Boil them in a proper quantity of water, and in about fifteen or twenty minutes they will be sufficiently done. When ready to be served up, pour over them some rice stewed in gravy, with salt and pepper; the rice should stew in the gravy till it become quite thick, and to this a particular attention should be paid.

Sauce for cold Partridge
Beat up the yolk of a hard egg with oil and vinegar. Add a little anchovy liquor, some Cayenne pepper, salt, parsley, and shalot, both chopped small.

Roast Turkey

MANSFIELD PARK (1814) by Jane Austen

"And you know what your dinner will be," said Mrs. Grant, smiling—"the turkey, and I assure you a very fine one."

While the novels of Jane Austen deal with social and moral problems, they are essentially entertaining. But *Mansfield Park* has at its center a serious subject, which does not lend itself to humorous treatment. It focuses on whether Mary Crawford, who despises the clerical office, will marry a clergyman. The mature Jane Austen uses her skill and power to organize a variety of ideas and motives against a backdrop of Mansfield Park society.

Fanny Price has been brought up at Mansfield Park, the home of Sir Thomas and Lady Bertram. Her own mother, the overburdened and impoverished Mrs. Price, made an unprosperous marriage, and was forced to turn for assistance to her sisters, Lady Bertram and Mrs. Norris. At Mansfield Park, Fanny is constantly reminded of her lowly status and made to feel uncomfortable, but compensations come in the kindnesses shown primarily by her cousin Edmund.

With the passage of time, her older cousin Tom develops into a carelessly extravagant young man, while Edmund chooses a clerical profession. He should have taken over the parsongage after Mr. Norris died, but Edmund must for a while help to pay for Tom's reckless spending.

After the death of Mr. Norris, the Grants move into Mansfield Parsonage. Dr. Grant, a man in his mid-forties, enjoys good food; and his young wife indulges him with rich dishes and an expensive cook, to the disapproval of Mrs. Norris, who seizes any reason for finding fault with them.

Mrs. Grant is the half-sister of Mary and Henry Crawford and the reason why the Crawfords have left London to stay for a while in Mansfield. Mrs. Grant invites Fanny and Edmund to dine at the parsonage. Turkey will be served, and she explains why. Although she would have preferred to save the turkey for Sunday when Dr. Grant could really have enjoyed it after a tiring day, the cook has warned that it will not keep until then; "cook insists upon the turkey's being dressed to-morrow." Dr. Grant responds that although he is glad there is "anything so good in the house," he does not care about a fine bill of fare. He is interested only in the fine company of Fanny Price and Edmund Bertram.

Lady Bertram expresses surprise that such a fine invitation should be extended to so poor a relation, and a great deal is made about whether she can spare Fanny. The odious Mrs. Norris arrives the next day to remind Fanny how fortunate she is to receive the invitation and to advise on proper deportment in view of Fanny's inferior social position.

Fanny, who has been mainly kept at home to act as companion to the selfish and indolent Lady Bertram, appreciates the rare social opportunity given to her and reflects that although she may be hurt by seeing Edmund together with Mary Crawford, she is happy to go. "Simple as such an engagement might appear in other eyes, it had novelty and importance in hers, for excepting the day at Sotherton, she had scarcely ever dined out before."

Unassertive and timid, Fanny remains reticent throughout dinner. But she feels compelled to speak up when Henry

Crawford expresses regret that her uncle's unexpected return from Antigua had put a stop to the theatricals:

> "As far as I am concerned, sir, I would not have delayed his return for a day. My uncle disapproved of it all so entirely when he did arrive, that in my opinion everything had gone quite far enough."

The effect of her angry words is to make Henry Crawford recognize her as a person of unique qualities, not a non-entity to be ignored. He reconsiders and expresses agreement with her. He tries to engage her in conversation and continues to be attentive to her from then on.

It is with no small thanks to a turkey dinner at the Grants' that the hesitant Fanny ceases to be a passive heroine. She has now entered the social circle and moves within it toward its center. Complications and misunderstandings ensue, but Fanny's integrity and devotion prevail. Predictably, all ends happily for her. Her patience is rewarded by marriage to Edmund. Even the untimely death of Dr. Grant intervenes in the penultimate paragraph to allow Edmund and Fanny to have the parsonage and a good income.

Roast Turkey

So crucial is the conversation that transpires at the dinner table, that no mention is made of the turkey that Mrs. Grant had earlier announced would be served. Nevertheless, an eighteenth-century recipe from E. Smith's *The Compleat Housewife* (1729) is one that might have been used.

To Roast a Turkey

Take a quarter of a pound of lean veal, a little thyme, parsley, sweet marjoram, a sprig of winter savory, a bit of lemon peel, one onion, a nutmeg grated, a dram of mace, a little salt, and half a pound of butter; cut your herbs very small, pound your meat as small as possible, and mix all together with three eggs, and as much flour or bread, as will make it of a proper consistence. Then fill the crop of your turkey with it, paper the breast and lay it down at a good distance from the fire. An hour and a quarter will roast it if not very large.

UPDATE: Roast in a moderate oven (325°) allowing three to four hours for a four- to eight-pound turkey, four and one-half to five hours for a twelve- to sixteen-pound turkey.

Quails

ANN VERONICA (1909) by H. G. Wells

*They were eating quails when they returned to the topic
of love.*

The topic of love on which the two diners converse is not about
the couple's love for each other. Rather, Ann Veronica is dis-
cussing the man she loves with Mr. Ramage, who has invited
her to dinner. Having left home to live alone in London, Ann
Veronica finds that her options are limited and turns to Mr.
Ramage for help.

Ann Veronica is an intelligent, attractive, and independent young lady. She had left home after her unreasonably
strict father refused to allow her to attend an unchaperoned
dance. Rebellious and resentful of the stifling and narrow
confines of her life, she defied the dictates of her father and
abandoned home to live on her own in London.

The lively heroine, in search of self-fulfillment, is dis-
couraged by the lack of opportunities available to women. She
accepts the help and friendship as well as a loan from Ramage,
an older, married man from her home town. He invites Ann
Veronica to dinner, feeling happily in love with her. But her
own mind is on the biology instructor she has met at the
college where she studies and with whom she is in love.

Over quails, they discuss love and its effects, and Ramage

asks why she believes that love makes people happy. She admits to confusion. Afterwards, at the opera, he confesses his own love and unnerves her greatly. Then she learns of her benefactor's real intentions when he attempts to seduce her.

Ramage—with a name that suggests "ravage"—is enraged to learn that the woman he has been helping is not willing to pay for that help. Did she not realize that he was giving, not lending, money for a purpose? Incensed by her total innocence and lack of worldliness, the thwarted Mr. Ramage tries to enforce his frustrated desires, but Ann Veronica manages to ward off the attempted rape.

On the rebound, she becomes a zealous suffragette and is arrested and imprisoned. She also becomes involved with a respectable suitor. Eventually, she returns to the man she loves, who has been separated from his wife, and runs off to Switzerland with him. But the progress of this emancipated woman ends when Wells conveniently gets rid of the unwanted wife, thereby enabling the pair to marry and enter the respectable middle class. She is reconciled with her family, and all ends happily. Or does it? There remains a lingering doubt as to whether the passion can survive within the confines of a conventional marriage.

Although Wells may be accused of capitulating at the end, the ideas were shocking in the England of 1909, and the scandalous novel was vilified. Preachers condemned it, libraries banned it, and the press attacked it. One reviewer called it "a poisonous book."

Wells had outraged Victorian propriety by championing sexual freedom and dealing with it openly in this novel. Sexual desire, he asserted, existed in women and was normal and acceptable. It was understandable for women to want more than the role of subservient daughter until marriage released them into the role of subservient wife. Although he weakened in the end by having the rebellious and independent heroine become a dutiful wife, he nevertheless broke new ground.

Quails

Just two years before the appearance of *Ann Veronica*, Escoffier published his *Guide to Modern Cookery,* which raised the level of cooking rather than Victorian eyebrows. Tasteful quails compensate for the distasteful episode which follows their appearance in the novel.

Quails

Quails should always be chosen plump, and their fat should be white and very firm. Besides the spit, which should always be used in preference to the oven for roasting, they allow of two other methods of cooking: they may be cooked in butter, in a saucepan; or they may be poached in excellent strong and gelatinous veal stock.

This last mode of procedure greatly enhances the quail's quality and is frequently used.

Meat Dishes

Veal Cutlets

DAVID COPPERFIELD (1850) by Charles Dickens

I never knew her more cheerful than she was, that very same night, over a veal-cutlet before the kitchen fire, telling me stories about her papa and mamma.

In this long autobiographical novel, David Copperfield begins with the beginning as he tells the story of his life. His father had been dead for six months when David was born. His mother eventually marries the heartless Mr. Murdstone, who sends the young lad off to school. David suffers further punishment and degradation but remains in school until his mother dies. Then Mr. Murdstone and his cruel sister rid themselves of the unwanted burden by sending David out to work in a rat-infested warehouse in London. Arrangements are made for the boy to lodge with Mr. and Mrs. Micawber.

In their shabby circumstances, the Micawbers are deeply in debt, hounded by creditors, and encumbered with children. They live from hand to mouth but seem able to bounce out of the depths of misery, especially with a treat of some delicate food speciality. David observes that despite her swooning after yet another financial setback, Mrs. Micawber finds herself recovered that same evening as she indulges in a veal cutlet and regales David with stories of her past.

David watches the foibles and eccentricities of the Micawbers and manages to pass the time with them in a relatively pleasant manner. He grows attached to the family. Even when Mr. Micawber is in prison, there is a sense of life and joy about him.

Everyone likes Mr. Micawber, including his creditors. The qualities of this leading character add humor and meaning to the story. But David's life with the Micawbers ends with the start of his manhood and fulfills the prophecy of the chapter title, "I begin life on my own account."

Veal Cutlets

Two dishes selected from *David Copperfield* are associated with the pleasant, if improvident, Micawbers. Both represent a Dickensian England filled with chops and joints and puddings. Both recipes are extracted from Eliza Acton's *Modern Cookery* of 1845. Appropriately, the loin of mutton (see page 187) is a practical and frugal dish, but I wonder whether Mrs. Micawber had the epicurean and "indispensable" mushroom sauce with her veal cutlet.

Veal Cutlets

Take them, if possible, free from bone, and after having trimmed them into proper shape, beat them with a paste roller until the fibre of the meat is thoroughly broken; flour them well to prevent the escape of the gravy, and fry them from twelve to fifteen minutes over a fire that is not sufficiently fierce to burn them before they are quite cooked through: they should be of a fine amber brown, and *perfectly done*. Lift them into a hot dish, pour the fat from the pan, throw in a slice of fresh butter, and when it is melted, stir or dredge in a dessertspoonful of flour; keep these shaken until they are well-coloured, then pour gradually to them a cup of gravy or boiling water; add pepper, salt, a little lemon-pickle or juice, give the whole a boil, and pour it over the cutlets: a few forcemeat balls, fried, and served with them, is usually a very acceptable addition to this dish, even when it is garnished or accompanied with rashers of ham or bacon. A morsel of *glaze*, or of the jelly of roast meat, should, when at hand, be added to the sauce, which a little mushroom powder would further improve: mushroom sauce, indeed, is considered by many epicures, as indispensable with veal cutlets. We have recommended in this one instance, that the meat should be thoroughly *beaten*, because we find that the veal is wonderfully improved by the process, which, however, we still deprecate for other meats, unless indeed we except pork chops.

12 to 15 minutes.

UPDATE: A dessertspoonful is equal to 2 teaspoons.

Loin of Mutton

See: DAVID COPPERFIELD (1850) by Charles Dickens, page 183.

Another debtor, who shared the room with Mr. Micawber, came in from the bakehouse with the loin of mutton which was our joint-stock repast.

David Copperfield visits Mr. Macawber in debtors' prison where Mr. Micawber waxes philosophical as he expresses economic wisdom. They dine on a loin of mutton, using a borrowed knife and fork, and David concludes that "there was something gipsy-like and agreeable in the dinner." In *Modern Cookery* (1845), Eliza Acton's directions are largely taken up in advising how to avoid waste in preparing this frugal dish.

To Roast a Loin of Mutton

The flesh of the loin of mutton is superior to that of the leg, when roasted; but to the frugal housekeeper, this consideration is usually overbalanced by the great weight of fat attached to it; this, however, when economy is more considered than appearance, may be pared off, and melted down for various kitchen-uses, or finely chopped, and substituted for suet in making hot pie, or pudding crust. When thus reduced in size, the mutton will be soon roasted. If it is to be dressed in the usual way, the butcher should be desired to take off the skin; care should be taken to preserve the fat from being ever so slightly burned; it should be

187

managed, indeed, in the same manner as the saddle, in every respect, and carved also in the same way, that is to say, the meat should be cut out in slices the whole length of the back-bone, and close to it.

Without the fat, 1 to 1 ½ hour; with, 1 ¼ to 1 ¾ hours.

Roast Mutton

THE TURN OF THE SCREW (1898) by Henry James

The roast mutton was on the table, and I had dispensed with attendance. . . "Come here and take your mutton."

In *The Turn of the Screw* Henry James produced a gripping ghost story that is entirely credible. The governess is the narrator of a story that the reader is maneuvered into believing even though a careful reading reveals that she is unreliable as a narrator and that her account is riddled with contradictions. James called his tale a trap for the unwary reader.

The governess relates how an English gentleman, the guardian of his young niece and nephew, hires her to care for the orphaned children. He stipulates that she must accept total responsibility and not disturb him with any questions or problems, regardless of magnitude. She is to make her own decisions in her position of supreme authority. Having fallen instantly—and hopelessly—in love with the fairy-tale bachelor, she accepts the position out of a desire to please him. Of course that means she will never again see the rich, handsome, and charming prince who seems to her to have come out of "a dream or an old novel." Her tendency to romanticize is exacerbated by an imagination active enough

189

to wonder about the unexplained and sudden death of her predecessor and to produce apparitions.

The young, inexperienced, and provincial daughter of a country parson arrives at the isolated country estate of Bly to take up her portentous position. She is greeted by the house-keeper, who seems to be inordinately relieved at her arrival. Mrs. Grose is a simple person who cannot read, knows her place, and is willing to accept what the governess tells her.

Emotionally overwrought and feeling great responsibility and loneliness, the governess immediately begins to suffer from insomnia. She fancies that she hears sounds in the night which include a light footstep in the passage outside her door and the distant cry of a child. Nevertheless, she is completely taken with her young charge and allows Flora to show her around Bly, envisioning it as a storybook castle. Then Miles is dismissed from school under mysterious circumstances, and hints of evil doings begin to build up.

The governess gives vent to her imagination as she fancies how delightful it would be to encounter, while strolling in the garden, a certain someone who would smile his approval. Suddenly, one afternoon, at twilight, she does see someone. But he is high up in the tower, and he is a stranger rather than her employer. The apparition is later identified as Peter Quint, the former valet who died when he slipped on the ice after leaving a public house in a drunken state. When she again sees him as he looks in through the dining room window, she knows for a certainty that he has come for the children.

Not long afterwards, when she and Flora are out of doors, the governess becomes aware of a figure on the opposite side of the lake. She concludes it is the former governess, Miss Jessel, and that the little girl also sees the figure.

Her suspicions of evil mount. When she catches Miles out on the lawn at midnight looking up, she knows that he is gazing at a person above her, the man in the tower. She becomes completely convinced that Peter Quint and Miss Jessel are trying to possess the children and is equally certain that the children respond to the ghosts and communicate with them. Peter Quint and Miss Jessel had been intimate in life and are somehow associated with depraved acts. Having corrupted the children with their ominous deeds, the pair return now from the dead to possess the souls of the innocent children. She must save them from the demons.

Flora, in search of freedom from confinement by her overprotective governess, runs off one day. When she is found, the governess demands that Flora tell her where Miss Jessel is, then screams out the answer herself, pointing across the lake: "She's there, she's there!" The child is convulsed with fear and begs and cries to be taken away. Delirious, she is comforted and removed from the scene by Mrs. Grose.

Left alone with the boy, the governess is determined to extort a confession from him. Her last interview with him is arranged over a roast mutton dinner. Miles "looked at the joint" and is told to "come here and take your mutton." He helps himself and tries to converse about his sister, while the governess remains obsessed with her thoughts about saving the boy: "Our meal was of the briefest—mine a vain pretence, and I had the things immediately removed."

She presses him for the reason for his expulsion from school. She shrieks to Peter Quint who appears at the dining room window that he shall possess the boy "no more, no more, no more!" She points out the spectre to the unseeing Miles. The horror of his trying to understand what she wants him to see, manifested in his agonized cry, has tragic consequences. Her demand for a confession and submission ends in his collapse from a shock too great to bear, and "his little heart, dispossessed, had stopped."

Readers have been manipulated into believing the ghostly aspect of the story with its theme of the supernatural. They often miss the fact that only the governess sees apparitions, and she alone explains their purpose. The tale is deliberately ambiguous and extremely clever.

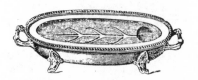

Roast Mutton

Some have called the tale a pot-boiler. Let us allow the pot to boil with the last dinner served to young Master Miles— roast mutton. Appropriate to a grand country house setting, this recipe, though not a figment and not ambiguous, was first conjured up by Mrs. Margaret Dods in *The Cook and Housewife's Manual* in 1826. It appears in exactly the same form some sixty years later, in the 1885 edition, with the same curious suggestions for dealing with unfresh meat and keeping off flies.

To Roast a Leg of Mutton.

Mutton intended to be roasted may be kept longer than mutton for boiling, as the colour is of less importance. Cut out the pipe that runs along the back bone, which taints so early; wipe off the mustiness that gathers on the surface, and in the folds and doublings of the meat, and below the flap. This and every other piece of meat may be lightly dusted with flour, or with pepper or pounded ginger, which, by excluding the external air and keeping off flies, helps to preserve the meat, and can be taken off in the washing, previous to roasting. A *leg*, a *chine*, a *saddle*, a *loin*, a *breast*, a *shoulder*, and the *haunch* or *gigot*, are the roasting pieces of mutton. Joint the roast well, whatever be the piece.

Roast Saddle of Mutton

THE FORSYTE SAGA (1922) by John Galsworthy

No Forsyte has given a dinner without providing a saddle of mutton. There is something in its succulent solidity which makes it suitable to people 'of a certain position'. It is nourishing and—tasty; the sort of thing a man remembers eating. It has a past and a future, like a deposit paid into a bank; and it is something that can be argued about.

Playwright and novelist John Galsworthy first introduced the Forsyte family in 1906 in *The Man of Property*, generally regarded as his best novel and the most widely read. He returned to the same characters in *In Chancery* (1920) and *To Let* (1921). When the three novels were published in 1922 in a single volume with the title *The Forsyte Saga*, Galsworthy's success and fame became firmly established. A good story-teller, he continued to return to the Forsytes in other novels and in short stories.

The Forsyte Saga presented a powerful expression of the anti-Victorian climate which was prevalent in the post-war period. It omitted the war years, jumping from 1901 to 1920, and dealt with evils and abuses of life and with the topic of the day, female emancipation. Galsworthy was fifty-five, and his popularity continued unabated for the rest of his life. By the time of his death early in 1933, shortly after he was awarded the Nobel Prize, he had left a large output including seventeen novels, twenty-six plays, and twelve volumes of short stories. In recent times, television has brought about a resurgence of interest in him.

The Man of Property takes place in London from June 1886 to December 1887 and introduces members of the Forsyte family by way of an "At Home" celebration on the occasion of the engagement of June Forsyte, old Jolyon's granddaughter, to Philip Bosinney. It tells of the unfortunate marriage of Soames Forsyte and Irene. Soames, ironically dubbed "the man of property" by old Jolyon, seeks to impose his will—the will of a Forsyte must not be resisted—on Irene. She comes to understand that to Soames she is like one of his portraits, a piece of property.

Early chapters give insight into Forsyte traits, which include close family ties, good living, and acquisitiveness. Gradually, family traditions are disclosed and British institutions are criticized. We learn about old Jolyon from his furniture and food—heavily carved mahogany and saddle of mutton.

The essence of the Forsyte family is described in terms of what is served at dinner. Basic traits are embodied in mutton. After a second glass of champagne, comes "the crowning point of a Forsyte feast—'the saddle of mutton'." Galsworthy enriches characterization by describing the favorite dish, and he makes a great point about the significance of saddle of mutton:

> To anyone interested psychologically in Forsytes, this great saddle-of-mutton trait is of prime importance; not only does it illustrate their tenacity, both collectively and as individuals, but it marks them as belonging in fibre and instincts to that great class which believes in nourishment and flavour, and yields to no sentimental craving for beauty.

194

Younger members of the family, Galsworthy continues with irony, would have avoided a joint altogether in favor of more imaginative, if less nourishing, courses. But such rebels were either females or males led astray by females. Wives and mothers who were forced to eat saddle of mutton throughout their married lives transferred their hostility towards it. So we have a classic within a classic—the classic English cut of lamb or young mutton within *The Forsyte Saga*.

Roast Saddle of Mutton

A traditional recipe to uphold Forsyte tradition as a saddle-of-mutton family is taken from another British institution, *Mrs. Beeton's Book of Household Management* of 1861.

INGREDIENTS.—Saddle of mutton, a little salt.

Mode.—To insure this joint being tender, let it hang for ten days or a fortnight, if the weather permits. Cut off the tail and flaps, and trim away every part that has not indisputable pretensions to be eaten, and have the skin taken off and skewered on again. Put it down to a bright, clear fire, and, when the joint has been cooking for an hour, remove the skin and dredge it with flour. It should not be placed too near the fire, as the fat should not be in the slightest degree burnt. Keep constantly basting, both before and after the skin is removed; sprinkle some salt over the meat, which send to table with a tureen of made gravy and red-currant jelly.

Time.—A saddle of mutton weighing 10 lbs., 2½ hours; 14 lbs., 3 ¼ hours. When liked underdone, allow rather less time.

Average Cost, 10 *d.* per lb.

Sufficient.—A moderate-sized saddle of 10 lbs. for 7 or 8 persons.

Seasonable all the year; not so good when lamb is in full season.

UPDATE: The saddle, the two loins together from ribs to tail, weighs about 10 pounds and should be roasted in a moderate oven for 20 minutes to the pound. It should be carved along the backbone.

Mutton Chops

THE WARDEN (1855) by Anthony Trollope

But a solitary dinner in an old, respectable, sombre,
solid London inn—what can be more melancholy than
a mutton chop and a pint of port in such a place?

Trollope is best known for his Barsetshire series, which consists of six novels portraying the clerical community of Barchester in the mid-nineteenth century. The first novel of the series, *The Warden*, portrays a quiet place and expresses affection for a world that is passing.

The gentle Reverend Septimus Harding is warden of a charitable foundation known as Hiram's Hospital. The position is attacked as a sinecure by John Bold, a young Barchester surgeon who seeks reform. Legal action is eventually taken on behalf of the inmates who are allegedly deprived of income that is rightfully theirs. The situation is complicated by the fact that John Bold is in love with Eleanor, Harding's younger daughter.

Honest and self-effacing, Mr. Harding is greatly distressed. His sense of morality suggests that the allegation may be correct. Furthermore, opposition to John Bold may damage Eleanor's chances for a suitable marriage. He worries and agonizes over his painful position, and the pain is exacerbated by the opposing stance taken by the intimidating Archdeacon Grantly.

When the diffident Mr. Harding goes to London to resign the wardenship, an independent and courageous act, he settles into a quiet and convenient inn where he has dinner in the company only of his troubled thoughts. In solitude, he partakes of a lonely and melancholy dinner consisting of a "mutton chop and a pint of port." After the mutton chop meal, Harding goes out to secure an appointment with Sir Abraham Haphazard to obtain legal advice. Given an appointment for 10 p.m. the next day, he remains in a state of trepidation lest he meet Dr. Grantly, whose support and advice he is now acting against.

Nervously passing the time prior to his late evening appointment with the barrister, Harding enters a shell-fish supper-house and again orders his customary mutton chop in an uncustomary setting. He is filled with anxiety as he dines in the squalid restaurant amid scents of lobster, oysters, and salmon. "His chop and potatoes, however, were eatable." Then, after coffee and a nap, he keeps his appointment, which confirms him in his decision to dissociate himself from the legal proceedings. His determination to resign gives him the comfort and confidence to now face Archdeacon Grantly.

After the resignation, the position of warden is left vacant, and the hospital falls into decay. The twelve old men who reside there are hurt by the reforms, and they lose the friendly care bestowed by their former warden. Eleanor Harding and John Bold marry. And the story continues in the next novel of the series, *Barchester Towers.*

Mutton Chops

If Mary Holland's 1825 recipe for mutton chops (in *Domestic Cookery*) cannot mask surrounding fishy smells, we learn something about Victorian sea-food restaurants.

Mutton Chops

Cut the back ribs or loin into handsome steaks, and flatten them; season with salt and spices, and stew bread crumbs over them. Put them in a frying-pan with a rich beef-stock, seasoned with ketchup and red wine. When it boils, put the whole into a close sauce-pan to stew. Dish it with cut pickles.

Mutton Cutlets

See: THE WOMAN IN WHITE (1860) by Wilkie Collins,
page 130.

*"I thought you liked boiled chicken better than cutlet,
Mrs. Vesey?"*

With Mrs. Vesey unable to decide whether to have
chicken or cutlet, the issue is decided by the compromise to
have both. And recipes for both are taken from *The English
Cookery Book* of 1856 by Frederick W. Davis.

Mutton Cutlets

Chop the leaves off half-a-dozen stalks of parsley, and a couple of
shallots, very fine; season with small quantities of salt and
Cayenne, and mix all together in a tablespoonful of Florence oil;
cover the cutlets on both sides with these ingredients, shake
them in finely-powdered bread crumbs, and fry in fresh butter,
turning them till quite done.

UPDATE: For Florence (or Italian) oil, use olive oil.

Cold Lamb Cutlets

PORTRAIT OF THE ARTIST AS A YOUNG DOG (1940)
by Dylan Thomas

"I do hope you like cold lamb."

Known and admired primarily as a poet, Dylan Thomas also wrote fiction of enormous merit. He was a great storyteller, particularly in pubs, and he could be very funny. Ten comic stories make up his most successful prose work, *Portrait of the Artist as a Young Dog.*

With a title that pays tribute to James Joyce's *A Portrait of the Artist as a Young Man,* Thomas produced an autobiographical collection that delves into the subject of growing up and into his Welsh childhood. The humorous and self-critical volume won for Thomas his first large reading audience. In each story, the boy is initiated into some aspect of adult life—love, friendship, madness, death—and a unified portrait of the young man emerges at the end.

"The Fight," one of the sensitive and observant stories of the *Portrait,* is based on the author's actual first meeting with a most important friend of his life, Dan Jones. A composer, writer, and scholar, Dr. Daniel Jones (a doctor of music who was later to compose the score for *Under Milk Wood*) has confirmed that the account is substantially correct. It was in the Jones home in Swansea that Dylan completed his literary education. Mr. Thomas had given his son a good foundation in the English classics. In the more broadly cultural home of his friend, Dylan learned about modern literature and foreign poetry. The boys met almost daily and read aloud to each other, supported each other, and exchanged criticism and dreams.

In "The Fight," the narrator describes his mischievous behavior as he awaits an opportunity to annoy Mr. Samuels, who complained regularly of being pelted by missiles thrown by boys from the school. Then the protagonist is himself accosted by a newcomer, and the two boys engage in a fist-fight. They are soon united in friendship, however, by mutual opposition to Mr. Samuels. They walk away together, proud of their bruises. Our hero sports the "best black eye in Wales" while his friend walks with coat flung open to display the bloodstains all over his shirt.

At home, the narrator, feeling like Tunney, sits silently over his sago pudding as he contemplates the situation and fantasizes before returning to school in the afternoon. In the evening, full of his own poetry, he calls on his new friend.

Dan is also a writer (who has already produced seven novels) and a composer who plays the piano and violin. They talk, they play a piano duet, they pay tribute to each other's creative endeavors, and they are called to supper.

At the supper table are Dan's parents, his aunt, and the Reverend and Mrs. Bevan. Mr. Bevan says grace hurriedly and plunges into his food. "He went at the cold meat like a dog." Mrs. Bevan, who "didn't look all there," feels reassured and begins to eat when the hostess says, "I do hope you like cold lamb." Mrs. Bevan, who is "off her head," asks for more meat. Our hero tries to impress the company by making himself a year older. Then he is discomfited when his host insists that he recite one of his poems, and the callow, derivative attempt is exposed.

By themselves after supper, the romantic thread is resumed. The boys discuss and try to understand Mrs. Bevan's form of madness before it is time for them to part. Dan must finish composing his string trio this evening, and the narrator must continue the long poem he is currently writing. They part to go to bed.

 # Cold Lamb Cutlets

The supper scene with cold lamb represents the adult world of cold reality. Mrs. Beeton provides a realistic way of preparing an excellent dish of cold lamb, but it might be more fun to indulge in a bit of fantasy over sago pudding (page 350), also provided in *Beeton's Book of Household Management* (1915).

Cold Lamb Cutlets (Fr.—Cotelettes d'Agneau à la Gelée.)

There are various ways of preparing this dish. The cutlets may be cooked in butter (sautéed or grilled) or braised and pressed. The former method is no doubt more simple, although braising is highly recommended on account of the fine flavour imparted to the meat by this method of cooking. The cutlets must be carefully pared, trimmed and flattened before they are cooked, and when cooked they must be pressed beneath a heavy weight, and kept thus until they are quite cold. To finish them, proceed as follows:—
Pour a layer of aspic in a sauté-pan, or large dish,; when set arrange the cutlets in it, cover with another layer of aspic jelly, and let this also set. Place the pan or dish on the ice for about 1 hour, then cut the cutlets out with a sharp knife, and arrange them in a circle on a round dish. Fill the centre of the dish with some kind of cooked vegetables—peas, beans, asparagus points, or macedoine—previously seasoned with mayonnaise or French salad dressing, and garnish with neatly cut cubes of set aspic jelly, and serve.
Average Cost, ls. to ls.2d. per lb. Allow 9 or 10 cutlets for 6 or 7 persons.

Curried Mutton

SILVER BLAZE (1890) by Arthur Conan Doyle

*The maid . . . carried down to the stables his supper,
which consisted of a dish of curried mutton.*

The mystery of an entire story, *Silver Blaze*, centers on a dish
of curry given to the stable boy. After supper, he has a drugged
sleep which enables the villain to remove the eponymous
horse from the stable in order to carry out his nefarious
scheme. The boy's curry had contained powdered opium, but
others in the house ate the same dish without ill effect. The
impeccable reasoning of Sherlock Holmes deduces that while
the taste of opium would be detected in ordinary bland food, "a
curry was exactly the medium which would disguise the taste"
of powdered opium. It follows that anyone who could not
possibly have a say in deciding the menu for the evening
supper is eliminated as a suspect. Elementary!

Curried Mutton

Here to underscore an enjoyable story is this recipe taken from *Mrs. A. B. Marshall's Cookery Book* of about the year 1890:

Curried Mutton
Peel six good sized onions, cut them up small, and put them into a stewpan with two ounces of fat or butter and two and a half to three pounds of boned scrag of mutton, or other part if preferred, cut up in neat pieces; season with a little salt, a pinch each of ground ginger, mace, cinnamon, and thyme, and two or three chopped bayleaves; fry all together till a nice brown colour, then add two tablespoonsfuls of flour, a tablespoonful of Marshall's curry powder, a tablespoonful of chutney, the strained juice of one lemon, and sufficient water or light stock to cover it, and boil very gently for one and a half to two hours, keeping it skimmed as the fat rises to the surface; dish the meat up in a pile in the center of a hot dish, in a border of boiled rice, and serve round the meat the gravy in which it was cooked.

Indian Curry

VANITY FAIR (1848) by William Makepeace Thackeray

His mouth was full of it; his face quite red with the delightful exercise of gobbling. "Mother, it's quite as good as my own curries in India."

Rebecca Sharp has been invited by her friend Amelia Sedley to spend a week at the Sedley home in Russell Square. She is delighted to meet Amelia's brother Joseph, who has just returned from India. Having learned that he is rich and unmarried, Becky schemes to snare him as a husband. Her ploy at dinner is to pretend to be very interested in India. Mrs. Sedley has prepared a "fine curry" for her fat son, and Rebecca remarks that everything from India must be good. Mr. Sedley, who has no difficulty in seeing through to her design, immediately offers her some curry.

Poor provincial Becky samples the unknown dish, and her delicate palate suffers from the effects of cayenne pepper. She is obviously feeling extremely uncomfortable to the amusement of both Joseph and his father, and Joseph compounds the cruelty by offering her a chili. Since chile suggests to her something cool, she eats it—then cries out for water. Joseph and his father enjoy their joke enormously and have a good laugh at the expense of the humiliated Becky, who has perhaps for once been properly punished for her deviousness.

Indian Curry

Becky Sharp was obviously not familiar with Eliza Acton's *Modern Cookery* of 1845. After supplying the following curry recipe, Eliza Acton offers this observation on the use of pepper: "Cayenne pepper can always be added to heighten the pungency of a currie, when the proportion in the powder is not considered sufficient."

A Common Indian Curry

For each pound of meat, whether veal, mutton, or beef, take a heaped tablespoonful of good currie-powder, a small teaspoonful of salt, and one of flour; mix these well together, and after having cut down the meat into thick small cutlets, or squares, rub half of the mixed powder equally over it. Next, fry gently from one to four or five large onions sliced, with or without the addition of a small clove of garlic, or half a dozen eschalots, according to the taste; and when they are of a fine golden brown, lift them out with a slice [sic] and lay them upon a sieve to drain; throw a little more butter into the pan and fry the meat lightly in it; drain it well from the fat in taking it out, and lay it into a clean stewpan or saucepan, strew the onion over it, and pour in as much boiling water as will almost cover it. Mix the remainder of the currie-powder smoothly with a little broth or cold water, and after the currie has stewed for a few minutes pour it in, shaking the pan well round that it may be smoothly blended with the gravy. Simmer the whole very softly until the meat is perfectly tender; this will be in from an hour and a quarter to two hours and a half, according to the quantity and the nature of the meat. Mutton will be the soonest done; the brisket end (gristles) of a breast of veal will require twice as much stewing, and sometimes more. A fowl will be done in an hour. An acid apple or two, or any of the vegetables we have enumerated at the commencement of this Chapter,* may be added to the currie, proper time being allowed for the cooking of each variety. Very young green peas, are liked by some people in it, and cucumbers pared, seeded and cut moderately small, are always a good addition. A richer currie will of course be produced if gravy or broth be substituted for the water: either should be boiling when poured to the meat. Lemon-juice should be stirred in before it is served, when there is no other acid in the currie. A dish of rice must be sent to table with it.

* Spinage, cucumbers, vegetable marrow, tomatas, acid apples, green goosberries (seeded), and tamarinds imported *in the shell*—not preserved—may all, in their season, be added, with very good effect, to curries of different kinds. Potatoes and celery are also occasionally boiled down in them.

Stew of Meat and Potatoes

THE MILL ON THE FLOSS (1860) by George Eliot

> *The men seated themselves and began to attack the contents of the kettle—a stew of meat and potatoes—which had been taken off the fire and turned out into a yellow platter.*

The young Maggie Tulliver harbors a deep love for her brother Tom and is so dependent on him that her demands for his attention become excessive. She feels ignored and neglected when Tom is enjoying the company of Lucy, a proper little girl. In a desperate state of passion, Maggie pushes Lucy into the mud. Tom slaps his sister before running to pick up and comfort the tearful Lucy.

The heartbroken Maggie determines to run off to the gypsies and find refuge in their world. After all, had she not been told that she was like a gypsy, that she was "half wild"? Her fault-finding family would never see her again. Tom would regret his cruelty.

Tired and hungry, she manages to make her way to the encampment of gypsies, who take her in and address her as "my pretty lady." But her dream soon turns into unpleasant reality. The gypsies dish out their meal of stew and eat with gusto. But Maggie feels discomfited in this uncongenial environment and has no appetite. She is unable to eat but does not wish to offend. Her romantic notions of gypsy life have been cruelly shattered. When the meal is over, she is happily returned to her Dorlcote Mill home and to the loving arms of her father by a gypsy who receives five shillings for his trouble. Gladly does she go back to the world of reality.

 # Stew of Meat and Potatoes

While it is easy enough to imagine a delicious stew enhanced by a pleasant outdoor setting, it is most unlikely that the gypsies referred to *any* cookery book for their repast. Nevertheless, Eliza Acton's Irish stew recipe of 1845, a simple dish that cannot fail to please, has been selected.

Stew of Meat and Potatoes (Irish Stew)

Take a couple of pounds of small thick mutton cutlets with or without fat according to the taste of the persons to whom the stew is to be served; take also four pounds of good potatoes, weighed after they are pared, slice them thick, and put a portion of them in a flat layer, into a large thick saucepan or stewpan; season the mutton well with pepper, and place some of it on the potatoes, cover it with another layer, and proceed in the same manner with all, reserving plenty of the vegetable for the top; pour in three quarters of a pint of cold water, and add, when the stew begins to boil, an ounce of salt; let it simmer gently for two hours, and serve it very hot. When the addition of onion is liked, strew in two or three minced ones with the potatoes.

Mutton cutlets, 2 lbs; potatoes, 4 lbs; pepper, ½ oz.; salt, 1 oz.; water, ¾ pint: 2 hours

Roast Sirloin of Beef

TOM JONES (1749) by Henry Fielding

*At his first arrival, which was immediately before the
entrance of the roast-beef, he had given an intimation
that he had brought some news with him, and was
beginning to tell. . . when the sight of the roast-beef
struck him dumb, permitting him only to say grace,
and to declare he must pay his respect to the baronet,
for so he called the sirloin.*

Mr. Allworthy, returning late one evening from a trip to
London, finds an infant in his bed. He decides to give it a home
and be the baby's guardian, while Miss Bridget Allworthy, his
unmarried sister, consents to be in charge of its care. Shortly
thereafter, Miss Allworthy marries the odious Captain Bilfil
and has a child. By a stroke of good fortune, her husband dies
of apoplexy. Master Bilfil and the foundling, Tom Jones, are
brought up together. The two lads clash frequently because
Bilfil is filled with malice and resentment. He is a hypocrite, a
liar, and a schemer whose misrepresentations and machina-
tions eventually succeed in having Allworthy evict Tom from
the house. Disgraced, the hero sets out on the adventures
which advance the plot, expose characters and mysteries, and
reveal the secret of Tom's birth. The great comic novel
concludes after Tom emerges as a character worthy of a happy
marriage union with his beautiful and beloved Sophia.

213

A great deal of dining goes on in *Tom Jones*. Fielding himself liked good, plain English food and castigated fancy French dishes such as Périgord pie, ortolans, and turtles. Simple hearty food is so basic to this novel that Fielding uses a roast beef simile to illustrate a point in one of the introductory chapters he wrote for each of the eighteen books which make up the novel. These introductory prefaces contain some of the author's best and liveliest prose and reveal his imagination in the form of an essay, commentary, or theory such as how the novel should be written. In the prologue to Book Six, a discussion on love defines that passion as involving esteem and gratitude and belonging to a high order, whereas, hunger, or "satisfying a voracious appetite with a certain quantity of human flesh," he equates with gross instinct. Fielding tells readers who may not agree with him that "love probably may, in your opinion, very greatly resemble a dish of soup, or a sirloin of roast-beef."

In just one incident involving food in the story itself, the character satisfies his gluttonous hunger with roast beef, and the dinner scene becomes the means by which the plot is thickened. Greatly impressed with Tom's abilities as a sportsman, Squire Western, Allworthy's neighbor, has made Tom a hunting companion and a regular guest at his table. He invites Tom to dinner after a session of hunting together. The young and beautiful Sophia Western presides at the table. But the occasion is spoiled by the arrival of the parson and the news he imparts after appeasing his prodigious appetite on a dinner of sirloin of roast beef.

It seems that the daughter of Squire Allworthy's game-keeper had disrupted the service and caused a bloody brawl because of her outlandish apparel. To the parson's horror, the wench is having a child out of wedlock. Tom makes a hasty escape, leaving his host to deduce that the young rascal is the father of the expected child. Western makes light of the matter on the grounds of normal youthful behavior. Sophia is discomfited and can only ask to be excused from the company.

Once again, fate has conspired, in the form of a meddling parson, to make Tom incur Squire Allworthy's immediate displeasure and give his benefactor one more reason for ejecting him.

Since roast beef had the effect of rendering the parson unable to speak, Tom's position might have been safer a while longer if the parson had continued gourmandizing on endless servings of this solid English fare to keep him in a state of permanent speech disability.

 # Roast Sirloin of Beef

That the parson paid "his respect to the baronet, for so he called the sirloin," is explained by an apocryphal anecdote on the origin of the word "sirloin": King Charles II, delighting at the sight of a huge and steaming loin of beef, exclaimed, "A noble joint! . . . It shall have a title!" He raised his sword over the meat, investing it with a knighthood and raising its status to Sir Loin. Despite the nobility of the story, the truth is that the word is undoubtedly a corruption of the French "surloin" meaning over or above the loin—that is, the upper part of the loin.

Hannah Glasse, in *The Art of Cookery Made Plain and Easy*, published directions for roasting a joint of beef in 1747, just two years before Fielding published *Tom Jones*.

Rules to be observ'd in Roasting.
In the first Place, take great Care the Spit be very clean; and be sure to clean it with nothing but Sand and Water. Wash it clean, and wipe it with a dry Cloth; for Oil, Brick-dust, and such Things, will spoil your Meat.

Beef.
To roast a Piece of Beef of about ten Pounds will take an Hour and a Half, at a good Fire. Twenty Pounds Weight will take three Hours, if it be a thick Piece; but if it be a thin Piece of twenty Pounds Weight, two Hours and a Half will do it; and so on, according to the Weight of your Meat, more or less. *Observe*, In frosty Weather your Beef will take Half an Hour longer.

Stewed Oxtail

THE NINE TAILORS (1934) by Dorothy L. Sayers

"What have we here? Stewed oxtail? Excellent! Most sustaining! I trust, Lord Peter, you can eat stewed oxtail."

In writing *The Nine Tailors*, Dorothy Sayers returned to the countryside of her childhood, the East Anglian Fens. The setting of the novel conveys an absolutely correct impression, although the author invented the village of Fenchurch St. Paul and its typically huge and impressive parish church. She did not, however, invent the technical details of bell ringing. For that, Dorothy L. Sayers did a great deal of study and research into the mystery and science of campanology. The title of her novel is a reference to the knell sounded to announce the death of a man.

In a blinding snowstorm, his car has become disabled, and Lord Peter Wimsey finds himself stranded in desolate Fen country on a cold and blustery New Year's Eve. Making his way to the village of Fenchurch St. Paul, he meets the Rector, whose cordial offer of hospitality at the Rectory is gratefully accepted.

By one of those amazing coincidences that mystery novels are heir to, Lord Peter just happens to know the art of bell ringing and agrees to ring Kent Treble Bob in place of the person who has just been taken ill in the current influenza epidemic. By staying up to ring bells from midnight until nine o'clock, he is in a position to return hospitality.

After a practice session, he and the Rector tour the church and the belfrey. The uncontrollable enthusiasm of the Rector causes them to arrive home a bit late. A dinner of stewed oxtail has been prepared by Mrs. Venables, the Rector's wife. It has a soporific effect, and Wimsey sleeps soundly in preparation for an active night of bell ringing. The long and exhausting bell-ringing session is followed by breakfast. Hospitality is wonderful at the Rectory, for Wimsey is invited to stay on for a lunch of shepherd's pie. Indeed, hospitality is so good that the Rector and his wife express concern about whether the meals being offered are of an acceptable standard. ("I trust you can eat stewed oxtail.". . . "Can you eat shepherd's pie?") The meals must have pleased Lord Peter, a notable gourmet, for he stays on long enough to become immersed in the intriguing story of the Thorpe family tragedies, beginning with the theft of an emerald necklace. He is later willing to return when events take a bizarre turn and his expertise is needed.

Lord Peter unravels the mystery and uncovers the murderer, thanks to the generous invitation issued to dine on stewed oxtail and on shepherd's pie. Had the meals not materialized, the murderer might still be at large.

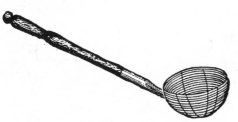

Stewed Oxtail

A stewed oxtail recipe is supplied by Mrs. C. F. Leyel and Olga Hartley in *The Gentle Art of Cookery*, 1925.

Stewed Oxtail

One oxtail, one large onion, one pound of tomatoes, bunch of herbs, two cloves, one dessertspoonful of lemon juice, butter and flour.

Cut up the oxtail and put into a casserole; just cover with water, and let it boil. Remove the scum, and add the onion in slices, and all the seasoning. Put on the lid and stew gently for two hours, then add the tomatoes, and let it simmer for another thirty minutes.

Strain off the gravy and add the butter and flour made into a roux to thicken; squeeze a dessertspoonful of lemon juice into it, and pour back into the casserole.

Boil the whole for another fifteen minutes, and serve in the casserole.

Shepherd's Pie

See: THE NINE TAILORS (1934) by Dorothy L. Sayers, page 217.

"You'll stay to lunch, of course. No trouble at all. Can you eat shepherd's pie?"

After a long bell-ringing session, Wimsey is invited to stay on at the Rectory for shepherd's pie, but not without concern about whether the fare is of an acceptable standard. ("Can you eat shepherd's pie?")

This shepherd's pie must be acceptable, for the following recipe derives from a newer edition (1915) of *Beeton's Book of Household Management.*

Shepherd's Pie

INGREDIENTS.—½ a lb. of beef or mutton, I lb. of mashed potato, I oz. of butter or dripping, ½ a pint of gravy or stock, I teaspoonful of parboiled and finely-chopped onion, salt and pepper.

METHOD.—Cut the meat into small thin slices. Melt half the butter or fat in a stewpan, add to it the potato, salt and pepper, and stir over the fire until thoroughly mixed. Place on the bottom of a greased pie-dish a thin layer of potato, put in the meat, sprinkle each layer with onion, salt and pepper, pour in the gravy, and cover with potato. The potato covering may be roughed with a fork or smoothed over with a knife: the latter method produces an appearance similar to that of ordinary crust. Before baking, the remainder of the fat or butter should be put on the top of the pie in small pieces, or when economy is not an object, the appearance of the pie may be improved by brushing it over with yolk of egg. Bake until the crust is well browned.

TIME.—About ½ an hour. Average Cost, 6 d. Sufficient for 2 persons.

Cow Heel

THE GOOD COMPANIONS (1929) by J. B. Priestley

*"But then sometimes when Father came back, I'd wake
up and go downstairs and he would be having his
supper and perhaps he'd give me some. He adored
cow-heels, done in milk and with onions—and so do I."*

With his long escapist story of adventures on the open road,
J .B. Priestley produced a colossal success which established
his name and reputation permanently. He has written scores
of novels and plays, but *The Good Companions* remains one of
his best-known works.

The novel is about a group of spirited characters who
leave their own world in search of new experiences. His main
characters exchange their unhappy or hopeless positions for
more fruitful lives. Miss Elizabeth Trant, one of his fugitives
from the real world, has cared for her ailing father for many
years until his recent death. Now financially independent at
thirty-seven, she impulsively sets off and becomes involved
with a touring group of actors. She meets Jess Oakroyd, who
has broken away from his nagging wife to be a carpenter and
handyman for the group, and Inigo Jollifant, an unsuccessful
schoolmaster with a Cambridge background, who now seeks
to apply his literary aspirations and musical ability to the
stage.

The leading characters come together when Miss Trant meets the Dinky Doos, a touring concert group who have been stranded by their manager. She takes over, financing the group and changing the name to the Good Companions—and we are on the way. We become involved in the lives and adventures of the members of the company before they disperse at the end, their experiences assimilated, to make new lives.

Miss Trant marries and becomes a respectable Edinburgh matron. Jess Oakroyd emigrates to Canada after his wife dies to be near his beloved daughter. Inigo Jollifant falls hopelessly in love with the pretty and talented leading lady of the Good Companions, Susie Dean. She, however, continues to devote herself to a stage career.

To give the characters identity, Priestley makes them part of the solid background to which they belong. Susie attains at the end the stardom to which she has aspired. But as she ruminates on her past, she thinks about her previous world, about her father and what he stands for. Her recollection of a particular food is a means of reaching for and illustrating the tradition that she is part of. She recalls cow-heels, a popular dish in the North, with a nostalgic longing that might make anyone wish to retrieve a bit of the past via an old-fashioned recipe and dash out for the nearest old-fashioned cookery book.

Cow Heel

Cow-heel is still an appropriate invalid diet in the North of England where it is considered a very nutritious dish and noted for its gelatinous nature.

In *The English Cookery Book* of 1856, Frederick Davis refers to the "mucilaginous nature" of cow-heel and calls it a "homely but excellent article." He offers a number of methods of preparation.

Cow Heel or Ox Feet

May be dressed in various ways, and are very nutricious in all.

Boil them; and serve in a napkin, with melted butter, mustard, and a large spoonful of vinegar.

Or boil them very tender, and serve them as a brown fricassee: the liquor will do to make jelly sweet or relishing, and likewise to give richness to soups or gravies.

Or cut them into four parts, dip them into an egg, and then flour and fry them; and fry onions (if you like them), to serve round. Sauce as above.

Or bake them as for mock turtle.

Elsewhere, Davis offers the following additional recipe, which illustrates just how incomplete and questionable a Victorian recipe can be; but the adventurous cook may wish to experiment.

Curry of Cow-Heel:
We think it is a mistake to devote dry meats to the purpose of a dish of curry. Rabbit, chicken, veal are all out of place. Lobster is passable, but the best material that can be used is the homely but excellent article cow-heel. Its mucilaginous nature absorbs the flavour of the Indian condiment; and the meat, being cut into small pieces, no one detects to what source they are indebted for so capital a dish.

Boiled Beef and Cabbage

JOSEPH ANDREWS (1742) by Henry Fielding

*He seemed to have the greatest appetite for a piece of
boiled beef and cabbage.*

Henry Fielding began his writing career as a highly successful
dramatist who wrote mostly comedies and farces. Among the
best known of the twenty-eight theatre pieces he produced for
the stage are *Tom Thumb* and *Rape upon Rape*. But his many
political satires criticized Walpole's government so effectively,
that the notorious Licensing Act of 1737 required all play-
wrights to obtain a license from the Lord Chamberlain.
Fielding's refusal to please the censor and omit political commentary from his plays brought his career as a dramatist to
an end.

He turned to law to support his wife and family and was
struggling to earn a living as a lawyer when Samuel
Richardson's *Pamela* appeared in 1740. Fielding disliked the
sentimentality of this remarkably popular work and was
aroused to parody it in *Shamela*. Out of this came his first
novel, *Joseph Andrews*, followed by such works as *The Life
of Jonathan Wild the Great*, *Tom Jones*, and *Amelia*. He
perfected the literary form of satire, which was little known
when he was born in 1707, and eventually earned for himself
the accolade, Father of the English Novel.

Pamela Andrews, the heroine of Richardson's *Pamela*, was a young servant girl who, by sheer goodness, managed to hold out against a lecherous squire until he capitulated and married her. Fielding saw the falseness of the story and wrote his own version in *Joseph Andrews*, his novel that inverted the central situation. Just as the heroine of Richardson's novel tried to escape the attentions of her master, so her equally virtuous brother, Joseph Andrews, shuns the advances of Lady Booby and is dismissed as her footman. Fielding produced a novel full of humor and vitality with human beings depicted as really alive for the first time in the history of English novel.

One of the best-known incidents is the discovery of Joseph naked in the ditch after he has been robbed, stripped, and left for dead shortly after he has left London, having been discharged from his position. On hearing Joseph's groans, the postilion stops the coach. The stage-coach passengers give themselves away by their reactions to his plight, as each offers an excuse for not coming to his aid.

The coachman, concerned only in running a profitable business, objects that they are already late. The prudish lady purports to be offended by a naked man but later peeks at him through the sticks of her fan. An old gentleman, on hearing Joseph's explanation and pleas for mercy, wishes to hurry on without becoming involved lest they too be robbed. A lawyer overrules objections on the basis of law, not charity. What if the poor creature should die and they are brought to account and indicted for murder? Only the postilion shows more kindness and compassion than all the gentry and saves Joseph by lending him his greatcoat.

Joseph is deposited at the Dragon Inn where moral shortcomings are again revealed by another assortment of characters and where help is again forthcoming from someone who is low on the social scale. Betty the chambermaid gets Joseph to bed, but the shrewish hostess of the inn rails at her for showing care and concern and at her henpecked husband

227

for supplying the poor naked guest with a shirt. The surgeon who is summoned goes back to sleep when he learns that it is not a gentleman but a mere pedestrian who has been injured. The totally incompetent clergyman, eager to join the company and the drink which await in the parlor, hurriedly announces that the sick man is light headed and is babbling nonsense.

Although the characters are revealed as self-interested and hypocritical, we know that Joseph is never in any real danger, and we are therefore able to be amused by the characters and their plights. Despite the surgeon's pessimistic prognosis for the wretched victim, we know that Joseph is not going to die. One certain clue is his healthy appetite.

By a happy coincidence, Joseph's old friend Parson Adams turns up at the inn. He is on his way to London where he hopes to sell some volumes of his sermons. He looks after Joseph, assures him of a speedy recovery, and offers a poached egg or chicken-broth. The hungry invalid cannot be hopelessly ill, for he expresses a desire for boiled beef and cabbage. Adams advises a lighter diet, and Joseph has either rabbit or fowl; the meal is not positively identified because the author, playfully cautious, will state only facts of which he can be absolutely certain, thus aiming for an effect of verisimilitude.

After Joseph's inevitable recovery, the pair travel together, for Joseph is returning to the country to be reunited with his beloved Fanny; and the curate must also journey homeward in order to retrieve the sermons which, it seems, he has absent-mindedly forgotten to take with him. The amiable Parson Adams is the agent of much of the good humor which pervades the novel and is one of Fielding's most delightful creations. He has within him something of the character of Cervantes' Don Quixote and becomes the real hero. It is useful to recall the full and expansive title of the novel: *The History of the Adventures of Joseph Andrews, and of his Friend Mr. Abraham Adams. Written in Imitation of Cervantes, Author of Don Quixote.*

228

As Joseph resumes his journey with the Parson, the work goes well beyond mere parody and becomes a masterful comic novel. Their rollicking adventures and encounters with a rich assortment of characters continue the sense of comedy which has already been established in this, one of the finest of English novels.

 # Boiled Beef and Cabbage

Although Fielding could not be entirely certain what his hero ate, it is absolutely certain that Joseph expressed a desire for boiled beef and cabbage; and that image is turned into solid fare by specific recipes from books with titles that have royal suggestions: Patrick Lamb's *Royal Cookery* (1731) supplies instructions for preparing beef, and Hannah Wolley's *The Queen-Like Closet* (1670) offers instructions for cabbage.

Rump of Beef boil'd
Rub it all over with common Salt, all Sorts of Pot-Herbs, Pepper and a little Salt-Petre, and let it lie three or four Days. Put it in a Pot with Water, among which put some Onions and Carots, Etc. Garden-Herbs, Bay-Leaves, Cloves, Pepper and Salt, Boil your Beef, and when it is ready, lay it in a Dish, garnish'd with green Parsly. So serve it hot for the first Course.

To make Cabbage Pottage
Take a Leg of Beef and a Neck of Mutton, and boil them well in water and salt, then put in good store of Cabbage cut small, and some whole Spice, and when it is boiled enough, serve it in.

Stewed Steak

RICEYMAN STEPS (1923) by Arnold Bennett

. . . the steak was stewed; it was very attractive,
seductive, full of sound nourishment; one would have
deemed it irresistible. . . .

One of Arnold Bennett's finest novels of his later years,
Riceyman Steps, is set in the Clerkenwell district of London.
Mr. Earlforward is a miser and an antiquarian bookseller
whose shop is located at the Riceyman Steps around the area
of King's Cross Road.

In his secondhand bookshop, in addition to novels, he has
done "quite a good trade in cheap cookery-books that professed
to teach rational housewives how to make substance out of
shadow." In fact, we first meet the heroine of the novel, Elsie,
when she tries to purchase a cheap recipe book for Mrs. Arb,
the proprietress of the confectioner's shop just opposite. Mrs.
Arb wants to expand her range to include sandwiches and
snacks.

A large, active, likable young person with a desire to serve,
Elsie serves Mr. Earlforward as charwoman. She tends to his
shop and to his less spacious living quarters at the back and
has recently begun to work also for the widowed Mrs. Arb.

The novel follows the friendship, courtship, marriage,
and deaths of Henry Earlforward and Violet Arb. Nothing

remarkable happens. They marry early in the plot and set up home together in his premises above the bookshop. She is angered by the miserliness which he cannot overcome although he wants things to be right for her. They visit Madame Taussaud's on their wedding day, and the festive day is cut short by his fear of extravagant spending. She arranges to give the premises a thorough spring cleaning using vacuum cleaners, and he is outraged by the expense. He scrimps on light, fuel, and food. They live. When they fall ill, they are cared for by the good-hearted and loyal Elsie.

Elsie brings warmth as she lights the fire. She dispels gloomy doubts as she flings rice on the newlyweds and presents them with the gift of a wedding cake. She promotes cleanliness and fresh air as she dusts and opens the windows.

Elsie's appetite for food parallels her appetite for life. She swallows cheese, cold potatoes, and raw bacon with gusto, to the consternation of her employers. A climax occurs when Elsie, unable to curb her appetite, devours the steak which her employer has rejected.

Shortly after Elsie has been reprimanded for gluttonously swallowing an egg, the evening meal is served. But Henry announces that he is not hungry. In an outburst of rage, Violet exclaims that she does not believe that he suffers from indigestion; she believes that he is denying himself the pleasures of an opulent steak. She gives vent to a furious tirade of complaints at his inconsiderate and cheap penny-pinching habits and stalks out of the dining room to retire early to bed.

Elsie, left to clear up, sees the uneaten steak on his plate and the fragment of steak on hers. There follows a battle with conscience. Guilty of the theft of an egg, Elsie must show remorse and never sin again. She must curb her greedy appetite. She must resist. But conscience cannot triumph after the suffering she has just endured. "The steak, during its cooking, had caused her a lot of inconvenience; the smell of it had awakened desires which she had had difficulty in withstanding; it had made her mouth water abundantly."

Well, she would have the fragment only, a mere mouthful. However, the effect of the taste is "more potent than brandy" and leads to the agonies of the alcoholic craving more liquor. She rationalizes, she struggles, she loses self-respect, she succumbs. The end of the chapter finds her weeping on her knees to Mrs. Earlforward, "Oh, 'm! I've gone and eaten the steak. . ."

The steak-eating episode is symbolic. Elsie, full of vitality and love, stands in contrast to Mr. Earlforward who dies, never having fully lived. In the impoverished world portrayed in the novel, Elsie has maintained enormous dignity. Squalid lives in a stifling neighborhood have been sympathetically presented. The understanding and compassion with which Bennett has portrayed the lives of ordinary people lifts the story up into the realm of the extraordinary.

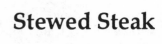

Stewed Steak

A recipe for stewed steak, taken from a 1907 volume named *High Class and Economical Cookery Recipes* by E. Roberta Rees, is just the sort of second-hand cook book that Mr. Earlforward might have stocked in his shop. And one particular word from its title—"Economical"—would certainly have appealed to him. Although Rees uses the rather untempting title of "Brown Stew," it is nevertheless a stewed steak recipe that might well account for the heroine's seduction to its smell and taste.

Stewed Steak (Brown Stew)

2 ozs. butter
1 ½ oz. flour
1 pint stock
1 lb. beef (stewing steak)
¼ lb. of mushrooms (if liked)

¼ lb. of tomatoes (if liked)
1 carrot and 1 onion cut into dice
A bunch of herbs
1 clove

Melt the butter and fry the meat in it till brown, take out the meat, fry the carrot and onion, add flour and fry till brown, add the stock, herbs, and clove, and stir till boiling, add the meat, also the mushrooms, and tomatoes peeled and sliced, and simmer gently for about two hours, or longer, if the meat is at all tough. Remove the herbs and clove, and dish on a hot dish.

Steak

THE PICKWICK PAPERS (1837) by Charles Dickens

A bit of fish and a steak were served up to the travellers.

In his work as a newspaper reporter for the prestigious *Morning Chronicle*, the young Charles Dickens was sent out into the provinces to report on elections and political speeches. He loved travel and the coaching inns which became an exciting part of his way of life. He relished the welcome produced by a good inn in the form of a blazing log fire and good food and wine in a friendly atmosphere. Dickens knew and appreciated the character of each of the variety of inns he visited—from the decrepit public houses to the posh hotels—and he wrote about them all in his diary, in his letters, and in his books. Whether he praised or castigated, his words immortalized the lodgings he wrote about.

Using his reporter's eye for detail, the young journalist adapted his travel experiences to his writing purposes and produced accurate and original accounts which eventually found an outlet in his first novel. Originally printed in monthly parts, a revolutionary practice in publishing, Mr. Pickwick's stage coach traveler's view of the country found a large reading public attracted to the hilarious adventures of amusing characters. With publication of *The Pickwick Papers*, Dickens had served his apprenticeship and was launched on an immensely successful career as a novelist. There followed such great classics as *Oliver Twist, Nicholas Nickleby, David Copperfield, Bleak House,* and *Great Expectations.*

In *The Pickwick Papers*, Dickens presents his views of actual inns with honesty. Many inns are mentioned and many meals are served in the novel, but the Great White Horse in Ipswich, where the gentlemen dine on steak in a private room, may be singled out for several reasons. It contains many amusing and oft-quoted scenes including the memorable one in which the hero becomes disoriented by the tortuous passages and enters the wrong bedroom only to find himself in the company of a strange lady with yellow curl-papers in her hair.

The section about the Great White Horse itself is unusual in that the author seems to malign everything about the inn—the facade ("some rampacious animal"), the interior ("labyrinths of uncarpeted passages"), the meal that is served ("after the lapse of an hour"), and the drink which follows ("the worst possible port wine, at the highest possible price").

The four hundred-year-old Great White Horse still stands in the heart of Ipswich. It is an attractive galleried inn with a timber-framed courtyard intact, with a gentle stone horse acting as a jolly signboard, and with the charm of age in its meandering corridors. There the traveler in Suffolk can still have a steak served up in a pleasant environment.

Steak

Actually, Dickens did not criticize the quality of the steak, and he did relent later in the story when he described Mr. Pickwick's "large double-bedded room" as "comfortable." In any case, a steak ordered at the White Horse in the present is bound to be acceptable if the chef prepares this simple steak recipe from the past. In *The Cook's Oracle* of 1822, Chef William Kitchiner adds a note of concern for achieving an attractive presentation as well as the most flavorful results.

Steaks

Cut the steaks rather thinner than for broiling. Pat some Butter into an iron frying pan, and when it is hot, lay in the steaks, and keep turning them till they are done enough.

Obs.—Unless the Fire be prepared on purpose, we like this way of cooking them; the gravy is preserved; and the meat is more equally dressed, and more evenly browned; which makes it more relishing, and invites the eye to encourage the Appetite.

Beef Steaks

WAVERLEY (1814) by Sir Walter Scott

Steaks, roasted on the coals, were supplied in liberal abundance, and disappeared . . . with a promptitude that seemed like magic, and astonished Waverley.

Born in 1771, Walter Scott was over forty-three when he published his first novel, *Waverley*. He had already achieved a great reputation as a poet. But fiction was not highly regarded in 1814, and he published the novel anonymously. It was an enormous success, and Scott produced novel after novel inscribed "by the author of *Waverley*" until 1827, when he came out of the closet and admitted authorship.

The *Waverley* novels, which include all of Scott's greatest works, deal with Scottish history of the eighteenth century. In the first of the series, Edward Waverley is advised by his uncle, who has partly brought him up, of his duty to follow the profession of his ancestors and join the army. Edward obtains a commission and leaves to join his regiment in Scotland.

His romantic and adventuresome disposition leads him to visit the Highlands and become involved in Jacobite causes and intrigues. When curiosity entices Waverley to make an expedition to a den of robbers, he is received with generous hospitality. From his comfortable position away from the oppressive heat of the charcoal fire, he marvels at the voracity with which the Highlanders devour steaks. Not only steaks, but whiskey too comes forth in great abundance.

Having been brought up on tales of heroic deeds of his ancestors, Waverley is prone now to expose himself to dangerous situations in these perilous times. He is to experience more feasts and undergo many more adventures, often of an ill-advised nature, before the actions of the plot are resolved. Waverley survives. He marries and settles down to a new order, for the old order has changed and cannot be recaptured.

 # Beef Steaks

Charcoal-cooked steaks might seem to be a modern idea. That they may be ascribed to Scott's time is supported by an excerpt from *A Complete System of Cookery* of 1813 by John Simpson, a chef who specialized in such public dinners as those given at the Guildhall.

Beef Steaks

Beef steaks should be cut from the rump and broiled over a clear charcoal fire; put a little shalot on the dish, a bit of cold butter, and a table spoonful of ketchup, and be very particular in sending them hot to table; all the other part of the dinner should be dished before the beef steaks are put on the fire; season them with pepper and salt.

Beefsteak and Oyster Sauce

TOM BROWN'S SCHOOLDAYS (1857) by
Thomas Hughes

*[Tom] heard with unfeigned joy the paternal order at
the bar, of steaks and oyster-sauce for supper in half an
hour. . . .*

When his son was eight years old, Thomas Hughes, concerned
about what to tell the boy before he went off to school, wrote
the story that was to make him a famous man of letters. He
began writing the book in 1856, and its publication the
following year was greeted with great enthusiasm and
acclaim from critics and from the general public. Although
there were some complaints about sentimentality and emphasis on moral and religious views, the merits outweighed
defects, and *Tom Brown's Schooldays* became a best seller. By
1890, England alone had nearly fifty printings, and new
editions continue to appear.

With *Tom Brown's Schooldays*, Hughes created a new
literary genre. He wrote the first fictional novel to present a
real world of boys in a real English public school setting.
Despite changes in literary taste and in educational modes, it
remains a vital work of fiction on that subject. Hughes wrote
a number of other books including a sequel, *Tom Brown at
Oxford*, but none achieved the high level of success of his first
and most important novel.

241

Hughes loved his own schooldays at Rugby but gave a picture of public school education in general. He made his hero the "commonest type of English boy of the upper middle class" and chose a name that would be appropriate for an ordinary schoolboy.

Young Tom Brown leaves his Berkshire home with his father one November morning in the 1830s to begin his new life at school. Their first stop is at the Peacock Inn, Islington, where they wait for the Tally-ho coach which will take Tom speedily and directly to Rugby. At the Peacock, they indulge in a supper treat. Tom enjoys "the beefsteak and unlimited oyster-sauce" as he listens to his father's excellent advice on good conduct. He must be truthful, brave, and kind; he must never use coarse or foul language or do anything that may cause him to feel shame.

It must surely be the stout that Tom is drinking for the first time, not the lecture, that has a soporific effect, and Tom begins to nod. The farewell scene, reminiscent of Polonius' advice to his departing son, supports the didactic purpose of the novel. But at least Tom has the advantage of a good supper which accompanies the moral treatise.

The simple message of the story is that one should be honest and self-reliant and fight evil, cruelty, and selfishness. Despite the preaching, the book became popular and influenced public schools to try to incorporate the ideals of the story and make themselves models of the vision presented by the author.

# Beefsteak and Oyster Sauce

A recipe for beefsteak with oyster sauce, which produced such joyful spirits in Tom, derives from Mrs. Rundell's *A New System of Domestic Cookery* of 1806.

Beefsteak and Oyster Sauce
Strain off the liquor from the oysters, and throw them into cold water to take off the grit, while you simmer the liquor with a bit of mace and lemon-peel; then put the oysters in, stew them a few minutes, add a little cream if you have it, and some butter rubbed in a bit of flour, let them boil up once, and have rumpsteaks well seasoned and broiled ready for throwing the oyster sauce over the moment you are to serve.

Ruth Pinch's Beefsteak Pudding

MARTIN CHUZZLEWIT (1844) by Charles Dickens

"In the whole catalogue of cookery, there is nothing I should like so much as a beef-steak pudding!" cried Tom.

All of Chapter XXXIX of Dickens' *Martin Chuzzlewit* is taken up with beef-steak pudding—from Tom Pinch's initial exclamation of a desire for this quintessential English dish to its subsequent preparation and final consumption.

Among the cast of various minor characters appearing in this complex novel which exposes greed and selfishness are such moral favorites as Sairey Gamp, Pecksniff, Todger, or the completely lovable Tom Pinch. But readers who share Dickens' own passion for good food will surely single out Ruth Pinch for her virtue and her unrivaled culinary skill.

Tom and his sister Ruth are praiseworthy characters who prepare a praiseworthy dinner in a jolly chapter, but not before Ruth, acting as Tom's housekeeper, expresses some concern about her ability since she has never before made a beef-steak pudding. What if it should "turn out a stew, or a soup, or something of that sort. . .?" They laughingly decide to proceed with the experiment, but not before Tom expresses the certainty "that it will come out an excellent pudding." Ruth—good housekeeper that she is!—cleans up and mends his frayed shirt collar before they go off to the butcher to buy steak.

Their shopping list is augmented by "some eggs, and flour, and such small matters," and they return to their lodgings to begin preparations. Tom writes a letter at the table while Ruth gathers together equipment and ingredients—flour, pie-board, eggs, batter, jug of water, rolling-pin, pudding-basin, pepper, salt. Happily and busily she works away, playfully disturbing Tom in order to explain why she butters the inside of the basin. ("How else do you think it would turn out easily when it was done?") She kneads, rolls out the crust, lines the basin with it, cuts the steak into small pieces, adds pepper and salt, places them in the basin, pours in cold water for gravy, and finishes with the top crust—just as John Westlock arrives.

He is charmed by the domestic scene and accepts an invitation to dinner. After imparting the good news of an employment opportunity for Tom, the two men go out, and Tom is successful in securing the position; they return to a dinner that is also predictably successful. They marvel that Ruth's first experiment in cookery "was so entire, so unalloyed and perfect, that . . . she must have been studying the art in secret for a long time past."

Ruth Pinch's Beefsteak Pudding

If there is any secret to beefsteak pudding, Florence White knew it, for she selected Eliza Acton's recipe from *Modern Cookery* (1845) to illustrate it in her own more modern volume, *Good Things in England* (1932). Ruth Pinch followed Acton, she explains, except for her use of butter instead of suet. These are Florence White's own words:

Ruth Pinch's Beefsteak Pudding
Miss Acton, 1845

Ruth Pinch is a well-known character in *Martin Chuzzlewit*. She used 6 oz. butter for the crust of her pudding instead of 6 oz. suet, and moistened the flour, etc., into a paste with the well-beaten yolks of 4 eggs, mixed with a little water (an extravagant young woman, that!). Otherwise the ingredients and directions for making are the same as in Miss Acton's recipe.

For a basin that holds 1 ½ pints of water the following quantities will be required:

INGREDIENTS: *Flour I lb., beef suet finely minced 6 oz.; (or if you are a Ruth Pinch 6 oz. butter); flour I oz.; salt ½ teaspoonful; water ½ pint (or the yolks of 4 eggs, and a little water); beefsteak 1 lb. (the 'skirt' makes an excellent pudding and is economical); salt ½ oz.; pepper ½ teaspoonful; water ¼ pint; mutton may be substituted for beef, and half a dozen or a dozen oysters interspersed with it.*

TIME: to boil 3 ½ hours.

METHOD

1. Grease a basin, put a large pot of water on to boil.
2. Make the pastry with the flour, suet (or butter), salt, and water (or eggs!).
3. Roll it out and line the basin leaving a piece for the lid.
4. Cut the steak into convenient pieces, flour and season them with pepper and salt; put them in the pudding.
5. Pour in the ¼ pint of water, and put on the lid.
6. Tie over with a floured cloth, and boil as above.

Beefsteak and Kidney Pudding

RUMPOLE OF THE BAILEY (1978) by John Mortimer

"I got an excellent steak and kidney pud and a very drinkable claret."

John Mortimer—playwright, novelist, and lawyer—has created a memorable character in Horace Rumpole, barrister at law. A series of fictional stories center around Rumpole of the Bailey, a lively if somewhat irascible and eccentric figure who is not without an enormous amount of wit and charm as well as an unsurpassed knowledge in the ways of crime. He refers to his wife as She Who Must Be Obeyed, spouts poetry (Wordsworth in particular), and argues and solves mysteries in the cause of British justice.

Horace Rumpole is usually too busy drinking (claret in particular) to be occupied with eating. Indeed, it is quite normal for him to enjoy "a glass of luncheon" at Pommeroy's Wine Bar. Occasionally he has the odd sausage roll. But he decries bad pub food such as "a particularly limp sausage roll." Or railway fare which features a brunch-burger, which he fancies might be eaten with a "suitable anaesthetic." So when he dines and has good, proper food, it is an occasion.

In "Rumpole and the Alternative Society," he has dinner at his client's residence in a community house named Nirvana by its young and free-thinking inhabitants. To his great surprise and delight, the house is extremely clean and comfortable, and dinner does not consist of the anticipated nut cutlet, but of a rather delicious steak and kidney pudding. From this thoroughly British dish for the thoroughly British Rumpole, the cannabis-peddling case is brought to a speedy and just conclusion.

Beefsteak and Kidney Pudding

From *Simplified Cookery* (1923) by A.E. Blockley and A.S.W. Edwards comes this simple recipe designed to bring preparation of steak and kidney pudding to a satisfying conclusion.

1 lb. Stewing Steak.
¼ lb. Ox Kidney.
½ tablespoon Flour.
Cold Water.
Salt and Pepper.

Suet Crust—
½ lb. Flour.
¼ lb. Suet.
½ teaspoon Baking Powder.
Salt.   Cold Water.

Method:
1. Mix half tablespoon flour, salt and pepper together.
2. Wash and cut the meat into thin slices, place a small piece of kidney and a little fat on each, roll and dip in the seasoning and flour.
3. Chop the suet, using some of the weighed flour.
4. Mix suet, flour, salt and baking powder together.
5. Mix to a stiff paste with the cold water.
6. Roll out thinly, and line a greased basin with the pastry.
7. Put in the meat and sufficient water to half fill the basin.
8. Wet the edges and cover with a piece of the pastry.
9. Cover with a cap of greased paper and steam for 2 ½ to 3 hours.
10. Remove paper, turn out, make a small hole in the pastry and add a little boiling water to make more gravy.
11. Serve very hot.

250

Boeuf en Daube

TO THE LIGHTHOUSE (1927) by Virginia Woolf

And she peered into the dish, with its shiny walls and its confusion of savoury brown and yellow meats, and its bay leaves and wine. . . . The Boeuf en Daube was a perfect triumph.

The best of Virginia Woolf's novels is by critical consensus *To the Lighthouse*. In it, Virginia Woolf addresses herself to the question of the meaning of life. What is truth? Reality? She uses an interior monologue technique as she passes from one consciousness to another.

Mrs. Ramsay, the dominant character of the novel, is surrounded by her eight children. She is a beautiful symbol of creation and motherhood. Her knitting is a symbolic activity; as she joins strands together into a pattern, so she joins people together.

At the Ramsay summer home at the seashore, Mrs. Ramsay is hostess at dinner to fifteen people. The inter-relationships of the houseguests with her family and with each other help to suggest the meaning of life. There is considerable anxiety on the part of Mrs. Ramsay, for several people have gone out for an evening walk and have not yet returned. Mildred has cooked her "masterpiece"—Boeuf en Daube—which has taken three days to prepare. It must be served immediately. "Everything depended upon things being served up the precise moment they were ready. The beef, the bayleaf, and the wine—all must be done to a turn. To keep it waiting was out of the question."

And what guests! In addition to the latecomers, Minta Doyle and Paul Rayley, there is William Bankes, for whom dinner is a waste of time when he might be working. Lily Briscoe thinks obsessively of her painting, thinks that she must move the tree further towards the middle. Charles Tansley is ill at ease with the rather snobbish family.

At least Mrs. Ramsay is pleased. "It is a French recipe of my grandmother's," she announces with pride. She has created a perfect triumph as she charms and presides over the guests, with Boeuf en Daube serving as the epitome of the celebration of a festival. Through her efforts, William Bankes is satisfied; and Lily attains a recollection of reality. The dinner, which provides the longest scene in the book, is among the most important dinners in all of literature.

Written in three movements, the novel conveys the passage of time in the very brief second part. Time elapses. Mrs. Ramsay dies, and her death is recorded parenthetically. Her personality continues to dominate even after her death. She appears in Part Three in the memories of various characters. Lily thinks of her as she finishes her painting with a single stroke of the brush and has the vision which closes the book.

E.M. Forster has stressed the importance in the works of Virginia Woolf of passages which describe eating. "They are a sharp reminder that here is a woman who is alert sensuously." Few writers have had her ability to make the reader savor dishes which "get right into our mouths. . . . We taste their deliciousness." Forster inevitably refers to the great dish of Boeuf en Daube which forms the center of the dinner of unison, "the dinner which exhales affection and poetry and loveliness, so that all the characters see the best in one another at last and for a moment, and one of them, Lily Briscoe, carries away a recollection of reality."

Boeuf en Daube

Appropriately, the famous French chef and author, George Auguste Escoffier, provides an excellent recipe in his *Guide to Modern Cookery* of 1907. Perhaps he obtained it from Mrs. Ramsay's grandmother.

Daube Chaude a La Provencale

Cut four lbs. of shoulder or cushion of beef into cubes weighing about four oz. each. Lard each piece of meat with a strip of bacon two inches long by one-half inch wide, and put the cubes or pieces into a bowl with salt, pepper, a very little spice, five or six tablespoonfuls of vinegar, and a glass of red wine. Leave to marinade for two or three hours, and toss the pieces, from time to time, in the marinading liquor, in order that each may be well saturated with it. Heat six oz. of grated bacon in an earthenware stewpan, and brown therein twelve small onions, fifteen carrots in the shape of olives, two sticks of celery cut into pieces of the same size as the carrots, and four cloves of garlic. Add the marinaded pieces of meat, which should have been properly dried; fry the whole, meat and vegetables, for a further seven or eight minutes, and moisten with the marinade and two glasses of red wine.

Complete with one-half lb. of fresh bacon rind, blanched and cut into square pieces of two-thirds inch side; a faggot made up of parsley stalks, thyme, bay, and, in the centre, a small piece of dry lemon rind. Set to boil, completely close the stewpan, and leave to cook in a moderate oven for six or seven hours.

When about to serve, remove the faggot, clear all grease from the gravy, and dish in a hot timbale, or serve the "daube" in the stewpan itself.

253

Irish Stew

THREE MEN IN A BOAT (1889) by Jerome K. Jerome

*It was a great success, that Irish stew. I don't think I
ever enjoyed a meal more. There was something so
fresh and piquant about it. . . .And it was nourishing
too.*

There are four on the boating expedition on the Thames—
George and Harris, the narrator and the dog. The comic
adventures that befall them, and the narrator's reflections,
have been amusing readers of this perennially popular
Victorian novel for over a hundred years.

Before embarking on their momentous voyage up the
River Thames, the three men breakfast on chops and cold
beef, a foreshadowing of the many meals to follow at camping
sites along the way. From the starting point of Kingston, they
pass Hampton, Walton, Weybridge, Staines, Old Windsor,
Maidenhead, Marlow, and arrive at Sonning, where Irish stew
comes into the picture.

It takes them twenty-five minutes to peel four potatoes, a
task which proves so difficult that they add some six more
without bothering to peel. They also add to the stew a cabbage
and half a peck of peas, and "all the odds and ends and the
remnants." George, their mentor and supervisor, advises of
the great advantage of Irish stew: "you got rid of such a lot of

things." They proceed, getting rid of half a pork pie and a bit of cold boiled bacon, half a tin of potted salmon, and a couple of cracked eggs. Even the dog offers a contribution as he returns from a brief foray with a water-rat in his mouth. But never having heard of water-rats in Irish stew, George rules in favor of precedent and against experimentation.

Irish Stew

The description of Irish stew in the novel has been subjected to great exaggeration for comic effect, but an actual Irish stew recipe in Williamson's *The Practice of Cookery* (1887), although humorless, has a positive culinary effect.

Irish Stew.

Take any thin pieces of mutton that have been cut off the loin or breast, and cut them in pieces four inches square, put them in a stew-pan and cover them with boiling water, add two dozen whole onions, pepper and salt, put on the cover close, draw it to the side of the fire, and let it boil slowly for one hour. Add a little boiling water to it. Wash and pare two dozen of potatoes, put them in the stew-pan amongst the mutton, and let them boil till quite soft. Stir the potatoes with the mutton till it becomes smooth, and dish it hot.

Collops

KIDNAPPED (1886) by Robert Louis Stevenson

Cookery was one of his chief fancies, and even while he
was greeting us in, he kept an eye to the collops.

The career of Robert Louis Stevenson as a novelist had its
inception one rainy holiday morning when he was helping his
twelve-year-old stepson with a map of an imaginary island.
Stevenson elaborated on the map drawn by the young boy,
labelled it "Treasure Island," and improvised an accompanying story. From this beginning, in 1883, was published the
book that established his literary reputation and made him
famous, *Treasure Island.* Three years later came publication
of *Dr. Jekyll and Mr. Hyde,* followed in six months by
Kidnapped, the book many consider his best.

A map figures also in *Kidnapped,* included in the first
edition to show the young hero's travels. The emphasis on
geographical detail lends an air of authenticity to the tale,
investing it with a strong local color atmosphere and nation-
alistic flavor. Set in the turbulent times of clan warfare in
eighteenth-century Scotland, some six years after the ill-fated
Jacobite rebellion of 1845, the historical background adds
additional weight to the splendid novel of adventure.

The young David Balfour, left alone and in poverty at the
death of his father, sets out for the home of his evil old Uncle

Ebenezer. Having illegally seized David's estate, Ebenezer plots to kill David. But he fails in the attempted murder and has the boy kidnapped on a ship bound for the Carolinas. On the journey, David encounters Alan Breck, who has been picked up from a sinking vessel. They become fast friends, and when the ship is wrecked on the rocks off the coast of Mull, David makes it ashore and begins the journey through the Highlands before being again united with Alan. At a crucial point, just after David has witnessed a murder which he is himself suspected of committing, Alan materializes to save him from being captured. They travel together through the Highlands and share perilous and exciting adventures.

Among David's various encounters with extreme danger is the flight in the heather. Pursued across the Highlands by vengeful clansmen and by the king's troops, the renegades flee for their lives. With suspicion hanging over David for the murder of Colin Campbell, the Red Fox, they are forced into the wildest regions of the Highlands and undergo a harrowing journey. Exhausted and hungry, they are overtaken by members of the clan of Cluny Macpherson. The exiled Highland chief extends hospitality to the two weary fugitives. After Alan is refreshed by sleep, he can look forward to "a dish of hot collops" which the messenger has reported will be forthcoming.

At Cluny's hiding place on a craggy mountain, the three enjoy a preprandial dram together before the meal of collops in which Cluny seems to take great pride:

> As soon as the collops were ready, Cluny gave them with his own hand a squeeze of a lemon (for he was well supplied with luxuries) and bade us draw in to our meal.

He focuses with equal pride on royalty and lemon as he continues to expound on the collops which, he says, "are such as I gave His Royal Highness in this very house; bating the lemon juice, for . . . there were mair dragoons than lemons in my country in the year forty-six." He continues during the meal to regale them with reminiscences of Prince Charlie's stay in his humble hut.

The incident with Cluny crystallizes aspects of Scottish culture and enables David to learn at first hand a bit of native history concerning the struggle for freedom and independence. He sees the enforced exile of a ravaged people who have lost their homeland.

The fortunate repast also makes it possible for them to resume the flight toward justice. A confrontation with Ebenezer and restoration of the estate which rightfully belongs to David bring the adventure to a happy conclusion.

Collops

Collops are thin slices of meat or escallops. As cooked
by Cluny in the Scottish wilderness, the meat, although
unspecified, is probably venison. Eliza Acton's 1845 recipe
uses collops of veal and prepares them with lemon juice, the
ingredient which Cluny expatiated on at great length and
with great pride.

Veal Cutlets, or Collops
Cut the veal into small thin collops of equal size, arrange them
evenly in a saute-pan, or in a small frying pan; dust a little fine
salt and white pepper over them, and grate over a small portion
of nutmeg, when it is liked; clarify an ounce or two of butter with
a gentle heat, pour it over the veal, and set the pan aside until the
dinner hour, then toss the cutlets over a clear fire till they are of a
fine amber-colour, which will be in from three to four minutes:
drain and dish them quickly. These are excellent, even without
any gravy, but some may be made in the pan quickly, by throwing
in a little of that which flows from roast meat, or a morsel of any
other jellied gravy, or stock, with a squeeze of lemon, and a little
cayenne.

3 to 4 minutes.

Roast Venison

PRIDE AND PREJUDICE (1813) by Jane Austen

"The dinner was as well dressed as any I ever saw. The venison was roasted to a turn—and everybody said they never saw so fat a haunch."

The most popular of all of Jane Austen's novels was begun in 1796 when the author was just twenty, but it remained unpublished. After *Sense and Sensibility* was accepted in 1811, Jane returned to *Pride and Prejudice*, originally titled *First Impressions*, and the revised form was published in 1813. The perfect blend of wit and drama makes a delightful novel.

With five unmarried daughters, Mrs. Bennet is obsessed with the need to find suitable husbands. Her first hopes for a union are shattered when Charles Bingley, a rich bachelor who has taken the nearby house of Netherfield, very suddenly leaves the vicinity and what seemed to have been a very promising relationship with Jane, the eldest of the Bennet girls. Bingley's friend Fitzwilliam Darcy is attracted to Elizabeth but offends her by supercilious behavior. Her dislike of Darcy is intensified by a false account of him given by George Wickham and by her deduction that he has played a part in separating Jane from Bingley.

When the unprincipled Wickham elopes with her sister Lydia, Darcy comes to the rescue and is instrumental in bringing about their marriage and respectability. It only remains now for the attachment of Jane and Bingley to be reinstated and for Elizabeth and Darcy, who obviously love each other, also to be joined.

On Bingley's return to Netherfield, he and Darcy call at the Bennet house, and Mrs. Bennet seizes the opportunity to invite the gentlemen to dinner on the following Tuesday. She overcomes the temptation to ask them to stay and dine that very day for, "though she always kept a very good table," her design to snare a man made her eager to impress with a more sumptuous spread than possible with only a day's notice. The theme and tone of the novel had been set by the famous opening sentence: "It is a truth universally acknowledged, that a single man in possession of a good fortune, must be in want of a wife." The novel that began with that witty and ironic statement comes full circle. Bingley and his friend are again at Netherfield, two single men in possession of good fortunes. Mrs. Bennet rises to the occasion.

The Tuesday evening dinner does turn out to be a success—but not yet for Jane or Elizabeth. It is a triumph for Mrs. Bennet who is extremely pleased to announce after all have left that "everything has passed off uncommonly well." Everyone enjoyed the haunch of venison, and even Mr. Darcy, who must have "two or three French cooks at least," complimented the meal.

In the course of the novel, the characters dine many times, nine times at Rosings, the mansion of Lady Catherine de Burgh. Dinner is intensely felt, and joints are carved. But specific foods are fleetingly mentioned or not named at all. That makes the passage quoted, with its detailed account, all the more important. It underscores the possibility for attaining the social level represented by the young gentlemen in question. Perhaps Mrs. Bennet is not quite so outrageously silly as she appears on the surface to be. Her design does in fact lead to resumption of romantic ties, to happiness for two couples, and to a satisfying conclusion.

Roast Venison

Mrs. Bennet may be the source of the old saying that the way to a man's heart is through his stomach, and it may be her only positive trait that she kept a good table. But it works! In her eagerness to impress on this particular occasion, perhaps she consulted Mrs. Frazer's *Practice of Cookery* of 1800, which gives the following recipe:

To Roast Venison

Lard and season it with mixed spices and salt, and let it lie four or five hours in some claret, lemon juice, or vinegar, turning it every hour; then spit and roast it at a gentle fire; baste it with the wine it lay in; take the drippings, add some gravy to it, and thicken it with butter knead in flour, and a little ketchup; boil it up, and pour it on the venison when it is dished.

Or you may prefer to follow this modern (1965) variation, from *The Art of British Cooking* by Theodora FitzGibbon:

Roast Venison

1 haunch venison, about 5 lb.	½ teaspoon cinnamon
8 rashers bacon	½ teaspoon ginger
1 sprig rosemary	1 teaspoon sugar
2 oz. butter	2 cloves
½ pint claret or burgundy	1 teaspoon vinegar
2 tablespoons breadcrumbs	salt and black pepper

For the Marinade:

½ bottle red wine
¼ pint olive oil
1 sprig rosemary

black pepper
1 sliced onion or shallot
1 bay leaf

Marinate the venison in the above marinade, overnight for preference. Take the joint out, dry it a little and wrap it in the rashers, then put it in the roasting-pan with the rosemary. Pour the wine around, also mix in the spices, cloves and sugar. Season well. Cover with grease-proof paper and roast in a moderate oven for 30 minutes to the pound.

When cooked strain off the gravy and put the joint on a warmed dish. Stir the breadcrumbs into the gravy, and when boiling add the butter, vinegar, and the juice and rind of the lemon. When it is all mixed put into a sauce-boat or pour over the joint, according to taste. Serve with red-currant jelly.

UPDATE: Since venison is a rather dry meat with very little fat on some joints, it is no wonder that Mrs. Bennet was pleased to hear people say "they never saw so fat a haunch."

The haunch is the best joint. Venison takes longer to cook than most meat but should not be hurried or it will be tough. To test for readiness, a skewer will go through the thickest part easily when the meat is done.

Boiled Rabbit

See: GULLIVER'S TRAVELS (1726) by Jonathan Swift,
page 134.

I laid in a stock of . . . Rabbits. . . .

To enable Gulliver to prepare rabbits for his travels,
The Queen-Like Closet of 1670 by Hannah Wolley comes to the
rescue.

To Boil a Rabbit.
Take a large Rabbit, truss it and boil it with a little Mutton
Broth, white wine and a blade of Mace, then take Lettuce,
Spinage, and Parslie, Winter-Savory and sweet Marjoram, pick
all these and wash them clean, and bruise them a little to make
the broth look green, thicken it with the Crust of a Manchet first
steeped in a little broth, and put in a little sweet Butter, season it
with Verjuice and Pepper, and serve it to the Table upon Sippets;
Garnish the Dish with Barberries.

UPDATE: A manchet refers to a fine quality bread loaf
or roll made of wheat flour. Sippets are small pieces of
bread cut into different shapes, fried and used for
garnish.

265

Roast Suckling Pig

THE SUN ALSO RISES (1926) by Ernest Hemingway

"We had roast young suckling pig."

The expatriate characters in *The Sun Also Rises* illustrate what Gertrude Stein called the Lost Generation. In the years following the First World War, disillusionment and rebellion against former ideals and values gave way to despair, cynicism, and hedonistic behavior. Hemingway's characters live in a post-war world full of human wreckage, having lost belief in goodness and adopted a skepticism of social institutions. Lady Brett Ashley leads a careless, promiscuous, pagan life as she travels about while awaiting a divorce before she can marry Michael Campbell. Robert Cohn, an American Jewish novelist, falls in love with her, but he is not liked by anyone in the group and eventually leaves. Jake Barnes is also in love with Brett, but their mutual love is doomed due to a wartime injury which has emasculated him. Brett falls for a young bullfighter and elopes only to return to Michael, one of her own kind. Mike, is a bankrupt and a drunkard. Brett and Jake are left together at the end to dwell on their fate. Not much happens. The members drink a lot, they travel on the Continent, and they are devoted to the bullfights, which offer a ritual spectacle of precision and order in a world full of disorder.

The last scene of the novel displays the understanding and concern existing between Brett and Jake. They dine and drink in a Madrid restaurant. For the final meal in what Hemingway alludes to as one of the great restaurants of the world, Jake partakes heartily of roast suckling pig. "My God! What a meal you've eaten." He also drinks quite a lot of red wine, *rioja alta*.

Afterwards, in the taxi, Brett laments about what a good time they could have had together. Jake's concluding words are, "Yes. Isn't it pretty to think so?"

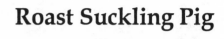

Roast Suckling Pig

An American novel of 1926 should call for an American recipe. In *The Boston Cooking-School Cook Book* of 1896, the principal of the School, Fannie Merritt Farmer, prefaces her chapter on pork with explanations of the different parts of pig or hog. She offers the information that "*Little pigs* (four weeks old) are sometimes killed, dressed, and roasted whole" and supplies this recipe:

Roast Pork.

Wipe pork, sprinkle with salt and pepper, place on a rack in a dripping-pan, and dredge meat and bottom of pan with flour. Bake in a moderate oven three or four hours, basting every fifteen minutes with fat in pan. Make a gravy as for other roasts.

However, the novel's feast is set in Spain, in a specific Spanish restaurant that Hemingway immortalized by writing about it. Casa Botin, which has actually been in existence since 1885, is located just a few steps from Madrid's main square or Plaza Mayor, in Calle Cuchilleros. It still features *Cochinillo Asado* or Roast Suckling Pig as a house speciality, and the manager allows diners to visit the kitchen, with its tiled oven that dates to 1725, to watch the roasting process. This is the way Sobrino de Botín's continues to do it:

COCHINILLO ASADO
(ROAST SUCKLING PIG)

1 3-week-old pig weighing approximately 6½ pounds (cleaned)
4-5 cloves of garlic, chopped
2 medium onions, chopped
a bunch of parsley, chopped
a sprig of thyme (or ½ tsp. powdered thyme)
1 bay leaf
½ cup dry white wine
½ cup water
½ lb. Lard
salt and pepper

Put bay leaf, thyme, chopped garlic, onions, and parsley inside pig. Salt and pepper outside of pig and place it in an earthenware dish. Pour in wine and water in equal parts (approximately ½ cup each) until bottom of dish is covered. Put lard in dish and roast in preheated moderate oven (350°) for 1 hour. Turn pig over, pouring off liquid which has formed. Brush skin with olive oil and return to oven. Continue baking until skin is crusty and golden brown. Baste frequently.

Leg of Pickled Pork

GREAT EXPECTATIONS (1860) by Charles Dickens

We were to have a superb dinner, consisting of a leg of pickled pork and greens and a pair of roast stuffed fowls. A handsome mince-pie had been made yesterday.

The plot of *Great Expectations* is off to a riveting start as the young orphan Pip, visiting the grave of his parents in the churchyard, and quietly trying to conjure up their appearance on the basis of the appearance of their tombstones, is suddenly accosted by a terrifying man in grey with an iron on his leg. The dreaded stranger, actually an escaped convict, threatens the frightened boy into returning to the sombre scene with food and a file snatched from home.

Pip lives with his strict and bad-tempered older sister who never lets the boy forget that she has brought him up at great sacrifice to herself. Her timid husband, Joe Gargery, is the village blacksmith. Among Joe's tools can be found the file required by the fearful stranger. Mrs. Joe's strict house-keeping habits render the pilfering of food a more difficult prospect, but Pip manages to secure both.

In the morning, Pip seeks out the limping criminal who is hiding in the marshes. Guns had been fired in the night to announce an escaped convict. Although filled with unspeakable terror, Pip also feels sympathy for the wretched creature, who gobbles up the food like an animal before beginning to work furiously at filing off the fetter.

Pip returns home to attend church with Joe while Mrs. Joe prepares dinner. On this Christmas Day, several guests are to join them for a dinner featuring a leg of pickled pork (later praised by a guest for being "plump and juicy") and a pair of roast stuffed fowls.

Pip feels overpowered by the august company at the table, who add their approval and support to Mrs. Joe's continual demands for gratitude. He is discomforted by the knowledge of his theft of food for the starving criminal. Not allowed to speak, he wishes to be ignored. He does not mind being given "the scaly tips of the drumsticks of the fowls" and "obscure corners of pork." But he does mind being also given bits of conversation directing and admonishing him to be moral, virtuous, and grateful. His only consolation is the extra gravy which Joe spoons onto his plate from time to time.

Dinner ends with the attempt to serve a savory pork pie—the very one which Pip had already appropriated for the starving fugitive. The dinner scene comes to a riotous conclusion of total confusion. Soldiers arrive with broken handcuffs which need to be mended at the forge by the blacksmith. A few civilians, including Pip and Joe, then join the soldiers in the hunt in the marshes. Two convicts are captured, and Pip is about to be exposed for his sinful deed. Suddenly, to his great fortune, he is unexpectedly exonerated when the captive confesses that he was himself guilty of the theft. Bonds of gratitude now exist between the two.

Theme and tone have been established in the dinner scene, described with much good humor. Dickens, selecting a leg of pork for Christmas dinner, allows Pip to refer to his portion as "those obscure corners of pork of which the pig, when living, had had the least reason to be vain." It is an important scene, for it establishes Pip's character. Full of self-accusation, he knows it is wrong to steal and to withhold

271

information from his elders. He knows he deserves to be punished, and he tries to reconcile his knowledge of acceptable social behavior with his socially unacceptable actions.

As the story of his life unfolds, he often rebukes himself as he seeks to know himself and to judge his behavior honestly. For example, he later feels ashamed of the good-hearted but socially inferior Joe and chides and dislikes himself for having those feelings. In showing his progress toward self-knowledge and spiritual freedom, the dinner scene exposes a vital aspect of the theme.

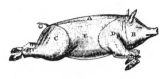 # Leg of Pickled Pork

For the vital elements of that Christmas dinner, leg of pork and roast fowls, let us turn to Charles Elme Francatelli's *The Modern Cook* of 1846. The fowls (see page 142) are provided with stuffing (see page 288) according to directions in *The Housekeeper's Guide*. For the "handsome mince-pie" that completes Pip's "superb dinner" see page 349.

Boiled Leg of Pork, A L'Anglaise
Saw off the shank bone of a salted leg of dairy-fed pork, then put it into a large braizing pan or stock-pot, fill this nearly full with cold water, and add six carrots, as many turnips, one head of celery, and an onion stuck with three cloves. Set the pork to boil gently by the side of the stove fire for about three hours—the exact time depending on its size. While the pork is boiling, trim a dozen and a half of small turnips and as many young carrots, boil these separately, and reserve them for garnishing the remove. When the pork is done, drain, trim, and dish it up; place the carrots and turnips alternately round the remove, pour some plain gravy under it, put a ruffle on the bone, and send to the table.

UPDATE: Removes, part of the practice of placing all the dishes for each course on the table, are the top and bottom dishes served to replace the soup or fish on ordinary tables. These usually consist of roast joints, turkeys, capons, etc.

Pork Cutlets

CAPTAINS COURAGEOUS (1897) by Rudyard Kipling

The boy handed him a plate full of pieces of crisp fried pork, which he ate ravenously.

The boy calling himself "the cook's helper" has given food to Harvey Cheyne, who has just been saved from drowning and taken aboard the *We're Here*, a fishing vessel from Gloucester. Harvey Cheyne is the spoiled and demanding son of very rich parents. After devouring his food, he insists that he be taken immediately back to New York with promises that a large reward awaits his rescuers.

But the world will not stop to meet the whims of a spoiled boy, even if he uses money as a bribe. Harvey needs to learn about life and to acquire a sense of morality and integrity. *Captains Courageous* is a moral tale, not highly regarded nowadays, although it was successful when it first appeared as a product of Rudyard Kipling's years in America.

Kipling resided in his wife's native country from 1892 to 1896. During his American period, he wrote the two *Jungle Books* and many short stories and poems as well as *Captains Courageous*. In Vermont, he developed a strong friendship with James Conland, the family physician, who had been to sea as a young man. His stories about the fishing fleets stimulated Kipling and opened up a new world to him. The two men made expeditions to Boston Harbor and to the fishing fleet in Gloucester, where Kipling learned the way of life of the vanishing world of fishermen in Massachusetts. He used the new material in his only book with wholly American characters and setting.

Kipling explained the writing of the novel in his autobiography, *Something of Myself*: "I wanted to see if I could catch and hold something of a rather beautiful localized American atmosphere that was already beginning to fade." The book can be thought of as his gift to America.

The story is simple. Fifteen-year-old Harvey Cheyne, the pampered son of a railway millionaire, is about to be taken off to Europe by his doting but injudicious mother. Shortly after boarding an Atlantic liner, the young hero alienates himself from other passengers by his insolent behavior. He is washed overboard and awakens to find himself lying in a dory on a pile of half-dead fish. He is saved, not only from the seas, but from a ruined life due to unearned riches.

Harvey's education begins on board the fishing schooner after he is offered a dish of fried pork. The physical and moral life of the microcosm represented by the vessel is impressed on the boy, who learns the hard life and discipline of the Gloucester fishermen and the art of "roughing it." He assimilates not only the meal, but the lesson to be learned on the evils of inherited money.

His father, having worked hard to earn his millions, is a self-made man who is entitled to his wealth. But Harvey has yet to acquire a correct moral outlook. The active, rugged, and splendid race of idealized fishermen transform and convert him to a life of work and responsibility. It is a regenerated, fine young man who is finally reunited with his parents.

Pork Cutlets

It is hardly likely that Harvey's plate of fried pork is based on Eliza Acton's cookbook—or indeed on any cookbook. But it is highly likely that a fried pork recipe from her *Modern Cookery* (1845) will deserve to be eaten ravenously.

To Broil or Fry Pork Cutlets

Cut them about half an inch thick from a delicate loin of pork, trim them into neat form, and take off part of the fat, or the whole of it when it is not liked; dredge a little pepper or cayenne upon them, and broil them over a clear and moderate fire, from fifteen to eighteen minutes, sprinkle a little fine salt upon them just before they are dished. They may be dipped into egg and then into bread-crumbs mixed with minced sage, then finished in the usual way. When fried, flour them well, and season them with salt and pepper first. Serve them with gravy made in the pan, or with sauce Robert.

Ham or Gammon

DUBLINERS (1914) by James Joyce

[On the table was] *a great ham* . . . .

Dubliners, James Joyce's book of short stories dealing with life in Dublin, contains one of the finest short stories in the English language. The last and longest of the stories—"The Dead"—is greatly admired and respected and is considered his earliest masterpiece. "The Dead" centers on the annual New Year's party given by Gabriel Conway's maiden aunts.

A somewhat pedantic and condescending literary man, Gabriel Conway arrives with his wife, Gretta. Aunt Kate and Aunt Julia depend on their nephew to perform certain duties, and he takes a leading part in the convivial affair. There is dancing, drinking, eating, and gaiety, but Gabriel blunders through a series of social encounters and loses his self-possession.

A teacher and writer of book reviews, who feels that his own Europeanized culture is superior to that of the provincial Dublin which surrounds him, he goes through a number of situations that expose his sense of superiority and egotism. As the evening progresses, his confidence disintegrates, and the evening ends in disaster for him.

The festive evening is filled with good music and good food. Aunt Kate and Aunt Julia confer on their nephew the role of master of ceremonies, and Gabriel performs his duties with good humor. He presides over the supper table and carves with aplomb, feeling comfortable at the head of the table. Plates of goose and ham and a wide assortment of holiday food are handed about amidst a scene of happy confusion. After the laughter and pleasant clatter of cutlery and corks, after the conversation and the supper have been enjoyed, Gabriel gives the after-dinner speech. His gracious speech about change is ironic, for he is about to undergo a severe change in himself.

Back in their hotel room after the dinner party, just when Gabriel believes that he and his wife are sharing a life of mutual happiness and desire, he learns that her thoughts are full of Michael Furey, not himself. A significant memory has been awakened in Gretta by a song heard at the end of the evening. The memory is of a boy, now dead, who had loved her. Gabriel discovers an inner life of his wife that he never knew she had. He can never share that experience with her and has never fully known her. He becomes aware of the world of the dead into which the living are passing. His own identity dissolves. Nothing is left but the dead and the dying, and he listens to the faintly falling snow which covers and unites all.

Ham or Gammon

A traditional New Year's feast is worthy of such traditional fare as offered by John Farley, a London tavern keeper who first published his recipes in 1783 in *The London Art of Cookery*. The title is misleading, for this recipe, from the 1801 edition, could be considered as belonging to the Dublin art of cookery, as served by the Misses Morkan and described by James Joyce.

Ham or Gammon.
Having taken off the skin or rind, lay it in lukewarm water for two or three hours. Then lay it in a pan, pour upon it a quart of canary, and let it steep therein for ten or twelve minutes. When you have spitted it, put some sheets of paper over the fat side, pour the canary, in which it was soaked, into the dripping pan, and baste it all the time it be roasting. When it be roasted enough, pull off the paper, and dredge it well with crumbled bread and parsley shred fine. Make the fire brisk, and brown it well. If you serve it up hot, garnish it with raspings of bread; but if cold, serve it on a clean napkin, and garnish it with green parsley, for a second course. Or you may do it thus: Take off the skin of the ham or gammon, when you have half boiled it, and dredge it with oatmeal sifted very fine. Baste it with butter, and roast it gently two hours. Stir up your fire, and then brown it quick; and when so done dish it up, and pour brown gravy into the dish. Garnish with bread raspings, if you serve it up hot, but with parsley if cold.

UPDATE: Canary is a sweet white wine from the Canary Islands, similar to Madeira.

Roast Kid

ROBINSON CRUSOE (1719) by Daniel Defoe

*I was resolv'd to feast him the next day with roasting a
piece of the kid; this I did by hanging it before the fire
in a string, as I had seen many people do in England,
setting two poles up, one on each side the fire, and one
cross on the top, and tying the string to the cross-stick,
letting the meat turn continually. This Friday admir'd
very much.*

*The Life and Strange Surprising Adventures of Robinson
Crusoe*, to give the novel its full title, is the best-known work
of Daniel Defoe. It is also the first truly great English novel.
Defoe embellished an actual event in which Alexander Selkirk
was put ashore on an uninhabited island in the year 1704 and
rescued some five years later. But in Defoe's convincing
account, the shipwrecked Robinson Crusoe remains on his
fictional island for over twenty-eight years and unfolds an
extraordinary narrative which appeals to the primal fears and
instincts within each of us. It is a tale of mythical proportions,
disclosing encounters with natural and supernatural forces.
Crusoe is a lonely and frightened individual, and every reader
can identify with his thoughts, feelings, needs, and sufferings.
Coleridge has called Robinson Crusoe "the universal
representative."

An observant narrator, Crusoe relates the hardships and dangers he endures as he makes efforts to survive and matches his wits with the forces of nature. He builds a house and a boat, domesticates goats, contends with the arrival of cannibal savages, and saves one of them from death. He names that native for the day of the week on which the event occurred and makes Friday his servant.

Friday, himself a cannibal, must be trained and civilized and converted from paganism. The resourceful Crusoe proceeds to teach him the repugnance of eating human flesh by arranging for Friday to partake of a meal of animal meat. He barbecues a kid and reports his success:

> . . .when he came to taste the flesh, he took so many ways to tell me how well he lik'd it, that I would not but understand him, and at last he told me he would never eat man's flesh any more, which I was very glad to hear.

Roast Kid

Roast kid, delicious enough to curb cannibalistic instincts, is also unique enough to be singled out by James Boswell during his tour of Scotland with Dr. Samuel Johnson. The new experience of eating kid, which takes place in Inverness, is recorded in 1773 in his *Journal of a Tour to the Hebrides*: "We had roasted kid, which Dr. Johnson had never tasted before. He relished it much."

Resorting to a seventeenth-century cook book enables us to follow Crusoe's example of serving basic British food. *Court and Kitchen of Elizabeth* is an early cookbook of 1664 by Joan Cromwell, who is fully identified on the title page: "Commonly called Joan Cromwel, The wife of the late Usurper."

This remarkable little book of recipes, written by the wife of Oliver Cromwell, was published by the Royalists. When Charles II was restored to the throne after the Cromwellian era of 1640-1660, the Royalists meant to discredit the Lord Protector with this book. Their aim was to show what a cheap and miserly household he had run. But the attempt at propaganda misfired. The book contained so many excellent recipes that it became a best seller.

The cooking of kid may not be altogether feasible nowadays, but we are given a lamb alternative in this interesting, old recipe replete with errors. Next to the unintelligible or unreadable word, I have placed in brackets the word I believe is actually meant.

To roast a Lamb, or Kid

Truss your Lamb or Kid, pricking the head backwards over the shoulder, laying it down, set it and lard it with Bacon, and draw it with time [thyme], and a little lemmon peel, then make a pudding with a little grated bread, a handful of sweet herbs, a handful of flower, and a little sassage [sausage] with time, made mince meat, season it with cloves, mace, cinamon, ginger, nutmeg, and salt, make it up into a tender body, with two or three eggs, and a little bran [cream], stuff it into the belly of the Lamb, and Kid, put some sauce [caul] of Veal or Lamb over it, so prick it up the belly, lolft [roast] the Lamb and Kid, and when it is enough, serve it up with Venison sauce.

Accompaniments

Apple Sauce

See: WUTHERING HEIGHTS by Emily Brontë, page 160.

He seized a tureen of hot apple sauce. . . .

It is a pity that the tureen of hot apple sauce is not seized by Heathcliff in order to be eaten. It would have made an excellent accompaniment. In a violent state of anger after insulting words are spoken by Linton, Heathcliff snatched "the first thing that came under his grip, and dashed it full against the speaker's face and neck." No real harm is done, however, and the hungry diners proceed with their feast, which features roast goose. Recipes for both goose and apple sauce appear in Elizabeth Raffald's *The Experienced English Housekeeper* of 1801.

To Make Sauce for a Goose.
Pare, core, and slice your apples, put them in a saucepan with as much water as will keep them from burning; set them over a very slow fire, keep them close covered till they are all of a pulp, then put in a lump of butter, and sugar to your taste, beat them well, and send them to table in a sauce-boat.

Stuffing

See: GREAT EXPECTATIONS (1860) by Charles Dickens, page 270.

We were to have a superb dinner. . . . a pair of roast stuffed fowls.

In *The Housekeeper's Guide* of 1834, Esther Copley provides a complete recipe for stuffing fowls to complete a superb Christmas dinner.

A Very Rich Stuffing for Veal, Poultry, or Game

Beef suet, chopped fine, two pounds, bread crumbs, one pound, chopped parsley a tea-cupful, of thyme and marjoram in powder a tea-spoonful, half a nutmeg, half a lemon-peel grated, half an ounce each of pepper and salt, mixed up with five whole eggs.

Bread Sauce

See: THE WAY OF ALL FLESH (1903) by Samuel Butler,
page 138.

*"I think we might have a roast fowl with bread
sauce..."*

The wedding dinner eaten by the newly-married couple
at an inn, with bread sauce as part of the main course, exposes
their character flaws. A bread sauce recipe is found in *The
English Cookery Book* of 1856 by Frederick Davis.

Bread Sauce
Put a tea-cupful of stale bread crumbs into a stewpan with a
small onion, pepper, mace, and as much milk as they will soak up;
let it boil, stirring well, and then simmer till stiff, and reduce to a
proper consistency by milk. The onion may be removed if not
approved of.

# New Potatoes

See: THE WAY OF ALL FLESH (1903) by Samuel Butler,
page 138.

*"I think we might have a roast fowl with bread sauce,
new potatoes and green peas. . . ."*

Although it seems gratuitous to offer a recipe for the simple boiling of potatoes, Eliza Acton makes that offer in *Modern Cookery* (1845):

To Boil New Potatoes

These are never good unless freshly dug. Take them of equal size, and rub off the skins with a brush, or a very coarse cloth, wash them clean, and put them, without salt, into boiling, or at least, quite hot water; boil them softly, and when they are tender enough to serve, pour off the water entirely, strew some fine salt over the potatoes, give them a shake, and let them stand by the fire in the saucepan for a minute, then dish, and serve them immediately. Some cooks throw in a small slice of fresh butter, with the salt, and toss them gently in after it is dissolved. This is a good mode, but the more usual one is to send melted butter to table with them, or to pour white sauce over them when they are very young, and served early in the season, as a side or corner dish.

Very small, 10 to 15 minutes; moderate-sized 15 to 20 minutes.

290

Mashed Potatoes

See: THE LITTLE MINISTER (1891) by J.M. Barrie, page 106.

Potatoes and salt fish. . . were his food.

This recipe (as well as that for salt fish) is taken from *The Practice of Cookery* (1842) by Mrs. Dalgairn.

Boil the potatoes; peel and mash them very smoothly; put for a large dish four ounces of butter, two eggs beat up in half a pint of good milk, and some salt; mix them well together, heap it upon the dish with a table-spoon to give it a rough and rocky appearance, or put it on the dish and score it with a knife; dip a brush or feather into melted butter, and brush over the top lightly; put it into a Dutch oven, and let it brown gradually for an hour or more.

To mash potatoes in a plain way, mix them with two ounces of butter, half a pint of milk, and a little salt. When mashed potatoes are not browned, it is a great improvement to add white pepper, salt, and one onion minced as finely as possible; heat the potatoes in a sauce-pan, and serve them hot.

Rice

See: ALMAYER'S FOLLY (1895) by Joseph Conrad,
page 88.

Almayer attacked his rice greedily.

Almayer eats hungrily in the happy belief that he is about to leave for a European life of luxury. He is unable to see that his dream of prosperity is doomed.

Martha Gordon includes a simple rice accompaniment in *Cookery for Working Men's Wives* (1889):

How to Boil Rice

½ lb. rice, a pinch of salt, a quart of water, and a tablespoon of dripping.

Put on a quart of water, let it boil. Wash the rice well. Throw it into the boiling water, with a pinch of salt. Boil for fifteen minutes. The rice must be soft, but each grain separate, drain it in a colander; and shake it well. Put the dripping into the pot, then put the rice back; and let it swell slowly near the fire for ten minutes. Serve hot.

Green Pease

See: THE WAY OF ALL FLESH (1903) by Samuel Butler, page 138.

"I think we might have a roast fowl . . . and green peas."

In her *Handbook of Practical Cookery* (1886), Matilda Lee Dods uses the old-fashioned spelling—"pease"—for the vegetable ordered by the honeymoon couple in the Samuel Butler novel. However, in addition to a change in spelling, I would recommend also a change in method—steaming rather than boiling the peas, reducing cooking time to five minutes, and using fresh, young peas which require no added sugar of any kind.

Green Pease

Green Pease.—One quart of shelled pease, one ounce of butter, one half tea-spoonful of powdered sugar, one tea-spoonful of salt, one half tea-spoonful of pepper, one sprig of mint.

Place the pease in a large sauce-pan of boiling water, in which should be thrown the sprig of mint, and covering, let them boil rapidly from ten to twenty minutes, as the age of the pease may require.

293

ACCOMPANIMENTS

The moment the pease are done, they must be taken from the water and drained, as overcooking spoils them. While the pease are draining, melt the butter in the sauce-pan in which they have been cooked, and when this is melted, throw back into it the pease, sprinkle over them the pepper, salt, and sugar, and covering the sauce-pan, shake it over the fire until the pease are very hot, taking care that they neither brown nor break.

Yorkshire Pudding

CRANFORD (1853) by Elizabeth Gaskell

We had pudding before meat; and I thought Mr.
Holbrook was going to make some apology for his
old-fashioned ways. . . . "When I was a young man, we
used to keep strictly to my father's rule, 'No broth, no
ball; no ball, no beef;' and always began dinner with
broth. . . .and the beef came last of all, and only those
had it who had done justice to the broth and the ball."

Mr. Holbrook invites the narrator Mary Smith, Miss Matty,
and Miss Pole to spend a day at his home in Woodley. At
dinner he indulges in the old-fashioned custom, still prevalent
in the North of England, of eating pudding before meat. He
explains and justifies the custom by quoting his father's
maxim: "No broth, no ball; no ball, no beef"—ball being a
dialect word for Yorkshire pudding. The idea was—and still is
in the North—to fill up on pudding rather than to appease
hunger on beef, a luxury course.

Thus are customs and manners revealed in a book about
customs and manners. *Cranford* was created because of a
request made by Charles Dickens. Elizabeth Gaskell's first
novel, *Mary Barton*, written in 1848, so impressed Dickens
that he invited her to contribute to his new weekly journal,
Household Words. Her short story "Lizzie Leigh" appeared in

1850, and for the next thirteen years some of her best stories appeared in periodicals he edited including the eight sketches which make up *Cranford*. Published in book form in June 1853, the delightful novel continues to please readers with its revelations of small town life.

For her focus, Mrs. Gaskell turned to the small country town of Knutsford in which she spent her childhood. Calling it Cranford, she detailed events and characterizations in extremely moving fashion so that the novel goes beyond period charm and nostalgia in its exploration of a dying way of life.

The chapter entitled "A Visit to an Old Bachelor" offers excellent insight into a traditional English food, which is nowadays a main dinner treat but was once a mere filler to forestall the consumption of too much expensive roast beef. Mr. Holbrook's adherence to unfashionable eating customs and coarse table manners indicates why he was considered inadequate as a match for Miss Matty. Cranford gentility looks at manners without giving enough credit to qualities of goodness and kindness.

In a poignant scene toward the end of the book, long after Mr. Holbrook has died, Miss Matty's brother recalls Holbrook's youthful attraction to his pretty sister. The romance did not reach fruition, and Miss Matty has had a lonely and empty life as a spinster. Her brother recalls the possibility that might have been and tells her, "You must have played your cards badly." What she feels is outwardly evinced by her shivers and by someone's direction to shut the window. What the reader feels goes toward explaining the enormous popularity of the novel.

A life has been wasted because snobbish Cranford characters judge people by such outward manners as eating Yorkshire pudding before roast beef rather than by important inner qualities.

 # Yorkshire Pudding

Things might have gone more happily for Miss Matty if characters had limited themselves to judging the goodness of Eliza Acton's Yorkshire pudding recipe of 1845 in *Modern Cookery*.

Good Yorkshire Pudding.

To make a very good and light Yorkshire pudding, take an equal number of eggs and of a heaped tablespoonsful of flour, with a teaspoonful of salt to six of these. Whisk the eggs well, strain, and mix them gradually with the flour, then pour in by degrees as much new milk as will reduce the batter to the consistency of rather thin cream. The tin which is to receive the pudding must have been placed for some time previously under a joint that has been put down to roast: one of beef is usually preferred. Beat the butter briskly and lightly the instant before it is poured into the pan, watch it carefully that it may not burn, and let the edges have an equal share of the fire. When the pudding is quite firm in every part, and well-coloured on the surface, turn it, to brown the underside. This is best accomplished by first dividing it into quarters. In Yorkshire it is made much thinner than in the south, roasted generally at an enormous fire, and not turned at all: currants there are sometimes added to it.

Eggs, 6; flour, 6 heaped tablespoonsful, or from 7 to 8 ozs.; milk, nearly or quite, I pint; salt, I teaspoonful: 2 hours.

Obs.—This pudding should be quite an inch thick when it is browned on both sides, but only half the depth when roasted in the Yorkshire mode. The cook must exercise her discretion a little in mixing the batter, as from the variation of weight in flour, and in the size of eggs, a little more or less of milk may be required: the whole should be rather more liquid than for a boiled pudding.

Cakes

and

Pastries

Apple Pie

THE OLD WIVES' TALE (1908) by Arnold Bennett

She hurried across the kitchen with a pie, which she whipped into the oven, shutting the iron door with a careful gesture.

A chain of six towns, incorporated in 1925 as the City of Stoke-on-Trent, make up an industrial conglomeration that has been named "the Potteries" for the work that is done there. Bottle-shaped kilns, now considered picturesque, once blackened the area with smoke as they did their coal firing to produce pottery and porcelain known to us by such names as Wedgwood, Spode, Royal Doulton, and Copeland. It was in this corner of North Staffordshire that Arnold Bennett was born in 1867.

Bennett achieved great success as a novelist with his discovery that he could use his native background for fiction. He gave artistic order to the shapeless sprawl of six towns, which he called the Five Towns, and first captured the essence of life in the Potteries in *Anna of the Five Towns*, published in 1902; Bennett continued to immortalize the area in such works as *The Card, Clayhanger, The Old Wives' Tale,* and *Helen With the High Hand.*

The Old Wives' Tale is generally regarded as his masterpiece. Although much of its action takes place in Paris, the novel begins and ends in the central square of Bursley, one of his Five Towns. As the story opens, Constance and Sophia Baines are young girls growing up together. Very early in the story, when the sisters are fifteen and sixteen, we are taken into the home and lives of the Baines family. We are made to feel the kitchen as Mrs. Baines bustles about one morning, busily making pastry. She catches her "little vixen" in the act of "stealing and eating slices of half-cooked apple" and tries to get Sophia to cooperate in the preparation of the pies. Sophia's independent spirit is revealed during the pastry-making scene in which the subject of her future becomes the topic of conversation.

At sixteen, Sophia is expected to leave school and work in the Baines family shop, the finest drapers' in Bursley. But Sophia aspires to be a teacher, and she challenges her mother's plans. Mrs. Baines, recognizing the danger of such defiance, is greatly perturbed by her obstinate daughter who will not heed parental reason or authority. She tries to cover up her emotions "by gazing into the oven at the first pie." At supper later, with this unresolved conflict still uppermost in the minds of all concerned, the family members are too agitated to relish any part of the meal, which includes the apple pie.

But the pie-making session has set the scene for the rebellious young Sophia to get away from the Potteries and venture into the world beyond the Five Towns. While the more conventional Constance remains contented in the world of Bursley Square, Sophia absconds from home, eventually settling in Paris. She returns to Bursley many years after her flight, when the sisters are about sixty years of age.

In the interim, the lives of many characters unfold. People mature, careers are experienced, deaths occur. Life has been presented.

Apple Pie

Mrs. Beeton first presented her cookery book to the world in 1861, and new editions have continually appeared. One adaptation, published the year before Arnold Bennett used a pie-making session as a clue to character, supplies instructions for apple pie: *Mrs. Beeton's Every-Day Cookery.*

Apple Pie or Tart

INGREDIENTS.—2 lbs. of apples, 2 tablespoonfuls of moist sugar, 4 cloves or ¼ teaspoonful of grated lemon-rind, short crust.

METHOD.—Peel, core, and cut the apples into thick slices. Roll the paste into an oval form a little larger than the top of the piedish, invert the dish in the centre of the paste, and cut round, leaving a ¼-inch margin on all sides. Line the edge of the piedish with the trimmings, put in half the apples, add the sugar, and flavouring ingredient, then the remainder of the fruit. Moisten the paste lining the edge of the dish with water, put on the cover, press the edges together, and notch them at intervals of about 1/8 of an inch. Bake in a brisk oven from 40 to 50 minutes, and when the paste has risen and set, brush it over lightly with cold water, and dredge well with castor sugar. This must be done quickly, and the tart immediately replaced in the oven. If the tart is to be eaten cold, directly it leaves the oven the crust should be raised gently with a knife, to allow some of the steam to escape, otherwise it may lose some of its crispness.

Cherry Tart

See: THE WAY OF ALL FLESH (1903) by Samuel Butler, page 138.

". . . we will see if they could let us have a cherry tart and some cream."

Once again, *Mrs. Beeton's Book of Household Management* (1861) supplies the recipes for both cherry tart and short crust.

Cherry Tart

INGREDIENTS.—1 ½ lb. of cherries, 2 small tablespoonfuls of moist sugar, ½ lb. of short crust, No. 1210 or 1211 (page 306).

Mode.—Pick the stalks from the cherries, put them, with the sugar, into a deep pie-dish just capable of holding them, with a small cup placed upside down in the midst of them. Make a short crust with ½ lb. of flour, by either of the recipes 1210 or 1211; lay a border round the edge of the dish; put on the cover, and ornament the edges; bake in a brisk oven from ½ hour to 40 minutes; strew finely-sifted sugar over, and serve hot or cold, although the latter is the more usual mode. It is more economical to make two or three tarts at one time, as the trimmings from one tart answer for lining the edges of the dish for another, and so much paste is not required as when they are made singly. Unless for family use, never make fruit pies in very large dishes; select them, however, as deep as possible.

Time.—½ hour to 40 minutes.

Average cost, in full season, 8d.

Sufficient for 5 or 6 persons.

Seasonable in June, July, and August.

Note.—A few currants added to the cherries will be found to impart a nice piquant taste to them.

UPDATE: Although Mrs. Beeton does not explain it, the purpose of the cup placed upside down in the dish is to keep in the juice.

Mrs. Beeton instructs that the stalks be picked from the cherries but says nothing about the stones. A bit of interesting, if impractical, advice comes from Mr. Samuel Hobbs in *One Hundred and Sixty Culinary Dainties* (1884): "You will find a quill pen an excellent instrument for stoning cherries."

Short Crust for Fruit Tarts

See: THE WAY OF ALL FLESH (1903) by Samuel Butler, page 138.

To make crust for the cherry tart that the newlyweds order at an inn, *Mrs. Beeton's Book of Household Management* of 1861 offers *two* recipes.

Very Good Short Crust for Fruit Tarts

1210. INGREDIENTS.—To every lb. of flour allow ¾ lb. of butter, 1 tablespoonful of sifted sugar, 1/3 pint of water.

Mode.—Rub the butter into the flour, after having ascertained that the latter is perfectly dry; add the sugar, and mix the whole into a stiff paste, with about 1/3 pint of water. Roll it out two or three times, folding the paste over each time, and it will be ready for use.

Average cost, ls. ld. per lb.

Another Good Short Crust

1211. INGREDIENTS.—To every lb. of flour allow 8 oz. of butter, the yolks of 2 eggs, 2 oz. of sifted sugar, about ¼ pint of milk.

Mode.—Rub the butter into the flour, add the sugar, and mix the whole as lightly as possible to a smooth paste, with the yolks of eggs well beaten, and the milk. The proportion of the latter ingredient must be judged of by the size of the eggs: if these are large, so much will not be required, and more if the eggs are smaller.

Average cost, 1s. per lb.

Batter Pudding and Jam

SONS AND LOVERS (1913) by D. H. Lawrence

The lad began hastily to lay the table, and directly the three sat down. They were eating batter-pudding and jam, when the boy jumped off his chair and stood perfectly still.

The third novel of D. H. Lawrence, *Sons and Lovers*, is a major achievement. It presents a deeply felt picture of industrial, working-class life set in the country outside Nottingham in which Lawrence grew up, and it presents characters based on the people Lawrence knew so well. The autobiographical narrative confronts the mother-son relationship and makes it the center of exploration of authentic human relations.

A full picture of colliery life in Bestwood shows its destructive effect on the Morel family. Walter Morel finds relief from his hard life as a coal miner only in escape to the pub. His disappointed wife craves something better and can only dream of escape to the middle class, perhaps through her children. Husband and wife are reduced to material struggle and inevitable conflict.

Paul Morel, whose name gave the book its first title, is the main characer. But in the first part of the novel, the incompatibility of the married pair forces Mrs. Morel to turn to her first-born child, William. We meet William when he is seven. The young boy rushes home at half-past twelve and breathlessly requests dinner so that he may leave for the fair which is due to begin in an hour's time. Bursting with childish anticipation, he is still eating the meal of batter-pudding when the sound of a merry-go-round emanates from the distance, and he dashes for his cap. "Take your pudding in your hand," his mother calls out to him, and William is off.

Later in the afternoon, Mrs. Morel, taking her little girl Annie along, joins William at the fair. A sense of enormous excitement pervades the fair grounds now that William has his mother. "He would not leave her. All the time he stuck close to her, bristling with a small boy's pride of her." After she leaves, he no longer enjoys himself.

Mrs. Morel has a strong hold on William and exercises complete control of him as long as he is at home. The love between mother and son is so strong that, after William's death early in the story, the mother's attachment is transferred to Paul, whose birth makes her vow to compensate for the sin of a child conceived out of a loveless relation. She derives from Paul the love denied by her husband.

The very first chapter, which includes the hurried dinner scene, exposed the problems and needs of the Morel family. The story opened with a typical childhood scene as William gobbled his food and rushed off to the fair. Walter Morel, generally ignored or slighted, is absent and uninvolved. Gertrude Morel has had her romantic dream of marriage shattered by the harsh reality of an inferior life style with a crude husband. Disillusioned and bitter, she has turned away from the husband she despises to the son whom she loved "passionately."

Batter Pudding and Jam

If it takes a batter-pudding dinner to reveal all, its ingredients ought also to be revealed. Frederick W. Davis, who was head cook of the Freemasons' Tavern, resorts to Mrs. Rundell's recipes of 1808 for his own volume of 1856. At least he gives full credit, both in the name of the recipe and in the lengthy title of his book: *The English Cookery Book, Comprising Mrs. Rundell's Domestic Cookery, Revised. With several Modern Dishes added thereto, Carefully Selected and Simplified.*

Mrs. Rundell's Batter Pudding

Take six ounces of fine flour, a little salt, and three eggs, beat up well with a little milk, added by degrees till the batter is quite smooth; make it the thickness of cream; put into a buttered pie-dish, and bake three quarters of an hour, or into a buttered and flowered basin, tied over tight with a cloth; boil one hour and a half, or two hours.

UPDATE: Batter pudding is served with sugar, butter, stewed fruit—or jam, as in *Sons and Lovers*. It is, therefore, included in the cakes-and-pastries section, even though it is a type of Yorkshire pudding. A note in the 1912 edition of *Mrs. Beeton's Cookery Book* explains that it is called Yorkshire pudding when cooked in front of the fire; when baked in the oven, the term 'batter pudding' is applied.

Cream Puffs

THE GARDEN PARTY (1922) by Katherine Mansfield

*That meant the cream puffs had come. Godber's were
famous for their cream puffs. Nobody ever thought of
making them at home. . . . "They look beautifully light
and feathery."*

A third volume of the short stories of Katherine Mansfield,
The Garden Party, was published in 1922. (Other collections
were to be published posthumously.) The deeply perceptive
and moving title story shows a remarkable talent.

On a perfectly beautiful morning, as preparations are
going on for a garden party, young Laura feels joy at the
beauty and promise of the day. She greets the workmen who
have come to set up the marquee and regrets that she has
come outside carrying her piece of bread and butter, as she
tries to affect adult behavior.

It is a bustling scene. The telephone rings, the florist
makes a delivery, the cook has questions about the sandwiches, and the cream puffs arrive from the baker. "Godber's
were famous for their cream puffs. Nobody ever thought of
making them at home." The cook offers them to Laura and her
sister. Although the idea of eating them just after breakfast
seems untenable, they are very soon enjoying the cream puffs
enormously and licking their fingers "with that absorbed

inward look that only comes from whipped cream." The cream puffs represent sheer delight in the midst of all this joyful activity and anticipation. Suddenly, a tragic accident is announced.

While preparations for a party are going on in one house, a sudden death has occurred in another. A poor carter from a small cottage just below the Sheridan house was killed that morning when his horse shied and he was thrown out on his head. He has left a wife and five children. The horrified Laura believes that the party must be stopped. To proceed would be callous.

But her sister tells her that to cancel the party would be absurd and extravagant, and her mother is annoyed and impatient with Laura's immature attitude. The party will not be called off. Laura is baffled by death, which happens at the wrong time. She must try to reconcile herself to such disorder and to the adult point of view which sees death as a natural occurrence, as a fact of life. After all, they are not the ones personally involved.

Later, when the festivities are over, Laura is made to bring a basket of leftover party food to the bereaved family. She goes, although she feels it is wrong. Still wearing her party dress and hat, feeling greatly upset, and needing to say something to the dead man, she sobs, "Forgive my hat."

Cream Puffs

The cream puffs have symbolized complete happiness, having been enjoyed before the intrusion of dreadful news. But they need not be purchased from a baker to excel, and surely somebody must have thought of making the delicacy at home, for here is one recipe taken from a 1912 pastry book, *The Art of Pastry and Confectionery Making* by Emile Herisse:

Baked Cream Puffs

Prepare a choux paste, drop it in rounds on a clean baking tin, sprinkle some chopped almonds mixed with sugar over the top, and bake the puffs in a moderate oven. When cold, they may be filled with whipped cream.

Choux Paste for General Use:

Take half a pound of flour, six ounces of butter, one pint of water, one dessertspoonful of castor sugar, a pinch of salt, and three or four eggs.

Put the butter, salt, sugar, and liquid into a saucepan over a gentle fire. When it rises to the top of the pan, add the sifted flour. Stir over the fire until the paste is smooth and dry, and will not adhere to the sides of the saucepan, taking great care that the paste does not burn. Take it off the fire, and keep stirring it. Next break the eggs, adding them two at a time to the paste. Keep the paste a medium thickness—not too soft, yet not too stiff—and, if necessary, add one more egg. If the paste is too stiff, it will not rise properly, and if too soft, it will make flat "puffs." Put the paste in a forcing bag, drop in small balls on greased iron baking-tins, brush them over with beaten egg, and bake in a moderate over. After they are baked, let them get cold, then fill them with whipped cream.

Chocolate Eclairs

BRAVE NEW WORLD (1932) by Aldous Huxley

*"Now, who wants a chocolate eclair?" she asked in a
loud, cheerful tone.*

A nightmare vision depicting the extremes of psychological
conditioning examines scientifically-controlled life in a brave
new world. Aldous Huxley's futuristic society, set in London
in the year 632 of Our Ford, has eliminated worry, suffering,
and tragedy to create a totally happy environment. People are
euphoric because they have been conditioned to like the roles
they must fulfill as members of a particular caste. They
readily accept orders and think of anyone who questions
authority as abnormal. They are kept too busy being happy to
have time to think. Thinking and feeling are taboo processes
which could lead to dissatisfaction or rebellion.

The opening scene describes an ominous visit to the
factory with assembly-line production of people who are being
created in bottles as needed—the requisite number of Alpha
Plus specimens, scores of Epsilons—before they are fashioned
into products with predictable responses.

A group of babies, hatched from bottles and decanted into
the world as members of a particular caste, are subjected to a
conditioning procedure. The infants are taught to hate books
and flowers by associating pain and fear with these objects of

opprobrium. Terrifying sounds of bells and sirens and electric shocks are applied as they crawl toward the formerly desired attractions.

A technique of hypnopaedia or sleep-teaching insures moral education of the bottle products. Recorded suggestion during sleep causes the children to imbibe determining attitudes and become completely accepting of their caste.

Occasionally something goes wrong, as in the case of Bernard Marx, a deviant intellectual of the Alpha caste whose blood surrogate may have been given a Gamma dose of alcohol when he was still in the bottle; consequently he is now a discontented misfit. In cases of mistakes or accidents, the escapist drug soma restores equilibrium and insures a steady state of euphoria.

Stability, the central aim of the new world, has been achieved at the expense of human experience. The synthetic society has eliminated poetry and art, human values and individuality. Without literature and without natural impulses, life is bland, sterile, and of no value.

An outsider enters this utopian world when Bernard Marx meets the Savage at an Indian Reservation inhabited by members of a pre-scientific society that was deemed unworthy to be incorporated into the new world. He brings the young man, John, back to London together with his mother, Linda. Born of a careless Beta Minus, John is an oddity whose strong individuality is enhanced by reading Shakespeare. He rejects soma and is made sick by the vast numbers of identical, mindless people. His is a gruesome view of the total dehumanization of the inhabitants of utopia, that marvellous world he had heard so much about from his mother.

John rebels and decides to opt out of the comfortable world, choosing life—the right to grow old, contract diseases, starve, and live in fear and pain. His choice of life is the road to self-destruction. Unable either to adapt to chemically-induced happiness or to retreat to the squalid Reservation, the

Savage kills himself. His suicide indicates his self-identity and his humanity.

Linda has a relatively peaceful end when she resorts to overdoses of soma for permanent escape. At forty-four, she is shunned in a world of youth whose inhabitants have never known old people and are revolted by her aged appearance. John becomes overwrought when he visits her in the special Park Lane Hospital for the Dying. Death has no significance for the brave new worlders, who had begun death conditioning at eighteen months. Each had spent two mornings a week in the Hospital for the Dying where the best toys are kept and special servings of chocolate cream come on death days to instill the idea of the end of life as a routine and natural event.

John is indignant when a group of ebullient eight-year-olds enter the ward with their noisy attitudes of delight and inquisitiveness, and he throttles one particularly offensive youngster. When he sobs uncontrollably upon Linda's death, the horrified nurse fears that his appalling behavior may undo the conditioning procedure. She counteracts any adverse effects by offering the most positive and desirable treat possible—chocolate eclairs. Screams of joy from happy faces smeared with chocolate indicate complete success in obliterating the risky scene from memory.

Chocolate Eclairs

Even though literature was forbidden in the brave new world, Mrs. Black's *Superior Cookery* of 1887 must have been somehow preserved to yield a method for making chocolate eclairs.

Chocolate Eclairs.

¼ lb. Flour.   2 oz. Butter.
½ pint Water.   1 oz. Sugar.
3 Eggs.

Put the water, butter, and sugar in a saucepan to boil. Have the flour sifted, and when the water is boiling, drop the flour all in and stir vigorously over the fire till it becomes a perfectly smooth thick paste, and leaves the side of the saucepan—it must boil five minutes at least. Remove the pan from the fire, and put it all away to cool for a quarter of an hour. When cool, drop in 1 egg, and with a wooden spoon beat till the egg is thoroughly mixed and quite smooth; then drop in another and do the same, and then the third. On this beating, and the previous careful boiling long enough, the success of the dish entirely depends. Put the whole of the preparation into a forcing-bag with plain tube, about 1/3 of an inch in diameter, and put the eclairs out on a buttered baking tin, in the length and thickness of finger biscuits. Put them in the oven to bake till ready (that is till they have risen a great deal and feel firm), about twenty minutes in a moderately hot oven. Take them out, and when cool, open them at the side or end, and fill them either with a puree of fruit, or the pastry cream that follows (if opened at the end, the forcing bag is used to fill them):—

Pastry Cream.

1 oz. Flour.   *½ pint Milk.*
1 oz. Sugar.   *2 Eggs.*
½ teaspoonful Vanilla Essence.

Beat up the eggs well, and make the whole into a perfectly smooth batter, which stir over the fire till it boils, and is a nice smooth paste. To this paste may be added a few ratafia biscuits broken up, or a few chopped almonds. With this fill the eclairs, and then ice them with the following.

Chocolate Icing

½ lb. Sugar.   *2 oz. Chocolate.*
1 teaspoonful Essence of Vanilla.

Put ½ a lb. of sugar and ½ a teacupful water in a small saucepan, and stir constantly till it boils a few minutes (three or five), until a little put on the fingers feels quite sticky, or till it is thick; then stir in the chocolate, grated, and ½ teaspoonful vanilla essence; stir till the chocolate is mixed and smooth. With this ice over the top of the eclairs, and leave to harden, and serve cold.

Cheese Cakes

THE HOUSE IN DORMER FOREST (1920) by
Mary Webb

"Cheescakes in the dairy!" . . . Now if there was a thing grandmother liked, it was cheescakes.

The House in Dormer Forest, Mary Webb's third novel, is about the stagnation of the spirit when wrong values rule. The house itself has an oppressive and malignant atmosphere and becomes worthless when uninhabited by the spirit of freedom and love; it is eventually burnt down.

The author is concerned with the problems of modern life and tries to show essential truths and the correct role for mankind. *The House in Dormer Forest* is a significant work, full of nature symbolism and mysticism in an all-important Shropshire setting. Its theme is the development of the individual soul and the search for wholeness. "Let the sleeping soul awake," is Mary Webb's inscription at the beginning of the novel.

Three generations of women reside at the house of Dormer, and each of the women seeks to dominate her world. Grandmother Velindre seeks to dominate by using religion and age. She quotes Biblical texts, often inappropriately, to support every act, even cruel ones. Her daughter, married to the gruff and insensitive Solomon Darke uses silence "like an iceberg silently pressing upon a ship." Catherine Velindre, a distant relative living in the house as a paying guest, uses her beauty and sexuality to gain power over men. She is unlike both Ruby and Amber, sisters who are also unlike each other. Ruby is sensuous but too naive to know that eloquent words of chivalry do not insure tenderness in marriage and too materialistic to understand that white satin does not compensate for the pain of a loveless marriage.

Only Amber Darke knows that power comes with love. Amber feels at home in nature—with birds, seasons, dawns over amethyst hills, and bunches of white violets. "These things were her home, not Dormer." Amber alone finds what she seeks—love. Although her looks are plain and sallow, Michael sees her inner radiance.

The natures of various members of the family who live at Dormer come to light with cheesecakes as a focal point. Early in the novel, there is "a large batch of successful cheesecakes in the oven" when Enoch, the hired man, comes into the kitchen after he has finished milking. The servant Sarah "opened the oven door and took out the cheesecakes." They converse, and she muses "dreamily, breaking off a bit of crust for Enoch." Her chosen one, she prophesies will "get plenty of these—a plenty." Later, cheesecakes are used to show diverse temperaments acting and reacting on each other and to expose the petty jealousies and mean dispositions of several of the main characters.

At the wedding of Ruby and Ernest, Catherine espies Peter and Marigold dancing by themselves in the dairy. Outraged that Peter ignores her in favor of a mere servant, the sly Catherine forms a plan to teach him a lesson. "Cheesecakes in the dairy!" she whispers to Grandmother Velindre with a malicious gleam in her eyes. She knows perfectly well that grandmother will go after the cheesecakes she is so very fond of and find and punish the culprits. The ruse works. They are caught by the old woman who thunders, "How dare you dance with a servant! Woman—go!"

Peter remains standing speechless and paralyzed with amazement. Why had grandmother come here to the dairy, a place she ventures to no more than twice a year? He works it out and recognizes Catherine's scheme. She loves no one but wants only to use him to arouse another. Peter plans his own vicious course of revenge against Catherine.

Through strange events, near tragedies, and comic scenes, the members of the Darke family pair off into couples. Marigold is dismissed from Dormer, but she and Peter eventually marry. Catherine ends up with Philip Arkinstall. But Amber Darke and Michael Hallowes meet and know instantly that theirs is the perfect relationship, that they have found everlasting love.

 # Cheese Cakes

This recipe, for cheese cakes better than mean old grandmother deserves, is given by Emile Herisse in his 1893 cookbook, *The Art of Pastry Making*.

Cheese Cakes

Take eight ounces of sugar, four ounces of best butter, two eggs, one ounce of finger biscuits reduced to a powder, the juice of two lemons, and a little milk. Break the eggs into a basin, add the sugar and melted butter, and stir until the mixture becomes light and smooth; then add the lemon juice, biscuit powder, and if necessary, a little milk. Next, line some tartlet pans with puff paste and fill up with the mixture; then bake in a quick oven.

UPDATE: Old recipes using cream and fruit juices were called "cheese" cakes because the mixture forms a curd and makes a flavored cream cheese.

Gingerbread

PRECIOUS BANE (1924) by Mary Webb

It was a merry scene, with ... the gingerbread as brown and sticky as chestnut buds.

Precious Bane is the last of the five complete novels of Mary Webb. When she died in 1927 at the age of forty-six, Mary Webb was virtually unheard of, and an intense period of creativity which lasted less than a dozen years came to an end with this, her most important work. Then Prime Minister Stanley Baldwin praised the quality of her writing in a speech at the Royal Literary Fund dinner, and his words of praise caused a surge of interest and popularity. Finally, posthumously, she received the public recognition and critical acclaim which she craved and which eluded her in her lifetime.

Precious Bane is a highly poetic love story, a story of love in all its aspects including the dark and savage side. The gentle Prudence Sarn tells the tale. Prue has a facial disfigurement, a harelip, which makes her an object of suspicion and scorn. But it also imbues her with a special beauty of spirit.

When her dour brother Gideon goes to market to buy oxen, Prue is pleased to accompany him, for she has hardly any opportunity to leave the farm. They are up at four on market day and arrive early at the festive scene where everything, it seems, is for sale. There are stalls selling cheeses, butter,

324

eggs, and poultry as well as stalls selling sunbonnets, toys, or gewgaws. And of course there is a stall for gingerbread. The festive market scene, based on the one Mary Webb knew in Shrewsbury, evokes the Shropshire world of the author.

Gideon conducts his business. As the story unfolds, he is revealed as being completely overcome by greed. His ruthless drive for wealth destroys others as well as himself. By contrast, Prue is rich in spiritual awareness. She has the "visitation" which, she says, changes her life and reconciles her to existence alone and unloved because of her physical defect. But her desire for a lover to whom she can give her whole being is fulfilled when she finds Kester Woodseaves, the weaver who appreciates her inner beauty.

The unfolding of Prue's love story is enhanced by the author's use of local legend and superstition, memorable characters, a rich and robust Shropshire dialect, and strong evocation of local landscape and atmosphere.

It all has a mystical, magical quality and brings out the beauty and aura of timelessness of the Shropshire world brilliantly. Prime Minister Baldwin summarized the author's power in a preface to the 1928 edition of *Precious Bane*: "Her sensibility is so acute and her power over words so sure and swift that one who reads some passage in Whitehall has almost the physical sense of being in Shropshire cornfields."

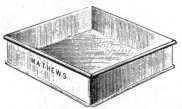

Gingerbread

Traditional gingerbread is a suitable food to select from a novel which gives a folk feeling of the past. Gingerbread has been for centuries eaten as a fair-day or festive treat and is very much a part of the Shropshire market authentically depicted by Mary Webb. The recipe is presented by E. Roberta Rees in *High Class and Economical Recipes* (1907).

Rich Gingerbread

3 eggs
½ lb. flour
¼ lb. ground rice
¼ lb. corn flour
6 oz. butter
6 oz. brown sugar
1 gill golden syrup
3 oz. crystallised ginger (sliced)

3 oz. candied orange or lemon
   peel (shredded)
1 teaspoonful ground ginger
½ teaspoonful carbonate of soda
½ teaspoonful ground cloves
½ teaspoonful ground cinnamon

Sift the flour, cornflour, and ground rice into a basin, melt the butter, sugar, and syrup, stir to the flour, etc. Sift the carbonate of soda and spices together, and stir them in with the crystallised ginger and candied peel. Beat the eggs well and stir quickly to the other ingredients. Bake at once in a lined and greased tin for about 1 ¾ hours.

UPDATE: A gill is equal to 5 fluid oz. or 100 ml.

326

Spice Cake

SHIRLEY (1849) by Charlotte Brontë

A 'spice-cake,' which followed by way of dessert, vanished like a vision.

Shirley, Charlotte Brontë's second published novel, appeared just two years after the hugely successful *Jane Eyre*. The public was eager to receive it, but the new novel lacked the passion of *Jane Eyre* and never achieved the same acclaim.

The author was in a state of grief and mourning over the deaths of Branwell, Emily, and Anne; her brother and sisters had all died during the composition of *Shirley*, and she alone was left living with her father in the Haworth Parsonage. It may be that her feelings of bereavement and of discontent with her own life were responsible for the failure.

The setting of the novel is the Yorkshire she knew so well, and the story, based on local history, takes place in the time of the Luddite riots of 1812. The author depicts with a sense of fairness the selfishness and the troubles of the mill owners on one side and the lawlessness of the workers on the other. She tries to reconcile the story of the Luddites with the love affairs of Caroline and Shirley, the latter character being a depiction of her sister Emily.

Charlotte incorporated personal feelings into the story and expressed her outrage about spinsterhood and the way unmarried women like herself were treated. Caroline faces life as a single woman and tries to find fulfilling occupation rather than accept a restricted life without purpose, one within the narrow confines allowed to women. But the feminist problem raised by the author is left unresolved, for Caroline is rewarded with marriage after all. The total effect is one of confusion and overcrowding of ideas.

The author's plan, infusing her own experience into a Yorkshire social history framework, was a formula for weakness. She tells a realistic story, avoiding use of her own powerful imagination and personal emotion. She did not enliven the historical account with the passion and vitality which made *Jane Eyre* a triumph. Nevertheless, there are moments and elements of greatness, as in her highly successful mockery of a trio of curates.

At the beginning of *Shirley*, she paints an unflattering portrait of three silly curates based on actual figures who frequented the Parsonage House at Haworth. Their appearances are comic and serve to enhance the theme of the uselessness of the clergy. The passages caused offense and were condemned by many.

The curates are described in the first chapter as having good appetites, and the eating scene sums up their arrogance, coarseness, and greed. They devour everything in sight—from tough beef to flat beer—without discrimination. They gobble bread, Yorkshire pudding, two tureens of vegetables, and cheese. But the disappearance of an entire spice-cake is particularly poignant, for it brings on the laments and tears of a six-year-old whose expectations are shattered when his mother brings back into the kitchen the empty platter.

Spice Cake

Fortunately, the platter may be refilled with a very traditional seventeenth-century spice cake from Robert May's *The Accomplisht Cook* of 1685.

Spice Cake

Take half a bushel of the best flour you can get very finely searsed, and lay it upon a large Pastry board, make a hole in the midst thereof, and put to it three pound of the best butter you can get; with fourteen pound of currans finely picked and rubbed, three quarts of good new thick cream warm'd, two pound of fine sugar beaten, three pints of good new ale, barm or yeast, four ounces of cinamon fine beaten and searsed, also an ounce of beaten ginger, two ounces of nutmegs fine beaten and searsed; put all these materials together, and work them up into an indifferent stiff paste, keep it warm till the oven be hot, then make it up and bake it, being baked an hour and a half ice it, then take four pound of double refined sugar, beat it, and searse it, and put it in a deep clean scowred skillet the quantity of a gallon, boil it to a candy height with a little rose-water, then draw the cake, run it all over, and set it into the oven, till it be candied.

UPDATE: In *The Accomplisht Cook*, Robert May entitles this spice cake recipe, "To Make an extraordinary good Cake." It must also make an extraordinarily large cake. With quantities like these, suitable for a large banquet, even the trio of curates could not have demolished the cake. Nevertheless, the amounts need to be altered and the instructions modified:

329

3 oz. butter
1 lb. plain flour
12 oz. currants
2 oz. sugar
½ tsp. ground cinnamon
½ tsp. ground ginger
¼ tsp. grated nutmeg
½ pint cream
*½ oz. dried yeast mixed with 1 tsp. sugar and ¼ pint warm
    water*

For glazing:

1 tbls. sugar
1 tbls. rosewater

Rub the butter into the flour, add the remainder of the dry ingredients, and mix in the cream and yeast to form a soft dough. Leave to rise in a warm place for about an hour, when it will double in size, then knead and place in a greased 8 inch cake tin. Leave to prove for 20 minutes, then bake at 425°F (220°C) for 20 minutes, then for 1 hour at 375°F (190°C). Melt the sugar in the rosewater over a low heat, and brush this glaze over the cake immediately after removing it from the oven.

Bride Cake

JUDE THE OBSCURE (1895) by Thomas Hardy

*Fawley's aunt being a baker she made him a
bride-cake. . . Of this cake Arabella took some slices,
wrapped them up in white note-paper, and sent them to
her companions in the pork-dressing business.*

First published in complete form in November 1895, *Jude the
Obscure* is the last—many would add the finest—novel of
Thomas Hardy.

Jude Fawley has been sent as a penniless, pitiful orphan
boy to his great aunt Drusilla to be cared for. With a passion
for learning, he tries to take his destiny into his own hands by
a process of self-education which he hopes will enable him to
go to the great university city of Christminster. Whether his
desperate desire to become a great scholar and a Doctor of
Divinity would have succeeded or not, the attempt is doomed
when Arabella intrudes herself into his life. Arabella is a
coarse and ignorant girl—"a complete and substantial female
animal"—in search of a husband. She tricks him into a
marriage which inevitably wrecks his intellectual aspirations
and career plans.

Everyone, including Jude himself, seems to know what a
very foolish thing he is doing by allowing himself to become
entrapped by Arabella. But he nevertheless decides to

sacrifice himself and do the honorable thing despite his full knowledge that "Arabella was not worth a great deal as a specimen of womankind."

The wedding is a travesty, and the prognosis promises only wretchedness. The wedding cake dramatizes the tension. Aunt Drusilla has baked the cake but not without a grudging and unkind reminder of Jude's luckless existence. That Arabella eagerly sends some of it to her pork-dressing companions with a self-congratulatory note referring to the sham she has just practiced so successfully is further commentary on the vulgar and unworkable association. The cake which ought to be celebratory becomes tainted, like the marriage, by Arabella's connection to the pig factory.

Bride Cake

It must have been in quite another frame of mind, filled with nothing but happy wedding thoughts, that Mrs. Beeton told her readers how to make a bride cake.

Rich Bride Cake

INGREDIENTS.—5 lbs. of the finest flour, 3 lbs. of fresh butter, 5 lbs. of currants, 2 lbs. of sifted loaf sugar, 2 nutmegs, ¼ oz. of mace, half ¼ oz. of cloves, 16 eggs, 1 lb. of sweet almonds, ½ lb. of candied citron, ½ lb. each of candied orange and lemon peel, 1 gill of wine, 1 gill of brandy.

Mode.—Let the flour be as fine as possible, and well dried and sifted; the currants washed, picked, and dried before the fire; the sugar well pounded and sifted; the nutmegs grated, the spices pounded; the eggs thoroughly whisked, whites and yolks separately; the almonds pounded with a little orange-flower water, and the candied peel cut in neat slices. When all these ingredients are prepared, mix them in the following manner. Begin working the butter with the hand till it becomes of a cream-like consistency; stir in the sugar, and when the whites of the eggs are whisked to a solid froth, mix them with the butter and sugar; next, well beat up the yolks for 10 minutes, and, adding them to the flour, nutmegs, mace, and cloves, continue beating the whole together for ½ hour or longer, till wanted for the oven. Then mix in lightly the currants, almonds, and candied peel with the wine and brandy; and having lined a hoop with buttered paper, fill it with the mixture, and bake the cake in a tolerably quick oven, taking care, however, not to burn it: to prevent this, the top of it may be covered with a sheet of paper. To ascertain whether the cake is done, plunge a clean knife into the middle of it, withdraw it directly, and if the blade is not sticky, and looks bright, the cake is sufficiently baked. These cakes are usually spread with a thick layer of almond icing, and over that another layer of sugar icing, and afterwards ornamented. In baking a large cake like this, great attention must be paid to the heat of the oven; it should not be too fierce, but have a good soaking heat.

Time.—5 to 6 hours. Average cost, 2s. per lb.

UPDATE: A gill is equal to 5 fluid oz. or 100 ml.

Oatcakes

FRANKENSTEIN (1818) by Mary Shelley

I still sat on the shore, satisfying my appetite, which had become ravenous, with an oaten cake.

As the daughter of the political philosopher William Godwin (*Enquiry Concerning Political Justice*) and the great feminist Mary Wollstonecraft (*A Vindication of the Rights of Women*), Mary Shelley was born in 1797 into fertile ground for herself attaining status as a writer. *Frankenstein* is the novel by which Mary Shelley, wife of the poet Percy Bysshe Shelley, achieved lasting literary fame.

Mary was not yet seventeen when she eloped with the poet. By the age of twenty, she had given birth to three children, all of whom died before she was twenty-two. The only child who survived into adulthood was born in 1819. Then, in 1822, Shelley himself died, drowned in a storm while sailing in the Gulf of Spezia. Having had great success with *Frankenstein*, the impoverished widow turned to writing for financial support. While the painful events of her life may have prevented attainment of her full literary potential, she nevertheless achieved, by the time of her death in 1851, a large and varied output including editions of Shelley's work, biography, travel pieces, articles, poems, numerous short stories, and four novels.

Shelley had encouraged her career as a writer. Indeed, *Frankenstein* would not have been written without the motivating influence of Shelley and his friends. A rainy summer holiday was spent in 1816 on the shores of Lake Geneva by a group consisting of Shelley and Mary, Byron and his eccentric friend Polidori, and Mary's stepsister Claire Clairmont (also Byron's mistress). At the Villa Diodati, they amused themselves with ghost stories and indulged in literary and philosophical discussions on such topics as gothic horrors, origin and principle of life, galvanism, and the Prometheus myth. Elements of all of these were to appear in *Frankenstein*.

Byron proposed that each of them write a ghost story. Mary describes herself, in the Introduction to the 1831 edition, as having an impasse until she became aroused by a particular conversation between Shelley and Byron on the origin of life. In an experiment conducted by Dr. Erasmus Darwin, a piece of vermicelli kept in a glass case began to move voluntarily. Obsessed with the idea, she dwelt on it throughout a nightmarish night and began her story in the morning: "It was on a dreary night of November. . ." Thus, with a line that lends itself to much literary spoofing, we have the genesis of the famous tale which was published in 1818.

Victor Frankenstein learns the secret of infusing life into inanimate objects. He constructs a creature in the semblance of a human being out of bones from the charnel house. Powerful and revolting, the creature inspires unmitigated horror and fear in those who see it. Basic human attributes, however, enable it to feel the pain of loneliness and rejection. Victor agrees to make a female companion but then withdraws from the task in a wave of remorse. The monster, in revenge and despair, kills its creator's bride. The monster has become malevolent, having been abandoned by his creator and by mankind and forced to live in isolation. Frankenstein pursues it to the Arctic in order to destroy the menace, but he is himself destroyed before his creation disappears into the icy wastelands.

Although the author considered it important that the demon be unnamed, it has in the popular mind taken on the name of its creator, thereby lending support to those who see in the novel a theme of the split personality. The wild Gothic tale can be read on many levels—the dangers of too much scientific knowledge, an attack on the stultifying effect of social convention, racial prejudice, the agony of loneliness, the parent-child relationship, and, in more recent times, the problems of identity concerned with organ transplants. But I very much doubt whether it has ever been read for the food or sustenance which Victor needs when he goes out in pursuit of the monster.

Out of fear that it may indulge in gratuitous violence and murder or propagate a race of evil beings, Victor Frankenstein destroys the partially-created mate he agreed to make. The violated contract obviates any hope for happiness for the heartbroken monster. Condemned to a miserable existence in a totally alien world, the demon howls in despair, threatens revenge, then swiftly escapes from the wilds of Scotland over the ocean.

Victor spends an agonized night considering the implications of the creature's flight. Then he goes into a deep sleep, a lifeless trance, and awakens refreshed but hungry. Before he can satisfy his craving for resolution, he needs to satisfy his craving for food. He eats an oatcake to appease his hunger before leaving the solitary island in the Orkneys in a small boat. He eventually pursues the destructive demon to the polar regions, where both perish.

Oatcakes

The great wonder of this gothic horror story may be how, not the monster, but the oatcakes, materialized. The conundrum is made even more baffling by an earlier description of the barren soil of the Orkneys which yielded only a scant supply of oatmeal for its deprived population of five emaciated inhabitants. Moreover, since oatcakes make such a nourishing and tasty repast, Victor Frankenstein might have avoided a great deal of trouble if his thoughts of creation were bent solely on oatcakes. After all, this is a story with a moral: At moments which call for decisive action, stop and eat an oatcake.

Elizabeth Moxon's *English Housewifry Exemplified* of 1758, still in use by noted chefs of our time, creates the following recipe for oatmeal cakes:

Otmeal Cakes

Take a Peck of fine Flour, half a Peck of Oat-meal, and mix it well together; put to it seven Eggs well beat, three Quarts of new Milk, a little warm Water, a Pint of Sack, and a Pint of new Yeast; mix all these well together, and let it stand to rise; then bake them. Butter the Stone every Time you lie on the Cakes, and make them rather thicker then a Pancake.

UPDATE: A peck is equal to eight quarts.

Here is a revised and modernized alternative that eliminates the old-fashioned errors of spelling and grammar as well as the unwieldy quantities:

Oatcakes

8 oz. medium oatmeal
4 oz. sifted flour
1 teaspoon salt
1 teaspoon baking powder
2 heaped tablespoons butter or lard

Put the oatmeal into a bowl and sift into it the flour, salt, and baking powder. Mix. Make a well in the mixture. Heat about 2 oz. water and add the fat, bring to a boil, and quickly pour into the well in the dry ingredients mixture. Work together rapidly, kneading lightly. If necessary, add a little water for holding the mixture together to form a stiff dough. Sprinkle the surface with more oatmeal and roll out thinly. Cut into three-inch rounds. Bake on a lightly greased tray at 350`F. for about 25 minutes or until pale gold.

Makes about 16 oatcakes.

Desserts

Syllabub

SYBIL: OR THE TWO NATIONS (1845) by
Benjamin Disraeli

"I wonder what the nobs has for supper". . . . *"syllabubs like blazes*. . . ."

The only Prime Minister ever to write novels became an author long before he was a politician. Benjamin Disraeli wrote his first novel (*Vivian Grey*) in 1826, when he was twenty-two, and went on writing fiction throughout his life. He produced a total of eleven novels, as well as short stories, poems, a biography, a play, and essays.

The so-called *Young England* trilogy of novels consisting of *Coningsby*, *Sybil*, and *Tancred* epitomize the ideals and objects of a group of bright, young, and dynamic Parliamentarians who made up the "Young England" movement. Greatly concerned with the well-being of man, the group called for past ideals to be applied to present Tory party principles. Disraeli described their aims in the trilogy, thereby extending his political ideology into the realm of imaginative writing. The novels deal with the socio-economic problems of the time.

Sybil, the most widely read of his novels, revealed the oppressed state of working people and exposed their hardships and sufferings. Disraeli expressed outrage at the abject

343

conditions of the laboring classes and indignation at the system of social injustice which permitted such conditions to survive. He presented an indictment of an aristocracy that neglects the struggling common people whose lives are deprived and hopeless. The polemical novel suggested how England could attain a political and spiritual rebirth by making a plea for idealism to do away with greedy materialism. Disraeli's remedy was a new and generous Toryism to close the gap.

The subtitle of the novel is a reference to the two diametrically opposed nations—the rich and the poor. Disraeli succeeded in giving his readers a picture of existing conditions by presenting contrasting pictures of those two nations. The reader is taken from scenes of idle and dissipated aristocratic life to scenes of degraded working-class life, from a sumptuous London club reminiscent of the opulence of Versailles to a squalid sweat-shop. As vignettes from rich and gilded life alternate with wretched and filthy life, vices of class distinction and abuses of capital are effectively exposed.

At the center of the novel is Charles Egremont, who becomes enlightened as he discovers the "other nation." While walking in the ruins of Marney Abbey, he meets Stephen Morley and Walter Gerard, the father of Sybil. The two strangers express bold and original views which give Egremont a desire to learn about conditions of England. He sees the squalid state of factory laborers and the sordid living places of the humble poor and is stunned by the realization that such conditions exist in England. He is initiated into ongoings of trade unions, Chartist agitation, and the riots of 1842. Morley and Gerard become the means through which he grows in awareness.

At the Abbey, when Egremont maintains to his new friends that the "Queen reigns over the greatest nation that ever existed," Morley asks, "Which nation? . . . for she reigns over two." He makes an elabaorate and articulate speech, which is an explicit statement on the two nations of the title and one of the most famous passages in English literature:

"Two nations; between whom there is no intercourse and no sympathy; who are as ignorant of each other's habits, thoughts, and feelings, as if they were dwellers in different zones, or inhabitants of different planets; who are formed by a different breeding, are fed by a different food, are ordered by different manners, and are not governed by the same laws. . . THE RICH AND THE POOR."

Fed by a different food. That phrase is more than a metaphor. One of the vignettes of life in England echoes the theme of the division between the wealthy and the poor by specific reference to food.

In contrast to the lights and fashion and music of a magnificent festival taking place in the splendid saloons of a great house fronting a royal park, a less luxurious party is taking place under the sky, in the light of the stars, on the grass. One adolescent of about fourteen conjectures to his friend on what the wealthy enjoy for supper and, reaching well into his imagination for what might be a stupendously satisfying feast, guesses that they indulge in "lots of kidneys." But his friend has the advantage of wisdom and experience that comes with the added age of a year or two and is quick to correct him, "Oh! no; sweets is the time of day in these here blowouts: syllabubs like blazes. . . ."

Syllabub

Syllabub is indeed a sweet or dessert that might grace the elegant tables of the wealthy. It is rich in ingredients as well as in tradition. The word is said to derive from the French town of Sille and "bub"—the Elizabethan word for drink. In Elizabethan times, syllabub was a bubbling drink of clear white wine with a frothy layer of cream on top. Before methods of whisking cream were discovered, froth was created by driving the cream through the air, allowing it to gather bubbles as it went. For sheer interest, consider this brief but complete recipe from an early book of the seventeenth century:

> Tak sack or white or Red wine & some Cream & some suger put in Together & let stand two hours Then milk it full from The Cow.

Now consider Eliza Acton's modern recipe in *Modern Cookery* (1845) for syllabub for *Sybil*:

Very Superior Whipped Syllabubs

Weigh seven ounces of fine sugar and rasp on it the rinds of two fresh sound lemons of good size, then pound or roll it to powder, and put it into a bowl with the strained juice of the lemons, two large glasses of sherry, and two of brandy; when the sugar is nearly or quite dissolved add a pint of rich cream, and whisk or mill the mixture well; take off the froth as it rises, and put it into glasses. These syllabubs will remain good for several days, and should always be made if possible, four and twenty hours before

346

they are wanted for table. The full flavor of the lemon-rind is obtained with less trouble than in rasping, by paring it very thin indeed, and infusing it for some hours in the juice of the fruit.

Sugar, 7 ozs.; rind and juice of lemons, 2; sherry, 2 large wineglassesful; brandy, 2 wineglassesful; cream, 1 pint.

Obs.—These proportions are sufficient for two dozens or more of syllabubs: they are often made with almost equal quantities of wine and cream, but are certainly neither so good nor so wholesome without a portion of brandy.

Pêches à la Melba

See: DECLINE AND FALL (1928) by Evelyn Waugh, page 157.

Mr. Prendergast ate two pêches Melba undisturbed.

To follow the braised pheasant served at dinner, comes this excellent dessert, taken from *Senn's Century Cook Book* (1923).

Pêches à la Melba

Halves of peaches, cooked in vanilla syrup, filled with vanilla cream ice, and dressed in pyramidal form on a border of Genoise or other light cake. The fruit must be sauced over with a rich raspberry syrup, and sprinkled over with almond chips.

Mince Pies

See: GREAT EXPECTATIONS by Charles Dickens (1860), page 270.

A handsome mince-pie had been made yesterday.

In *The English Cookery Book* of 1858, John Henry Walsh tells us that "mince pies are made in small patty-pans, which are lined with puff-paste, and, after putting in some mince-meat, covering them over with more paste, and baking."

To Make the Mince-Meat.—Take three pounds of suet finely chopped and sifted, two pounds of currants, three pounds of raisins, and one pound of apples, all chopped very small, three pounds of moist sugar, three-quarters of a pint of red and white wine mixed, a glass of brandy, the peel of two small lemons, the juice of one, two ounces of candied peel, cut; mix all together with a quarter of an ounce of cinnamon, a quarter of an ounce of mace, and one small nutmeg, all finely powdered. Keep it in a close covered jar, and, if kept a twelve-month, it may require the addition of a little more wine.

UPDATE: Mince-meat pies are named for the meat they originally contained. It was a way of preserving meat to be eaten in winter in a form other than smoking or salting. Only beef suet remains in "modern" recipes as a reminder of this fact.

349

Sago Pudding

See: PORTRAIT OF THE ARTIST AS A YOUNG DOG
(1940) by Dylan Thomas, page 201.

I sat silently . . . over the sago pudding.

Before returning to school, the narrator sits contemplating and fantasizing, over his sago pudding, about a new friendship that will have great influence in his future life. In *A Handbook of Cookery for a Small House* (1923), Jessie Conrad provides a recipe for sago pudding that will surely bring happiness. In the Preface to his wife's cookery book, Joseph Conrad lauds his wife's good cooking of simple food which, he says, has been increasing his own daily happiness.

Tapioca or Sago Pudding

Put the tapioca or sago about an inch thick at the bottom of the pie-dish. Pour boiling milk on to it to about half a dishful and leave it to soak for about half an hour. When cold add a beaten egg, sugar to taste, and fill up the dish with cold milk. Put a little grated nutmeg over the top and bake for two hours in a slow oven.

UPDATE: Sago, a farinaceous food obtained from palms, is native to Malaysia and means "bread" in Malay. The starchy pith is extracted from stems and beaten in cold water to separate granules from woody filaments. Moist sago is dried for export.

Banana Fritters

MEMOIRS OF A FOX-HUNTING MAN (1928) by
Siegfried Sassoon

She handed me a plate with two banana fritters on it.

With his reputation firmly established as a powerful war poet, Siegfried Sassoon turned in his middle years to prose. He had fought on the front, sustained wounds several times, and been awarded the Military Cross for heroism on the field. But he acquired a hatred for the war with its stupidities and enormous waste of lives and expressed in verse the loathing and bitterness he felt. The disillusioned Sassoon needed to examine his disturbed inner self in his writing, and he turned to prose.

George Sherston is introduced in Sassoon's first prose work, a semi-autobiographical novel called *Memoirs of a Fox-Hunting Man*. Sherston becomes a representative figure of the lost generation. This first novel, an integral part of a trilogy, follows the events in the hero's life up to the beginnings of the war. The fictional sequence is continued in *Memoirs of an Infantry Officer* and *Sherston's Progress*. The horrors of war have a disrupting effect on Sherston, who becomes a compassionate and anguished figure as he revolts against military authority and receives treatment as a shell-shock case in a military hospital.

351

Sassoon was a lover of the hunt, as is George Sherston, who first appears as a young boy. When Master George is given his first pony, he begins his progress toward fox-hunting, eventually becoming an active participant in the sport. He enthusiastically reports one day at the dinner table the hunting events of that day, and his Aunt Evelyn worries about the effect on his health, while Miriam worries about his safety. She issues a warning on the inherent dangers of the hunt—he might break his neck—as she serves him a dish of banana fritters. But the pre-war world of horses and flower shows and village cricket is soon to be shattered by the advent of the Great War; concern for safety is shifted to the young men whose lives are threatened by the War.

Banana Fritters

Before everything changes for him, and before he goes into the changes wrought by the war, Sherston had been enjoying a happy life as a fox-hunting man—enjoying it no doubt as much as the plate of banana fritters, which may be traced to a pre-World War I cook book, Charles Elme Francatelli's *The Modern Cook* of 1911.

Banana Fritters (Sweet)

Remove the skin from six not overripe bananas, cut each in half crossways, and then divide in halves lengthways. Put the bananas thus prepared into a pie-dish, sprinkle with castor sugar, a little ground cinnamon, and a liqueur-glass of kirsch or maraschino. Allow to stand for about fifteen minutes. Have ready some frying batter. Coat each piece of banana with batter and drop into very hot frying fat. When of a golden colour and crisp, take up and drain the fritters on a cloth or paper. Dish up, dredge with fine sugar, and serve hot.

Frying Batter, for all Sorts of Fruit Fritters

Put into a basin four ounces of sifted flour, one ounce of fresh butter (melted), one wine-glassful of Curacao, and a very little salt; mix these gently together with a wooden spoon, gradually pouring into the basin about half a gill of bitter ale. When the batter becomes mixed to the thickness of double cream, set it aside while you whisk the whites of two eggs into a substantial froth, and instantly incorporate this with it.

DESSERTS

Many prefer such fritters as pineapple, peach, apricot, or plum, fried with a plainer kind of batter, in making which water is substituted for ale.

UPDATE: Half a gill is equal to 2 ½ oz. or 50 ml.

Soufflée

BLISS (1920) by Katherine Mansfield

"This is a very admirable soufflée!"

Katherine Mansfield, one of the most respected and influential writers of the short story, might have found complete happiness in her writing and in her marriage to John Middleton Murry in 1918. But she contracted tuberculosis in 1917, and ill health demolished the possibility for a happy and contented life; her premature death came at the age of thirty-four in 1923.

Bliss is her second book of collected stories. The title story is one of her many mature works and is an artistic triumph in its presentation of a world of beauty suddenly tainted by the entry of something evil. Fate is adversely changed in a world indifferent to human suffering.

In "Bliss," a young woman feels the perfection of a spring day and is in a state of bliss, like the flowering pear tree in the garden. She has the feeling that something wonderful will soon happen and goes through the evening in a state of extreme happiness. Her euphoria reaches a peak when, as hostess at a dinner party, her husband compliments the dessert in particular. She anticipates the moment when the guests will leave and she can be alone with him. But the whole world toward which she had felt so tender is cruelly shattered, and her hopes and happiness are suddenly destroyed as, inadvertently, she sees her husband embracing another woman. Only nature, symbolized by the pear tree, remains untouched and as "lovely as ever."

Soufflée

So successful was the *soufflée* which was served at the height of the heroine's happiness, that she feels like weeping with pleasure. Indeed, it is a party dish that ought always to be associated with festive occasions.

This recipe for chocolate *soufflée*, taken from a 1912 edition of *Mrs. Beeton's Cookery Book*, may not guarantee lasting happiness; but it will undoubtedly elicit positive comments from grateful guests.

Chocolate Soufflée

Ingredients.—2 oz. of finely-grated chocolate, 3 oz. of flour, 1 oz. of sugar, 1 oz. of butter, ½ pint of milk, 3 yolks of eggs, 4 whites of eggs, ½ a teaspoonful of vanilla essence, custard, or other suitable sweet sauce.

Method.—Place the milk and chocolate in a small stewpan, and simmer gently until dissolved. Melt the butter, stir in the flour, add the chocolate mixture, and boil well. Let it cool a little, add the vanilla, sugar, the yolks of eggs one at a time, give the whole a good beating, then stir in as lightly as possible the stiffly-whisked whites of eggs. Turn into a well-buttered mould, and steam gently from 45 to 50 minutes. Serve the sauce round the dish.

Gooseberry Wine

See: THE VICAR OF WAKEFIELD (1766) by
Oliver Goldsmith, page 163.

*As we lived near the road, we often had the traveller or
stranger visit us to taste our gooseberry wine, for which
we had great reputation.*

At the high point of their success, the Primroses serve
gooseberry wine regularly. When their fortunes decline, they
move to a new home in a community of simple farmers where
they continue to serve it to selected guests. Neighbor
Flamborough continues to partake of the famous gooseberry
wine. The landlord of the estate, Squire Thornhill, is invited
in for "a glass of her gooseberry." Their good friend Mr.
Burchell, who had saved Sophia from drowning, is also offered
generous guantities of gooseberry wine. Instructions for
making it are found in Elizabeth Moxon's *English Housewifry
Exemplified* of 1758.

To make Gooseberry Wine of ripe Gooseberries.

Pick, clean and beat your Gooseberries in a Marble Mortar
or Wooden Bowl, measure them in Quarts up-heap'd, add two
Quarts of Spring Water, and let them stand all Night or twelve
Hours, then rub or press out the Husks very well, strain them
through a wide Strainer, and to every Gallon put three Pound of
Sugar, and a Jill of Brandy, then put all into a sweet Vessel, not

very full, and keep it very close for four Months, then decant it off till it comes clear, pour out the Grounds, and wash the Vessel clean with a little of the Wine; add to every Gallon a Pound more Sugar, let it stand a Month in the Vessel again, drop the Grounds thro' a Flannel Bag, and put it to the other in the Vessel; the tap Hole must not be over near the Bottom of the Cask, for fear of letting out the Grounds.

The same Receipt will serve for Currant Wine the same Way; let them be red Currants.

UPDATE: For a Jill (or gill) of Brandy use 5 oz. or 100 ml.

Author Index